THE DEPARTURE LOUNGE:
TRAVEL AND LITERATURE
IN THE POST-MODERN WORLD

JOHN NEEDHAM

The Departure Lounge

Travel and Literature in the Post-Modern World

CARCANET

First published in Great Britain in 1999 by
Carcanet Press Limited
4th Floor, Conavon Court
12–16 Blackfriars Street
Manchester M3 5BQ

A CIP catalogue record for this book is available
from the British Library
ISBN 1 85754 443 9

The publisher acknowledges financial assistance
from the Arts Council of England

Set in Sabon by XL Publishing Services, Tiverton
Printed and bound in England by SRP Ltd, Exeter

Contents

Preface

The only systematic things about these theoretic wanderings are the generous encouragement they were given by Michael Schmidt, who first published them in *PN Review*, and my belief that travel brings the theorist down to earth. I began by accident in Los Angeles, and though I usually had a rough idea of my intellectual destination, I was never quite sure how I'd get there, and was sometimes surprised – often pleasantly so – when I eventually did. I hope the reader, too, will find some pleasure in the journey.

John Needham
26 February 1999

A Brief Excursion into Hotel-Theory

Being an infrequent traveller it was only recently that I found myself with a belated opportunity to look at the Westin Bonaventure, the Los Angeles hotel and shopping complex analysed by Fredric Jameson in the opening chapter of *Post-modernism*. History of course has already been rather unkind to both Jameson and John Portman, the architect. Racial conflict has damaged Los Angeles tourism almost as much as the Soviet collapse has damaged academic Marxism, and Portman's work in general has lately been labelled banal, but though neither the hotel nor the essay are as much frequented as they once were, I felt they might still have something to tell me about contemporary aesthetic theory, so off I went.

Since Jameson's thesis is that the post-modern structure of the Bonaventure undermines our fundamental perception of space and since his first piece of evidence for this is the uncertain location of the entrance, it seems appropriate that I should have some difficulty in finding the building at all. My tourist pamphlet describes it as being on South Flower Street, but my map contains only a Flower Street, so I make my way to that, and head experimentally south. The road-side buildings rarely rise more than two storeys and I will surely have little difficulty in sighting the Bonaventure's thirty-five-floor bulk. But the further south I drive, the less likely it seems that the deteriorating urban scene will suddenly disclose a luxury hotel, even one intended as a post-modern stunt. These are clearly localities in which the indigenes might well exact summary economic retribution from any transient sybarite. Realising that this might apply to me too and that I am reaching the limits of my map, I execute a rather cowardly U-turn. The downtown tower blocks gleam dully in the haze from the burning hills and the congested city; the Bonaventure seems a receding mystery; and it is purely by chance that I eventually come upon it, at the very northern end of (South?) Flower Street, right in the city centre.

I swerve into a basement car-park, hand over my car to a squad of vehicular valets, and make my way up to the street. Composing myself for the architectural encounter, I am relieved to find that the *outside* of the hotel, at any rate, isn't too disconcerting. In fact its symmetrical dark glass cylinders seem almost reassuring amongst the glittering monoliths that loom over it; one soaring thin wedge of bronze glass in particular looks poised to sheer over and slice its way into the bowels of the earth. And the street between me and the hotel is empty of distraction. The shops are all secreted in basements or mezzanines, and the only human being in sight is a solitary middle-aged black, sitting with his legs stretched out across the pavement and his back propped up by the Bank of America. He sits at ease, as though the pavement were grass and the bank a tree, but his face has a look of dull resentment, and there is an implicit criticism in his very presence; his shabby clothes, his dusty skin and hair, and his evident lack of occupation, seem to say, 'This glittering world exists by excluding me.' But he doesn't look at all diminished by the buildings. On the contrary, he seems a reminder that common things like trees and grass, exclusion and resentment, will outlast the most imposing edifice.

Jameson, I then discover, has somewhat exaggerated the mystery of the entrance. From Flower Street you simply walk up three steps, and push a great rectangle of plate-glass, which smoothly yields to admit you to what is evidently the hotel-lobby. Nor are you then confronted by any of the stock post-modern jokes – dropped keystones, functionless columns, and so on – that make an obvious assault on your sense of structure. In fact there seems nothing to upset any conservative accountant's expectation that a big hotel will mainly confer a certain dignity. Tracts of grey carpet recede into the distance. A matching grey light, already filtered by the haze outside, is filtered again through the dark glass and then discreetly toned up by spotlights as unobtrusive as stars in the high heavens of the atrium. In the centre rises a great column surrounded by a pool, which is flanked in turn by more columns, with wall-climber lifts gliding up like space capsules into the dim heights and then disappearing through the roof and scaling the residential towers. There is a general effect, reinforced by the air-conditioning, of being on a cooling planet. The pool is half-girdled by a broad belt of low tables and deep armchairs, and the clerks at the arc of reception desk in the perimeter wall survey the scene as from a distant shore. In the only occupied armchairs, four middle-aged business-men, with red faces and loosened collars, are evidently drinking the afternoon away. The sound of their voices breaks faintly in the bay of the entrance, and I suddenly sense that this might be an attempt at boisterousness – which in these grey spaces would defeat the convivial powers of a Cossack regiment.

But then a slight feeling of oddity sets in. Overhead for instance, perhaps suspended from – or supported by? – the central column, looms the great disc of a mezzanine floor, and at intervals on its circumference are a number of oval appendages; though clearly of considerable weight and bulk, they seem as lightly attached as petals on a flower-head, suggesting some extremity of the engineer's art, like those advertisements in which an elephant is shown hanging by a drop of super-glue. The atrium is circled by yet more columns, each with a broad concrete spiral staircase. Climbing one of these I find myself in a shopping gallery on a level with the mezzanine, and see, across the dividing chasm, that the suspended disc is in fact another lounge, and that the petals are circular alcoves lined with upholstered seats. Alcoves, usually corners enclosed by all the reassuring logic of structure, are here attachments that look in danger of crashing to the ground – or floating up into the heights, where there are further mezzanine-discs and alcove-petals. At the edges of all this the relation between the circles of shops and the central cylinder of the atrium dissolves into uncertainty; it seems that the spiral staircases on the fringe may belong to other structural principles altogether, unseen, and that the great central column might not really be supporting anything. In short you begin to see Jameson's point.

On the other hand, his account strongly suggests that he wilfully courted disorientation, shooting up through the ceiling in one of Portman's 'people-movers' and traversing the glassy surface of one of the residential towers, before plunging his sensorium back into the enigmatic spaces of the lobby. Little wonder he found on his return that 'it is quite impossible to get your bearings'. Conservative accountants, or other likely denizens of such a hotel, clearly wouldn't waste their time in such perceptual profligacy. Still, it may be that their sense of space is *subconsciously* disrupted. But cogitation of this intensity begins to make me hungry. In the restaurant that occupies a further segment of the ground floor I order lunch and then try to discover what effect, if any, the building has on the waiter, who presumably spends the major part of his waking existence in it. He is a sturdy, middle-aged Hispanic, with hard-faced good looks, and he is clearly capable of noticing things – he has already been appraising me in turn with an aplomb that verges, I feel, on impertinence. I open with the usual remarks about the bush-fires, then steer the conversation round to matters architectural. When at length I insinuate that the building may possess mind-altering powers, his appraisal becomes even more pointed. He is clearly wondering whether I will have to be restrained from attacking the fittings. But

I persist, throwing in the occasional polysyllable to ballast my credibility, until at length he grunts non-committally, 'It's big.' And this evidently exhausts his stock of ideas about the architecture. A fruitless enquiry, it seems. But as I finish lunch and my next need makes itself felt, I see his point of view. The wash-room, often so elusive for the anxious tourist, is strikingly easy to locate, and I am reminded that people in hotels co-ordinate their space with reference to their practical needs (bar, restaurant, lounge, toilets, etc.) and that this will easily over-ride any disorienting effect of the architectural style. In fact it is the same principle as that which applies to the cloverleaf junctions on the city's freeways, where the motorists (unless intent on suicide) orient themselves with reference to their need to get in lane and avoid the other cars, not with reference to the beautiful but baffling three-dimensional geometry of the flyovers. And there is nothing post-modern about the basic perceptual skills at work here; they are the same as those exercised, for example, by a horde of cavemen charging down a rocky slope. In the Bonaventure lobby it isn't the guests who feel disoriented but the cultural critics. Not content to get their bearings in relation to the facilities, they need to identify the style. And since they regard style as a reflection of deep socioeconomic change, they are in effect trying to locate not the washroom but their position in world-history – and this without benefit of any reference to the more permanent features of human behaviour.

This is confirmed when I re-ascend, fortified by lunch, to the upper regions. Airing my critical vocabulary in the shopping galleries, I find that the complex structural coding is being contradicted by signs coming from an altogether different referential order. Subverting the dominant text there are inscriptions in fat red, white, and blue neon, announcing 'NICK'S DELI', 'FRESH SUBS', or 'AL'S BURGERS', and clamouring for the cultural analyst's attention. They are clearly not jocular post-modern allusions on the part of the architect, nor even resolute refusals to be textually marginalised on the part of Al and Nick. They are simply the consequence of allowing shopkeepers to rent a space and do their thing. And again I have a sense of the more enduring perspectives. This isn't to imply some human absolute. It is merely that the commercial instincts, along with trees, resentment, and alimentation, exist on a somewhat longer cycle than any particular aesthetic style.

It is, I reflect, no coincidence that Jameson works at the same academic institution as Stanley Fish, another theorist who flourishes by ignoring the longer perspectives. Fish's big idea of course is that we each belong to an 'interpretive community' and that this determines how we look at works of art, or anything else. There is little to be gained, he thinks, from dispute with rival communities. Sensible reader-response critics accosted by a new historicist will simply say, 'We don't talk like that around here.' This advice clearly reflects one of the most common weaknesses of recent aesthetic theory – its absurd exaggeration of the effect of history and culture on human perception and behaviour. Fish is at the academic end of a spectrum whose popular end is occupied by Barnum-and-Bailey trend-hounds with their apocalyptic analyses of the contemporary world. In the field of architectural criticism even a book as perceptive and well-informed as Deyan Sudjic's *The Hundred Mile City* is written in a breathless style that intermittently betrays the same tendency. As for Jameson's own central claim that late-capitalism creates a sensory world that 'transcends all the older habits of bodily perception', it collapses as soon as we actually think about physical experience. A gallop along a country road in a coach and six on a stormy night, for instance, is surely as dizzy-making as a stroll across the carpets of the Bonaventure hotel. The simple truth is that people have always enjoyed an occasional whirl; and Jameson himself evidently gets a kindred thrill from imagining the treacheries of post-modern space drawing us inexorably towards some unknown pinnacle or abyss of human experience. Giddiness of course is often harmless enough, but it can be dangerous, and in Jameson's case it is disastrous. His excitability, together with his neglect of the ordinary human continuities, robs his sense of history of all sense of proportion.

On the descent back to the floor of the atrium, an elementary continuity is easy enough to feel. The large alchemies of space and weight and shape and light are comparable with those of any lofty interior, even those of a cathedral. Of course they serve a different purpose here, and it may be said that the mystery and grandeur evidently lack real conviction, serving in fact only to undermine the sense of conviviality or luxury that a hotel ought to express; perhaps the Bonaventure is thus a failure of judgement that tells us something about contemporary culture. But these questions can be pursued only in the longer perspectives that Jameson and Fish ignore; the perspectives in which conviviality, grandeur and mystery are persistent features of human experience. A masterpiece in fact can be simply defined as a work in which a period style opens onto these perspectives; Shakespeare, for instance, not only employs the conventions of Elizabethan comedy, but also makes you really laugh. Of course contemporary aesthetic theory is largely founded on the denial of such permanences; and the denial rests in turn on the neo-Saussurean claim that all language (and this is metaphorically extended to include buildings, clothes, and so on) is an arbitrary code radically unconnected with any kind of reality, let alone a reality that endures. No serious critic, I think, would now advance the neo-Saussurean claim explicitly, but it remains the implicit foundation of much high-rise theory. The occupants increasingly suspect that the structure is unsound, but since they don't know where else to go, they simply close the doors on the recognition that the great artists are those capable of revitalising the relation between their artistic medium and an enduring human nature. The irony is that the laager of 'interpretive community', alleged to protect us from the tyranny of value-judgements and an unreal 'reality', is in fact the instrument of a far more oppressive and unreal credo – that artists can only reflect their socio-economic systems, that critics can only echo their peer-groups, and that questions of artistic merit are thus merely political.

The development of value judgements is a much more free and flexible process. On my way back to the car-park I naturally discover that looking at the Bonaventure has made me, for the time being at least, more receptive to essential values of proportion and space; more critical of their absence but also more appreciative of their presence. I claim no certainty of judgement, nor would I do so even if my knowledge of architecture were less minimal than it is. As I walk along I would be happy to 'converse', in both the ordinary sense and Richard Rorty's, with anyone who might care to question my reactions. I certainly wouldn't want to turn away murmuring, 'We don't talk like that around here.' I might well find of course that my interlocutor had radically different notions, and that there was no prospect (if Rorty is right) of translating our respective critical languages into a neutral third. But even so, there is obviously something to be learned, in the ordinary way of give and take, from talking to almost anybody; it is still possible – pointing and gesticulating no doubt as well as talking and listening – to engage in the kind of activity that clarifies and deepens our perceptions of a common world. Needless to say, I can't parcel this world out neatly into 'subjective' and 'objective' elements, but then, in this context, the subject-object dichotomy is in more need of sceptical scrutiny than the world of perception itself. I believe in this world just as I believe that the sign saying 'Public Parking', over there on the street-corner, will lead me back to my car; it is this sort of belief that makes 'conversation' an exploratory pursuit, not just a conventional game. And in a few moments of course, round the corner and down a concrete staircase, there the car is, with a smiling vehicular valet waiting to be paid.

Further Excursions and Alarms

Sydney, September '94. A brilliant spring morning; through the window I can see the big ferries sliding in and out of Circular Quay and the sun is already standing up over the great shell-cluster of the opera house. A young man with a shaved head and a pleasantly harsh Sydney voice is talking about the Russian avant-garde painters of 1917. He is busy rejecting the view that their modernist ideas about art naturally drew them towards the autocratic end of the political spectrum after the revolution. I ought to be paying more attention. This afternoon my own paper will argue that *post*-modernist *writers*, at any rate, accustomed to the manipulation of what they regard as arbitrary signs, are indeed that much more likely to approve the exercise of arbitrary power. But the speaker's words echo a little amongst the marble pillars of the conference hall and my mind is only half drawn into their web; the other half strays out along the busy waterfront. As I lose the thread, I begin to doubt my own conviction that signs, so far from being arbitrary impositions on an inscrutable reality, follow from things that actually go on in the world. I take off my glasses and turn down my hearing aids – one of my routine procedures for semantic testing. My reality immediately turns vague and soundless, like underwater, and evidently no words I choose to impose could materially alter this; if they could I wouldn't need all this sensory technology. After a few moments I effect prosthetic re-engagement; the silent blur turns back into an articulate man, further reassuring me that my perceptions are radically free of language. Then the man suddenly falls silent again; he has finished, leaving me in clear possession of my own ideas but not of his.

Before the morning break there is one more paper, given by a dark thick-set man with a fixed gaze and dramatic monotone. His concern is whether the abstract painter Reinhardt's artistic impersonality is a kind of nihilism. I think of Dr Johnson's remark that though Shakespeare is apparently indifferent to poetic justice he none the less 'thinks morally' because he 'thinks rationally'. It seems that the speaker may be moving, in some obscure way, towards a similar conclusion. But his manner is disconcerting. In his faintly menacing monotone and intermittently Gallicized syntax, he incessantly rotates his key words – 'painting', 'nothing', 'profundity', 'final' (attached to any of the substantives) – until he seems to be intoning a mantra. Reinhardt 'never made anything of anything', he tells us: 'Would this then constitute a final painting? And of what? Of nothing? Or is it itself nothing? And is this a final profundity?' I'm no longer making much of anything myself, and finally I can think of nothing but coffee.

During the break, tribal gravitation draws me into conversation with two other delegates whose conference tags betray their New Zealand origin – a radiantly obtuse young woman who announces that she 'likes playing with Derrida', and an elderly man who surprises me by turning out to be an uncle of one of my post-graduate students. In itself this isn't a very remarkable coincidence, but I am rather struck by its chiming with another theme of my own paper – the nature of chance in narrative. I intend to rivet the conference with an analysis of 'the aleatory' (as I shall tactically call it) in Vikram Seth's *A Suitable Boy*. The novel tells a number of stories, each following a perfectly logical progression in itself but also intersecting with the other stories at unexpected points; these chance intersections are sometimes rich in consequence, sometimes not; sometimes they loom portentously but then, sadly or happily, just fail to materialise. Perhaps there is something Indian here; or perhaps Seth is dramatising chaos theory. Anyway, my own intersection with my student's uncle will doubtless prove inconsequential. None the less, since my theory of chance is part of a more general theory of suspense, I can invest even trivial junctures with a degree of excitement.

The uncle – an arts administrator – is soon telling me, in a faintly aggressive manner, that all the exciting work in the New Zealand arts is now being done by women and Maoris; white males are finished. But I refuse the provocation. He resembles – and in fact turns out to be – a retired accountant, and this is perhaps making him over-anxious to affirm his commitment to marginality. It's that sort of conference. He may also be flattering the young woman; at any rate his words intensify her dull glow. But I must confess that I too have been cultivating a mildly marginal image, by gracing the social side of the conference in the company of D—, a rather glamorous-looking Chinese who is the daughter of an old friend. She now makes a living in Sydney dealing in antiques, and was happy to lend me moral support, especially when I told her that the conferees would think of her as a 'visible site of alterity' rather than a 'token coloured woman'; but this morning she has gone to an auction. In any case my wisp of marginalist cover will be blown when I give my paper. Though I have peppered it with words like 'aleatory', 'discourse', and 'deconstruction', it blatantly rests on the proposition that not only words but plots too, so far from being the arbitrary creations of the patriarchs and capitalists, are largely determined by our natural perceptions of the world.

I brood intermittently over this during the next paper – 'Malevich and the Liberation of Art from the Bondage of Subject and Object'. Freedom in the visual and verbal arts, incidentally, is the official theme of the conference, so a rather derisory attitude to artistic realism is taken for granted; and it has been proving contagious. Even my early morning walk from the hotel – a perfectly respectable establishment but in the heart of King's Cross – seemed a rather post-modern sequence, presenting, in rapid succession, a Bardolphian drunk with a malt-worm-ravaged face, staggering past shuttered shops; three huge men with tattoos lounging in a sunny doorway; a curiously dilapidated ATM designed perhaps to dispense soiled banknotes for nefarious use; trees casting dappled sunlight on a host of Amazonian girls streaming towards an old red-brick school; the city's tower-blocks standing beyond it like shining toys; a dock with a sleek destroyer moored alongside a decaying wooden hangar; then, past a motorway, the botanical gardens where a marquee suffused with light and brilliant with orchids is being prepared for the Annual Show; and all the way, glimpsed here and there above the trees or buildings, the great arch of the harbour bridge, one of the icons of my Imperial British childhood. Everything delightfully disjunct, and made a little strange by the unfamiliar trees and light.

We have learned that Malevich's suprematist abstractionism still left its practitioners in thrall to the world and are now exploring Gabo's belief in the purer freedoms of constructivism; but the speaker, warily skirting the minefields of current theory, himself seems a subject in bondage to too many objects; his anarchic Russians would surely have felt that when the manoeuvres of freedom grow so complicated it is time for the revolution to move on – perhaps even in the direction of restraint.

At lunchtime I emerge gratefully into the foyer and as I wonder whether to stay here for quiche and deconstruction or drift along the waterfront in search of fish and chips, I am suddenly accosted by a tall, good-looking young man with a pale face and a politely diffident manner. To my astonishment he announces himself as someone I last met when he was seven years old. My sense of chance is vividly renewed. But of course there is a simple logic at work. His father, an

old colleague who went off long ago to work in Canberra, has seen
my name in a conference brochure and has asked the son, who works
in a Sydney law-office, to drop in and say hello. As we·walk along
Circular Quay and take an outside table at an oyster bar, my contradictory sense of chance and design persists. The young man's story,
as he briefly recounts it, is perfectly familiar, given his time and place:
a degree, a couple of years work and travel in Europe, then back to
Australia to make a career. And of course to meet him after so many
years makes me even more conscious of the larger shapes of lives,
both his and mine. But I still feel the surprise of our meeting, and as
he tells me something of his plans and hopes, sitting there on the
sunny quay, I have an acute sense of life's hidden possibilities, 'the
lips parted, the new ships'. And then a sense of shipwreck too, when
he goes on to say that his parents are in the throes of divorce. I had
heard rumours of it. And so it is true. At their age! Which is my own.
I glance round at the tourists and office-workers under big striped
umbrellas. Enjoying their sea-food, talking, and laughing, they offer
much that is delightful to contemplate, but nothing really disjunct,
only tangled life-lines, if one knew.

An obscure sense of this general truth seems to lie behind the anxieties of the young woman with beautiful red hair who presents the
first paper after lunch. She is developing an analysis of the current
dress styles of Sydney's radical youth. Their sartorial 'transgres-
sions', it appears, tend to be either nostalgic or futuristic, looking
towards past or future revolutions. The speaker's worry is that
'transgression' has become so normal that 'to be truly radical
requires an almost counter-transgressive desire'. More deeply – for
she is clearly a woman capable of energetic thought and feeling – she
betrays an uneasy sense that none of this, whether 'transgressive' or
'counter-trangressive', seems anything more than a question of *style*.
Her own radical style is undeniably very good. 'Beware, Beware, her
flashing eyes and floating hair,' I find myself thinking, as she makes
an emphatic point, flourishes her notes, and makes a dash from the
microphone to the overhead projector. But clearly she is in something of the same plight as her sartorial transgressors; her radical
style is thin in radical substance. It is of course a current problem.
The alliance with radicalism that gave 'theory' its initial lift-off is in
fact falling apart. The Marxists are in disarray, the new historicists
have returned to empiricism, and the feminists, their cause securely
based on a demand for justice, have never regarded aesthetic theory
as more than an optional extra. But of course the most crucial development is that the genuine article – a radicalism both righteous and

dynamic, exulting in its power to frighten the populace and trans-form the world – is now the property not of the academic left but the economic right. And in this context academics are clearly part of the frightened populace, perpetually alarmed by threats of cuts in government spending. In short they are people with a radical style but conservative needs. Many of them still contrive to ignore this chasm between style and content by believing that since the world consists of signs then style is all there is. But the speaker is clearly too earnest for that. For people like her there are only two possible solutions. Either they must recapture the radical high ground – and there is scant hope of that, while the right wing has its heavy artillery on the economic summits – or else they must change their rhetoric to suit their needs; and here of course the speaker herself is entirely typical; she finds the idea of a conservative style – an acquiescence in a 'counter-transgressive desire' – quite repugnant.

Well, that's her problem. Mine, in a few minutes, will be to exploit any 'counter-transgressive desires' that may be lurking in the conference's collective breast. In brief I hope to persuade them that a conventional realist narrative like *A Suitable Boy*, in which the characters follow their own inner logic, serves human freedom far better than an 'experimental' narrative like *The French Lieutenant's Woman*, in which the characters are grossly manipulated in the name of a *theory* of freedom (in this of course they resemble the unhappy subjects of the self-righteous dictators who have infested modern history). Moreover I am employing a frankly 'counter-transgressive' critical method; my analysis will marry Empson with Aristotle, so to speak; it will focus on suspenseful points of the action and relate the multiple possibilities of the dramatic outcome to the multiple meanings of the diction. It is a method with no direct bearing on the text's hidden agenda or its relation with 'the historic moment'; even worse, it claims to promote judgements of value, helping us to decide whether a narrative is an artistic success (*A Suitable Boy*) or a botched piece of work (*The French Lieutenant's Woman*.) Glancing round the audience (there is no sign of the shaved head) I comfort myself with the thought that here at any rate my counter-transgressive desires may be genuinely transgressive; but this only makes my mouth go dry.

Luckily there is a break before my session starts, so I can wet my whistle. More important, my visible site of alterity, together with her partner (domestic and business), arrives to give me support. When I finally begin to read my paper I find my eyes alighting with some frequency on her intelligently sympathetic countenance (she tells me later that she didn't understand a word of it), but the audience at large remain inscrutable; they might be rapt with attention or asleep with their eyes open. The shaven avant-gardist, like many of the delegates whose interests are visual rather than verbal, has evidently decamped. As it turns out my nervousness adds energy to my delivery and to my relief I find myself still convinced by my own argument. Not so the audience. At question time I am soon being told that the 'closures' of conventional narrative radically deny the freedom of the *reader*. But this of course is something I had anticipated. I counter that the doctrine of reader-freedom reaches its apotheosis in 'hyper-fiction', where it also produces narrative crudity and character manipulation of the grossest kind; then I argue that suspense and chance in conventional narrative reflect not some theoretic freedom but the ambiguous freedoms of life itself, where free will jostles with both the contingent and the predetermined. But what chiefly strikes me about the discussion is the receptive temper of the questioners. Perhaps they are just being polite to someone too far 'out of the true' to be worth prolonged opposition. But I think not. The questions chiefly come from two young women – including the one with red hair – who seem too lively and too thoughtful to be mere prisoners of current theory, even though they are evidently recent graduates. Behind their questions I sense a distinct interest in possible ways out.

My impression, I should add, runs contrary to that enshrined in the report on Academic Standards in English, recently commissioned by the Australian Vice-Chancellors' Committee. Its authors would have us believe that today's young academics are 'a generation whose allegiance is to the new discourses, and that these discourses will remain entrenched for at least two or three decades'. The style of this is revealing, coming from those who claim a peculiar insight into 'discourse', especially into its tendency to impose illusory structures on the world. And it is a style that pervades the whole report. A 'discourse analyst' of the old I.A. Richards school would describe it roughly as follows: genre – committee-speak; tone – authoritative; feeling – complacent; purpose – maintenance of the status quo; sense – questionable. What is particularly questionable is the blank assumption that argument will change nothing; that change will only come about through some mystic process of exhaustion (when the exponents of the 'new discourses' reach retiring age). The report is in fact further witness to the old truth that Jonathan Culler has shrewdly pointed at Stanley Fish: when radical sceptics get into power their scepticism immediately becomes an instrument of 'entrenchment'.

But my point is that the 'entrenchment' here is in any case an illusory structure. The young academics facing me in the conference hall are clearly open to argument. And in this respect they are like most of my own graduate students, who are just as likely to feel that Derrida and company are obscurantist pedants as to accredit them with profound insight. So far from being safely entrenched, the theorists are already in retreat and simply concealing it with the manoeuvre analysed by Raymond Tallis in *PNR* 98 – that is, continually shifting trenches without acknowledging it.

Question-time finished and the day's proceedings ended, I suddenly realise why freedom is so notoriously difficult to define; it is not so much an idea as a feeling; and it is coming strongly upon me as we leave the conference-hall. Tomorrow is Sunday and we are spending the night with a friend of D—'s, a retired antique dealer who lives in the bush, fifty miles up the coast. By dusk we are negotiating the back-roads and we arrive at dinner-time. After an oddly desultory discussion someone drives off to the take-away next to the local petrol pump. They return with the worst Chinese food I've had since I stood on the sacred summit of Mt Tai, in the days when the East was still Red, and ingested what seemed a concoction of Ching dynasty dish-water and snow melted in urine. But Tino, our host, is a delightful man, and his house is filled with the fascinating residue of his time as a dealer in collectables. There are clockwork toys – cars, motor-bikes, and aeroplanes with leather-helmeted and be-goggled pilots – that take me straight back to my childhood, though they are in fact more finely wrought and highly finished than anything I remember from the Coronation Streets of the 1940s. He paints too; in a spare room an easel holds a half-finished portrait of a middle-aged woman, done with photographic realism and conspicuous skill.

Finding myself like this in an art-world so neatly opposed to that of the conference hall, I again have that curious sense of both chance and design. Tino's ruling deities are conventionality, value, and the past. Of course they are somewhat fallen. Value tends to be calculated in dollars, and the calculation drags in both history and convention; the older and the more exemplary the piece, the higher the price. None the less, while Tino is showing me his things – things he hasn't wanted to part with – he still radiates something of the delight in creative excellence that is a central meaning of words like 'art' and 'poetry'. Needless to say it is a meaning that was completely absent from the conference hall, where it was assumed as a matter of course that judgements of value are simply political. And in this respect at least the report on Academic Standards in English makes salutary reading; by spelling out the grounds of the assumption it inadvertently reminds us how untenable they are. Since no literary values are 'absolute' or 'universal', the argument glibly runs, it's no use worrying about them at all. This line of reasoning, as I recall, used to be the refuge of smart fifth-formers who hadn't done their homework. It is richly ironic to find it in a policy document on university standards. Would the authors risk applying it to fields of endeavour in which the general public takes an urgent interest – food, for instance, or football?

But these thoughts, as usual, are beginning to agitate me. I tell myself that most academics don't actually believe such nonsense, although they sometimes fall in with it because it might seem illiberal to demur; then I fill my glass and bend all my attention on Tino's scheme for making a fortune by shipping a container-load of European antiques from Argentina to Australia.

Next morning is as brilliantly sunny as ever. Drought is becoming a daily headline. The dream-like quality of the Australian out-back that D.H. Lawrence captured so vividly seems largely an effect of dryness; as though the whole country might evaporate into air and light; and in such an atmosphere its vastness becomes a vagueness. So different from New Zealand, where you raise your eyes to dark hills and feel a coast beyond and a complete land defined by the great seas. When I go out walking with D— after breakfast and we talk about her family back home across the Tasman, the hard glare of the soil underfoot makes me suddenly long for the ferns, the moss, and the cool damp earth of the New Zealand bush. Tomorrow I'll be there.

It's a Monday morning flight so my taxi to the airport has to negotiate the rush-hour traffic. The driver is from Ghana. He tells me that he came to Australia ten years ago and that Sydney has a small Ghanaian community. We soon fall to talking about the football final (rugby league), played the day before. When I tell him that even after many years in New Zealand, I still think that 'football' really means 'soccer', he agrees delightedly, and we are soon enthusing over Nigeria's performance in the World Cup. So when he abruptly asks me whether Tom Jones is an Englishman or a Scot, I am momentarily at a loss, until I register the voice on the car-radio urgently requesting someone to knock three times on the ceiling if she wants him. 'Welsh,' I reply, 'they're good at singing.' The driver nods sagely, and goes on to confide that Jones and Engelbert Humperdink are still his favourite singers. At this point he has to brake sharply when a young man in a BMW switches lanes. He reacts automatically and simply carries on talking, but when I ask him whether there are many bad drivers about, his black face darkens, and he mutters something about the futility of getting involved in quarrels. It doesn't need much imagination to see that in a city like this there will inevitably be incidents, sometimes with a racist issue. And this must be one reason for the evident pleasure he is feeling just now, sharing a common culture – albeit only that of international entertainment – with a middle-aged, middle-class white. Of course I take pleasure in it, too, but for him it is different. From his point of view any passenger is a part of his real daily life. From my point of view, despite my fleeting glimpse into something of the form and pressure of his days, he is in danger of seeming just a patch of local colour. Travel is too disjunctive; I need to get back home and pick up my own tangled life-lines.

An Excursion to a New Jerusalem

For the hundredth time, it seems, since we left the main highway, the switchback road reaches the top of a hill then veers abruptly into a steep descent; but this time the trees on the shoulder thin out, and down below we catch our first glimpse of the church, standing on a slope above the river. Though the road is scarcely wider than the car, we stop to look. The river in front of the church seems as broad as a lake; above it rises an amphitheatre of rugged bush-covered hills. Scattered round it are perhaps a score of houses; some of them, we find later, are in rather poor repair, but from here they all seem idyllic, looking out from amongst the trees; and the weatherboard church itself, its bronze-painted spire glittering faintly in the sun and a gleam on its pale-gold walls, might be made of precious metals. So this is Jerusalem – in Maori, Hiruharama. It seems a fitting location for today's theoretical project – resurrection (or, at least, a query about 'the death of the author').

Driving on we come upon a man with a bulging supermarket bag standing in front of a crude roadside shelter. Inside there are other figures, keeping to the shadows. The man outside is rather dusty and fat, but has the leonine look you often see in older Maori men; square jaw and brow, thick mane of greying hair, and the lion's tawny eye, looking straight at you, untroubled, perhaps indifferent. The poet's grave, he says, in answer to our question, is up there, on the hill behind the church. He gestures towards a grassy side-road. I would like to talk to him, but the only remarks that come to mind feel absurdly literary, so the moment passes, and after a little silence we drive on.

The side-road runs prettily up between over-arching trees and ends in a grassy space in front of the church. As we get out of the car, the throb of cicadas bursts on the ear like the pulse of summer, but it quickly drops away again as our attention is caught by a row of wooden crosses. About five feet high, set amongst pansies and roses, they line the gravel path to the church-door. They look at first like the stations of the cross; but there are fifteen of them, each one carrying a painted wooden picture of some event in the story of Christ. An omen for our enquiry perhaps, since he is clearly an author whose works have always been inseparable from his life. Of course we only know the life from the texts – of one kind or another. In front of me, for instance, nailed onto a wooden cross, is a picture of him nailed onto a wooden cross; enough to launch any passing theorist into a disquisition on the ubiquity of signs and the unavailability of the real. The latter, one must admit, isn't available here. The Christ in the wooden picture seems to be swooning over the scent of the roses rather than dying in agony, and you can't even remotely believe in the nails. But of course in some paintings of the crucifixion you can. The criterion of the the 'real', whatever its defects for the philosopher, remains indispensable for the critic who wants to distinguish between images that give you a sense of a life and images that don't. The question remains of course whether our sense of an *author's* life, however vivid, is really relevant to the works. But my companion – a literary biographer rather than a theorist – seems anxious to move on.

With its cream paint standing out against the green of the bush and its bronze spire against the burning blue of the sky, the church makes a vivid impression, but the interior seems devoid of 'atmosphere'. Not that it's bare. Though airy and light it has plenty of things to look at, some of them striking; the Maori piece that supports the communion table, for instance – a long, low, heavy carving, in pale wood, of convoluted spirit-figures with glaring eyes, full of power and danger. Or the big old rata growing outside one of the tall clearglass windows and filling it with bursts of orange-scarlet blossom. It all looks cared for but it doesn't add up, any more than the odd assortment of ancient pews and modern chairs, or the office-desk standing next to the organ. Seeking some unity of impression you find yourself left only with the gathered light and silence, deepened by the distant chirr of the cicadas. And in a while this begins to seem enough, that all the objects in the church are simply there, in a strange resonance – sanctity almost – of the ordinary.

Still under this little spell, my eye is caught by a framed photograph of our quarry – 'James Keir Baxter, 1926-1972' – hanging in a corner along with a brief 'life' on a typewritten sheet. A leading poet of his generation, Baxter ran a commune here at Jerusalem on the Wanganui River in the last three years of his life. Staring from the pages of the recent biographies, the long-haired, bead-and-bangle-festooned 'drop-outs' who gathered round him look irretrievably sixtyish at first glance, but it's easy enough to recognise the abiding human types – the gregarious and the lonely, the idealist and the opportunist, the desperate and the brave. Baxter himself, it is said, was a mixture of all these; but the photograph on the church-wall is just an undistinguished snap-shot, without expression. And the whole flimsy memorial – two scraps of paper and a wooden frame – might well seem ordinary to the point of meanness; New Zealand's egalitarian spirit sometimes shows this less attractive side. But no, the curious resonance remains. I think of the ancestral shrine in a Chinese home; just a photograph on the wall, with a shelf beneath for a bowl of fruit and a stick of incense; a memorial woven into daily life. And a Chinese countryside grave gives the same impression; a grey stone box with an inscription and an urn, looking down from a patch of scrub above a rice-paddy, and set in its due place between earth and heaven by the local geomancer. The Maori too have a strong feeling for their particular earth – and for poetry. Did they choose Baxter's burial place, I wonder?

Before climbing the hill to look for it, we decide to eat our lunch at a picnic table under a lemon tree by the church. Naturally my biographer friend – from a new literary generation, weary of 'pure textuality' and stirred by post-colonial impulses – is also interested in poetry and place, so it's no surprise when he pulls from his bag, along with his sandwiches, a copy of Baxter's *Jerusalem Sonnets*. He turns up some passages that mention things we can actually see – the church, the old convent, the Maori meeting house; but I'm soon disconcerted to find that, so far from being enriched by the locality, the words seem to be losing all their meaning. The mid-day sun has filled the trees and the hills with a brooding weight, the air itself feels almost tangible, and in this intensely physical atmosphere even the book is turning into a mere *thing* – a dazzling white rectangle crowded with black marks; its power to fall away and let you through into an imagined world has gone; as though the poems and the actuality they spring from, exist in mutually exclusive realms.

Before I can try this anti-biographical sentiment on my biographer friend, actuality becomes still more insistent. A young Maori woman appears through a gateway pushing a rotary mower, and starts noisily mowing the lawn. But why do it in the noon-day heat? And in fact something in her manner suggests that she has been prompted by our arrival (my companion is young and good-looking) rather than the state of the grass. In a moment an elderly nun in a dark blue habit with a knee-length skirt appears from a nearby house and advances across the sward. As she passes our table she stops to greet us. She knows about Baxter, we discover, but her pale grey eyes remain guarded, occasionally glancing towards the mower. 'I have to get petrol for the girl,' she murmurs at length, and makes off. The nuns of Baxter's day of course often felt that his moral fervour lagged alarmingly behind his spiritual insight, especially with regard to sex-and-drugs on the commune. Perhaps our nun feels that Baxter-seekers are likely to share their idol's imbalances.

As she steers 'the girl' away 'to get petrol', an ancient car noses slowly round the bend and parks next to ours. The driver, a stocky, balding European of fifty-something, turns out to be a retired wood-work teacher from Sheffield, contriving to 'see the world on a small pension'. But why see this particular bit of it? The scenery, appar-ently. He has heard nothing of Baxter. When we tell him, he seems pleased that someone of public note has lived here but a little disap-pointed that it should be a poet. He himself, he says with emphasis, is a practical man; he has driven all round Australia, is now doing New Zealand, and plans the same treatment for the United States – in cheap second-hand cars maintained by himself. But when he strides off to look inside the church, he seems quite eager; and I suddenly imagine him back in Sheffield, airing his traveller's tales in the pub, and recalling, with affable condescension, the 'little place up the Wanganui River, that turned out to be a sort of Stratford-Down-Under'. The fancy pleases me. People with no understanding of poetry should at least retain some notion – however vague – that it matters. This is one of the uses of literary tourism. The links it creates between poetry and society are admittedly of the humblest kind; but on the other hand, the impossible ideals erected in this area by Leavis and company were a discouragement rather than an inspi-ration. They made one's best endeavours in the classroom seem a futile gesture in the face of an irresistible tide of barbarism. What they said about modern culture may have been true enough; 'dull Saturnian days of lead and gold'. But those words are Pope's of course, and the sentiment is timeless; the cultural world, like the world at large, is at any time largely a standing witness to the defeat of intelligence and the triumph of money. And Leavis should have acknowledged this; it might have made the weaker brethren like myself less prone to attitudes of militancy or despair. Anyway, that's all done. On this sunny afternoon, I can take my cultural pleasure without thought of the thousands elsewhere allegedly ruining their sensibilities watching the afternoon soaps or playing bingo. No man is an island, but the erection of fences is perfectly legitimate – and even effective up to a point.

Here in Jerusalem there seem to be fences everywhere. Together with the overhanging trees and the narrowness of the paths, they make the way to the grave surprisingly hard to find; and the place feels deserted in the noon-day heat. But at length we come upon a Maori in jeans and work-shirt, walking along with a hoe on his shoulder. His dreadlocks stick out from under an old felt hat, and his seamed and sun-tanned face radiates so much unfocussed good-will that one can't help wondering what sort of crop he is off to cultivate. But he readily points us in the right direction, and we are soon climbing a flight of rough steps cut into the clay of the thickly wooded hillside.

The grave (the Baxter scholars say) is on private ground, and the owners (they indignantly add) expect a '*koha*', or donation. Since the scholars themselves make a comfortable living out of dead poets I'm not sure that they ought to complain about the lower orders of the industry, and when we come to a patch of level ground with a fence, a gate, and a house beyond, I'm quite ready to contribute my five dollars; but there seems to be nobody home. The door is open and the verandah has all the signs of daily life – boots, boxes, trikes, and, more oddly, a full-length mirror, ornately framed, leaning against the wall – but nothing stirs. Over to one side, through some trees, we can see a small graveyard.

As we stand wondering what to do, a car pulls up beside the house (the hillside is evidently a maze of hidden roads and paths) and a woman gets out. A little dark-haired European of forty-something, she turns out to be the house-holder, and when we explain our busi-ness she clearly has no thought whatever of a *koha*. Admittedly her mind doesn't seem crowded with thoughts of any kind. Yes, she has lived here for twenty years; yes, she has two children who go to the local school, and so on. When we remark on the quietness of the neighbourhood, she ponders, then replies that it's noisier when the children come home, and she seems to feel this as a conversational height. There is another pause, filled with the stillness of the summer afternoon. I am fleetingly conscious of a sensation that might turn out, if it lasted, to be either deep contentment or infinite boredom. And this suddenly brings Baxter a little closer; his *Jerusalem Sonnets* are often troubled by doubts about 'the country and the city' – empti-ness and fulfilment, obscurity and fame. In one poem he listens to a wicked magpie telling him that he ought to leave the backwoods and become a roaring literary lion, then he carries on doggedly building a wall of grass-sods.

The gravestones seem to beckon, however, and with the woman's leave we make our way across the garden. The graveyard is on a slightly higher level, through a further gate, and just before we reach it we come upon two other graves, amongst the trees. One of them is simply an enormous slab of what appears to be concrete. According to the inscription it covers the mortal remains of a husband and wife, but it looks more like a seal for nuclear waste. The other grave is Baxter's. It has only a head-stone – a natural stone from the river, whitish in colour and slightly irregular in shape, with the inscription 'Hemi' (the Maori version of 'James') and the full name and dates in smaller lettering underneath. In front of it grows one of those small, slender-leaved fuschias with flowers like elongated blood-drops about to fall. We take photos of each other by the grave, then stand and look rather aimlessly about; there's little to see, but we're reluctant to leave so quickly having travelled so far. And then again comes the curious resonance of the ordinary. The stone, the clay, the grass, and the blood-red flowers take on an elemental look, but so unassumingly that you might not notice. When you do, however, the sheer existence of things, against the blankness of death, strikes you with an almost physical shock. Even the awful concrete slab begins to look like a rock of ages. Oddly enough it makes me think of Sartre. Why did he feel the need to reduce our wonder at the world to a mere nausea at the 'in-itself'? Perhaps because wonder tends to make talk superfluous. At any rate we just stand for a while in silence, then turn away and start back down the hill.

We get lost again of course in the maze of paths, and have to ask directions from two young Maori men sitting at ease on their front porch. Their dogs – a white pit bull terrier and a huge dark-headed Rottweiler – prick up their ears at our approach, then display a marked absence of hostility or even interest. Walking on we pass a vegetable garden where the man with dreadlocks is hoeing a patch of innocent pumpkins. His good-will shines on and we stop to talk, but we are soon reduced to the garden and the weather. They get mild winters here, he tells us, gesturing towards the encircling hills. I nod. The ordinary is beginning to feel just ordinary again. By the time we get back to the car we are discussing a critique, just published in a 'very nineties' magazine, of Baxter's 'sixties attitudes'; Jerusalem is already receding into the background.

Driving back along the river-road, however, we pull in at the first 'Scenic Lookout' to take a last look. The ground drops away steeply from the road, almost a cliff, and at its base, down through a grove of pines, the river's silver ribbon winds away round a bend. But back along the valley there is already nothing to be seen except a rolling sea of bush. And being invisible Jerusalem seems touched by mystery again. As we stand wondering which green undulation hides it, a camper-van pulls in behind us, and a man and woman get out, followed in a moment by a young girl. The woman and girl are fair, a bit watchful, the man is darker, Mediterranean-looking, and seems more at ease. It turns out that they are tourists from New Caledonia, where (they hasten to add) they are only working on contract – they are really from Marseilles. My mind still running in its literary groove, I tell them that a poet once lived down there – I wave towards the sea of green. My French is too rusty even to get started and their English is rudimentary, but they respond readily to 'commune' of course, and to 'hippie' and 'marijuana', so these words become the mainstay of the faltering conversation. At length they climb back into their van obviously pleased to have made significant contact with the natives, and in a moment they have disappeared round the bend, taking with them a singularly orgiastic impression of modern New Zealand poetry.

And I suddenly regret having given them such a gross stereotype of such a complicated man. How much easier life must be, I find myself thinking irritably, for those who have discovered that any connection between language and the world is in any case purely arbitrary. No need then for the laborious chemistry of feeling, perception, idea, and word that exercises the unenlightened. Just toss your arbitrary effusions in the intertextual soup and leave the rest to the reader's powers of digestion. But luckily this thought calls up Pope's image of the pure textualists as a circle of porkers contentedly feeding on each other's excreta, and my annoyance dissolves.

As we drive home, our talk is desultory, and when I finally drop the biographer at his front door, the day's impressions seem to have receded even further. In the evening, however, I take the *Jerusalem Sonnets* down from the shelf. I simply want to check some matters of fact, but the strong voice of the poems soon compels a full attention. Baxter was not only a bearded, bare-foot 'holy man', but also a product of the modern literary academy, and his keynote is a distinctive blend of subtlety and simplicity. This evening I seem to be hearing it more clearly than usual, and it reminds me of Jerusalem; yet when I try to put my finger on it, the poetry and the actuality seem just as incompatible as they did earlier, under the midday sun, except that now it's the poems that stand self-sufficient, leaving no room for the actual world they describe.

I put the book down and walk out onto the verandah. From any rational standpoint the deep gulley that runs past the back of my house is an arboreal catastrophe. About forty years ago, after some fool had cleared the native bush, it was planted with gum-trees to prevent erosion. The gums are now seventy feet tall, far too big for their place, and with a strange medley of undergrowth. But from the verandah they're not at all oppressive. The house stands at the mid-levels of the tree-world, and in the evening the sun's rays slant under the canopy of foliage, turning the trunks and limbs to silver, then filtering down into the bottom of the gulley and kindling here and there a green glow of leaves or a yellow flare of dry twigs. The whole place seems rather magical.

As I stand and look, my feeling about Baxter's keynote grows more distinct, and I realise that it too is a pleasure of locality; in the poems the sense of place is a sense of *voice*, giving the words a full human context. And it seems to me more than ever strange that literary critics should have been so bullied by the neo-Saussurean catch-cries about 'logocentrism' and 'the privileging of the spoken word.' In fact Saussure's radical deficiency was that he simply excluded voice from his semantics. This was why Ogden and Richards, in *The Meaning of Meaning*, dismissed his ideas as useless for any practical purpose – and why Richards himself went on to develop an account of meaning that gives voice a central place. Of course Richards lacks the neologistic polysyllability currently favoured by the theorists, but he still points in the right direction – towards voice as relatedness. 'Tone', he insisted (and he stuck to this most common of words for the speaker's relation with the audience), is an aspect of *meaning* as crucial as it is obvious. If the words 'What are you doing?', for instance, are voiced sympathetically, they mean 'I take an interest in you'; but voiced angrily they mean, 'You bungling fool'. And Richards's insistence of course was consciously geared to Eliot's revolution, conferring prestige and influence on poets with subtly dramatic voices. But the emotionalities of tone were inconvenient for Saussure's scientific ambitions, so out they went. And the neo-Saussurean achievement has been to elevate the master's tin ear into a philosophical principle. Voice, they say, is simply a comforting illusion for those unable to face the facts of unmitigated semiosis.

Well, those that have ears to hear... And what they will hear in poetry is not some 'metaphysical centre' or 'presence', but a voice richly located. An ear sufficiently acute of course can locate virtu-ally any voice. Empson, a mathematician as well as a poet, could detect complex emotions in the voice of Euclid's theorems. And even the deconstructive monotone, droning through the academic stratos-phere, places itself by the creaking of its puns and its tendency to rise to a purr of conceit. But it's a dull location, the haunt of pedants through the ages. The evening song of the blackbird, just starting to transmit from its usual station on a corner fence-post, though (I suppose) on a lower intellectual frequency than the voice of deconstruction, seems far more vividly located. And in any case it clearly illustrates what is at issue here. Its paradoxical note of serenity and urgency isn't to be found simply in my ear, or my brain, or my heart, or in the bird's throat or instincts, or in the intervening air; it exists between all these points. In a complex event like this, as Whitehead insisted, the idea of a simple location, or a 'centre', is indeed a fallacy, but the idea of a rich location is a necessity.

I stand locating the song with some complacency – especially since it's 'our' blackbird – until it occurs to me that the odd Marxist critic still in practice might respond to my sentiments about voice and place with dark reminders of Heidegger and Hitler, the mother-tongue and the father-land. But surely my affection for my back-garden – whether literally or nationally speaking – doesn't make me a Nazi, any more than my enjoyment of a drink makes me a besotted wife-beater. In a moment I prove this point to my own satisfaction by going back inside, pouring myself a beer, and savouring to the full my sense of belonging.

The odd Marxist, I suppose, would see this as merely confirming my frivolity – especially if he happened to know that Jerusalem is more noted for its connection with colonial war than modern poetry. And coincidentally enough this evening's television news has shown Maori demonstrators gathered only a few miles down-river, occupying land they say was taken from them unlawfully. The occupation is an earnest of much bigger land-claims. There is talk of 'Maori sovereignty', an uncertain phrase designed to raise both constitutional questions and racial temperatures.

In this context, my own sort of concern with 'place' may seem the mere maundering of an aesthete. And it would indeed be foolish to sentimentalise the issue. The Maori of course are as aware as anyone else that land means money and power, and of course some of their leaders are busily converting ancient colonial injustice into modern political advantage. But for some it also remains true that the land is their earth-mother. I think especially of the older folk who were shown earlier on television. Even gathered in protest they looked patient, almost passive, as if there on sufferance. A hostile witness might say they're just clinging to the land because they have nothing else; if they could get their share of modern wealth, they'd join the modern world – and the sooner the better. Which is to assume that what finally matters – as the Marxists used to lament and the derivatives dealers now proclaim – is money. But sooner or later of course even the lords of the universe will have to acknowledge the elementary truth felt by these old men and women sitting on the grass under their makeshift shelters: what finally matters is the earth. And it's a 'sense of place' that makes this a truth not just of prudence or necessity but of love.

But elevated thoughts always make me nervous. Finishing my beer, I myself come back down to earth in the *Jerusalem Sonnets*, and notwithstanding my feelings about place and voice in general, I still have to admit that the poems feel self-sufficient, free of their source in actuality. I turn to a poem in which – so it's usually said – Baxter's real-life tendency to see himself as a latter-day Jesus leaks embarrassingly into the text:

> I read it in the Maori primer,
> 'Ka timata te pupuhi o te hau' –
>
> The wind began blowing; it blew for a century
> Levelling by the musket and the law
>
> Ten thousand meeting houses – there are two of them in the pa,
> Neither one used; the mice and the spiders meet there;
>
> And the tapu mound where the heads of the chiefs were burned
> Will serve perhaps one day for a golf course – yet
>
> Their children fear te taipo,
> The bush demon; on that account
>
> They keep the lights burning all night outside their houses –
> What can this pakeha fog-eater do?
>
> Nothing; nothing! Tribe of the wind,
> You can have my flesh for kai, my blood to drink.

Any reader who knows the untranslated Maori words (roughly speaking, 'pa' means 'fort', 'pakeha' means 'European', 'kai' means 'food') will no doubt find this rather embarrassing – if taken straight. As one commentator solemnly remarks, 'an offering of oneself for what is implied as eucharistic consumption seems theologically most questionable.' But surely the voice isn't straight. An ironic note is clearly sounded by phrases like 'the musket and the law' and 'the

mice and spiders meet there'; and at the end this modulates into
Baxter's comically vexed admission that all he's good for in
Jerusalem is to be served up for dinner, like the stew-pot mission-
aries in the old cartoons, food for the flesh, not the spirit. But besides
smiling at his own Jesus-pretensions, he is also reminding us that the
eucharistic symbolism itself has 'primitive' roots; and this in turn
complicates the reference to 'the bush demon' – of which Baxter
records his *own* fear in other poems. Altogether the voice here has
a deep and complex resonance; to hear only the religious exhibi-
tionist who may have sometimes held forth in real life, is to lose the
poem.

Biography that reduces poems to bits of the author's life, and inter-
textuality that reduces them to bits of other poems, have always been
the two main routes for the evasion of poetry. Of late, and somewhat paradoxically, both have been busier than ever, with the
publishers pouring money into biography at almost the same extra-
vagant rate that the inter-textualists have been shouting 'death to the
author'. Poetry itself of course lies between the two bypasses; it is
the place where the particularity of a life and the generality of the
word come together to make something new – in this case a new
Jerusalem, not just Baxter's but any reader's.

A Day in the Capital

The old man scrutinising the Lowe cartoons on the gallery wall could be a cartoon himself. Tall, thin and stoop-shouldered, with a hooked nose and a sharp grey eye, he looks like a stork in the shallows, poised to strike. The 'belt' holding up his white flannel trousers seems to be a tie – regimental, probably, or collegial – and his linen jacket and straw boater, though well-kept, seem rather worn. A retired army officer perhaps – though, in appearance at least, the reverse of a Colonel Blimp. He would have looked at home in Tonbridge Wells half a century ago.

My perception of him is evidently influenced by the works on display – Lowe's classic anti-fascist cartoons of the nineteen-thirties, with their planes, tanks, and propaganda, and great dictators; all the modern machinery of wars and lies. They seem almost to sum up 'the twentieth century'. And Lowe's own style, stripped down to a few bold strokes, seems quite in keeping.

My historicising impulse was triggered even as we approached the exhibition hall – the New Zealand National Library – by the striking contrast between its modernist walls, with their serried concrete wedges, and the old parliament buildings across the road, with their newly restored Victorian-classical marble pillars. We – I'm with a friend whose current occupation is literary biography – have just failed to penetrate the latter. A trail of builder's ramps and walkways, led us to a side entrance with plate-glass sliding doors, where we were accosted by a security guard. He agreed affably with my observation that the building had been 'officially opened' (by the Queen, no less – I saw it on TV), but it wasn't, he added, yet open to 'the public'. A smooth young man, but beneath the PR veneer, his blue eyes gleamed with the perennial steel of authority. And in fact, despite the difference of period-style, both library and parliament buildings are clearly meant to express the power of the capital.

The stork has now fixed his gaze on a cartoon depicting a giant fist and forearm. In the shelter of the forearm stands a diminutive Neville Chamberlain evidently stiffening at last into some resistance; at the end of the fist, recoiling in alarm, are the pygmy figures of Hitler and Mussolini. Emblazoned in capitals along the arm are the words WE SHALL FIGHT. Provoked beyond endurance, we are to infer, the people have spoken, and the puny politicians had better listen.

The image still has an impact. It expresses the idea with a fine economy, and the idea itself remains valid. 'The people' at the time, admittedly, seem to have been largely indifferent – or even sympathetic – to the great dictators, but when the popular will to resist really is aroused, it must evidently be heeded. The cartoon, however, can't really stand without the history. That Hitler is a frightened bully, for instance, isn't fully conveyed by his face and posture. Lowe's Stalin, curiously enough, is usually a more free-standing image; even to someone who knew nothing of the man it would convey a vivid idea of jovial cruelty and cunning.

I walk back to consult Lowe's potted biography on the wall in the foyer, leaving the stork – who himself may well have fought in the Western Desert or in Crete – looking more like a cartoon than ever, as he stands eye-balling a life-sized caricature of the Duke of Edinburgh. Lowe was born, I discover, in 1891, and this further quickens my historical sense. We've come to Wellington in fact to look at Katherine Mansfield's birth-place – the Lowe exhibition just happens to be on. Mansfield was born only three years before the cartoonist, but, dying as she did in 1922, she seems of another age – seems almost to have missed 'the twentieth century' altogether.

Her birth-place is just round the corner from the National Library. A cream-painted two-storey weatherboard villa, with green doors and window-frames, it looks across a lawn bordered with agapanthus, lavender, and roses, onto a busy city street. It's a solid middle-class structure built by her father, an energetic businessman who eventually became Governor of the Bank of New Zealand – and gave his daughter a quite liberal allowance. 'Solid' of course is relative. Weatherboard isn't meant to weather. You keep it painted, replacing the occasional rotten board, and the house seems eternally to have been built last week. When you first see Wellington's painted wooden houses on the bright windy hills above the harbour, you feel that a real gale might blow the whole project into the sea. But of course you can grow to like its lightness more than Europe's accumulated weight of brick and stone.

Mansfield herself, it seems, was born in the night, with the house shrieking and groaning in a storm from the Antarctic. I like to link this with her streak of recklessness, and as I pay my fee to the brisk Scotswoman in the entrance-hall, I'm pleased to see the Mansfield tee-shirts on display, emblazoned with with her slogan 'Risk

Everything'. After this the downstairs rooms are a little disappointing; no sense of freedom here, just Victorian domestic clutter – too much furniture and bric-a-brac, too little space and light.

The house in her story 'The Garden Party', though said to be based on one like this, has no such feeling. In fact the story has no 'clutter' of particularity at all. My biographer-friend, a New Zealander who did his MA in London, tells me that his fellow-students there had so little sense of the locale of Mansfield's New Zealand stories that they were simply unaware of the antipodean provenance. They were being a bit imperceptive, evidently, but less so, I think, than the post-colonial critics currently scouring Mansfield's work for historic premonitions of a 'New Zealand identity'.

One of these 'new' historicists quotes a remark by Coleridge that Mansfield copied into her Journal: 'I, for one, do not call the sod under my feet my country. But language, religion, laws, government, blood-identity in these makes men of one country.' Having copied it, Mansfield adds laconically, 'The sod under my feet makes mine.' This seems admirably clear and suitably down-to-earth, but the post-colonial critic finds it 'hard to understand what idea of country or nation or indeed sod Mansfield could have had in mind when she wrote that entry.' The doubt about 'sod' might sound vaguely jocular, but it refers simply to the fact that Mansfield had been away from New Zealand for some years and was on French soil at the time of writing.

Having thus declared her mystification, the critic feels free to claim that Mansfield meant the reverse of what she said, and was really agreeing with Coleridge. The 'New Zealand' of the stories, we are told, is really a political and historical construct, a celebration in fact of the 'new liberalism' of the 1890s, a liberalism with serious flaws, admittedly – especially with regard to women and the Maori – but an advance at least on class-ridden old England. Nothing like this idea actually appears in the stories, to be sure, but the critic surmounts this obstacle by arguing that it's implicit in the 'gaps'. This rests in turn on the assumptions that Mansfield was a modernist and that gaps are a primary feature of modernist art. What is one to make of all this?

I mount the staircase, a broad, open structure that seems meant for a bigger house, and discover that the upper floor, less furnished and better lit, is altogether more attractive. Mansfield was born in a small back-bedroom. Through its window now comes the muffled roar of a six-lane motorway, a great canyon through the city; beyond it are warehouses, the railway, the docks, and the sea enclosed by rugged green hills. The hazy glimmer on the far shore is Day's Bay, the setting for one of Mansfield's best-known New Zealand stories, 'At The Bay'.

In its opening pages Stanley Burnell – chief vehicle for the alleged new liberal spirit – dashes across the beach for his morning swim, over 'the big porous stones, over the cold, wet pebbles, on to the hard sand that gleamed like oil'; and later, his swim finished, he wades back through the shallows, 'pressing his toes into the firm, wrinkled sand'.

It's easy to see why students in London failed to notice the antipodean locale. This is any sand, under any feet, universal because immediate; the metaphor makes you feel the 'wrinkles' pressing into his-your toes. Here surely is Mansfield's 'sod beneath my feet'. She's advancing the artist's traditional claim to citizenship in a human world of sense and feeling that transcends nationality.

In the stories of course this world is a linguistic creation. Just before Stanley's early morning swim, a flock of sheep appears at the edge of the sea-side village; 'they were huddled together, a small tossing woolly mass, and their thin stick-like legs trotted along quickly as if the cold and the quiet had frightened them.' In 'little pattering rushes', they pass through the sleeping settlement, then 'pushing, nudging, hurrying, they rounded the bend and the shepherd followed after out of sight'.

'Pushing, nudging, hurrying'; the verbs are clearly differentiated from each other, and from what they would mean if this were a crowd of people. What Saussure called 'difference' is clearly at work. But of course that's only half the story. To say that 'nudge' *isn't* push, or shove, or knock, or squeeze, and so on *ad infinitum*, will never tell us what it positively means; the reader is also checking the words against the developing 'image'. Exactly how the mind processes its stored clusters of words and sense-perceptions remains completely mysterious of course, but when words are used as Mansfield uses them, two things are evidently happening; we say, 'Yes, that's what sheep look like', and 'Yes, that's what these words mean'. She purifies the language of the tribe.

Saussure himself tried to exclude 'what sheep look like' from the account because it was too messy for his 'scientific' theory of meaning, but his literary followers have been more political than scientific. Suggest to them that the interaction of word and perception in 'pushing, nudging, hurrying' creates a vivid image of sheep moving about, and they'll tell you it's an illusion created by the ruling class – for some purpose that a 'new' historicist might bring to light.

Artists themselves of course tend to regard the friction between word and perception, between medium and experience, as the chief source of their creative pleasure and pain. In Mansfield's case the pleasure has a late nineteenth-century feel. She found life exciting in itself, but even more so as the raw material of her art – which can accordingly become somewhat overwrought: 'The breeze of morning lifted in the bush and the smell of leaves and wet black earth mingled with the sharp smell of the sea. Myriads of birds were singing. A goldfinch flew over the shepherd's head and, perching on the tiptop of a spray, it turned to the sun ruffling its small breast feathers.'

In a pioneer society like that of Mansfield's childhood of course the general tendency is rather towards the underwrought. Just up the road from her birthplace is a steep and thickly wooded cemetery, with crumbling statuary amongst the great gnarled trees. The grave-stones, many of them dating from around the time of Mansfield's birth, now look their age, as grave-stones should. And the elegiac effect of a material richly worked by human hands and deeply marked by the march of time is peculiarly striking here because it's so exceptional. This is still largely a weatherboard world, and since weatherboard doesn't weather, the only way to enrich it is to add a little fretwork; Mansfield's house, as it happens, has none, and though well-proportioned enough, looks rather bare and box-like.

So all in all, the occasional bit of fretwork in her style might seem forgivable. But it has been long felt as an embarrassment. In the half-century after her death of course literary fret-work, along with 'illusionism' and 'sentiment', was seen as a symptom of the reduction of art to bourgeois entertainment. And one can indeed understand why the mere thought of, say, a theatre-full of well-fed Europeans complacently laughing and crying over reflections of themselves in the mirror of 'realism', sent people like Walter Benjamin into paroxysms of disgust; though with the benefit of hindsight one may also feel that if he had seen plays purged of all fret-work, illusion, and sentiment – as during the Chinese Cultural Revolution – and audiences applauding merely through political fear or ambition, he might well have been less impatient with the 'bourgeoisie'.

In due course the contempt for fret-work reached New Zealand, and it seemed to the critics that the best defence of Mansfield was to play down her 'Dickensian' modes and play up her 'modernism', her 'fragmentariness'. We were told, for instance, that her 'new method' of telling a story, of which she herself spoke so excitedly, was an abandonment of 'plot'. Unfortunately 'Je ne Parle pas Français' – the story in which she says the method first came to her – has even more plot than usual; but never mind, said the critics, though more abundant, the plot is essentially irrelevant.

Bill Manhire, the Wellington poet, has written an elegantly engaging post-modern narrative called *The Brain of Katherine Mansfield*. I'll be seeing him later in the morning. I must ask him what he thinks about her 'modernism'.

But a crowd of schoolgirls have just come milling up the stairs to the natal bedroom. They stand chattering and pointing out landmarks through the window, evidently more excited just to be out of school than to be in the birthplace of a genius. But there's the usual exception – a tall, pale girl with heavy fair hair; her dark blue eyes are drinking in the room's every detail. I wonder what she's thinking? That she too might one day become a writer, run off to Europe, and have love affairs with artists? In a year or so she'll be at university, I suppose, learning how to excavate politically incorrect sub-texts.

The biggest upstairs room has a display of photographs – events and people from Mansfield's life, with quotations appended from her works. I stop in front of a section featuring D.H. Lawrence and Frieda. I've seen the pictures before, in various Lawrence biographies, but the quotations from Mansfield are mostly new to me. I peer at the photo of her and Middleton-Murry after their wedding, standing outside the registry office with the Lawrences. In their dark, stuffy, European clothes, in the dark, stuffy, London street, all four of them seem so embedded in their era. Photography, with its undiscriminating eye for detail, has evidently played a great part in the modern hypertrophy of the 'historical sense'.

I look out of the window. The street below, with its wooden houses, rests so much more lightly on the earth than London's great urban accretions. I think of Lawrence here in Wellington in 1921, perhaps in that identical suit, sending Katherine Mansfield a postcard, before travelling on to the deserts of New Mexico to meet the thoroughly modern Mabel Dodge and the earth-ancient American Indians. I turn again to the photo, and read the quotation beneath: Lawrence, says Mansfield, once proposed that he and she should swear an oath of eternal friendship. I knew of Lawrence's enthusiasm for the idea in general, but not of this particular instance. Mansfield evidently declined. It was not until years later, she says, that she realised what an important proposal it was. Her words, so unexpected and so patently sincere, jolt them both out of their historical frame; in their human need and failure they seem suddenly very near.

So is our time for meeting Bill Manhire; but so too is his house, and we soon find ourselves looking down onto its irregular cluster of roofs from a green wicket-gate in a quiet cul-de-sac above the cable-car's top terminus. The hill-side below is scattered with other houses, half-hidden amongst the trees; above the green shoulders of the hills the light is silvery through the cloud-cover; the day is turning warm and humid. A crooked flight of steps takes us down to an open side-door that looks into a hallway and corridor, with other doors all ajar, some leading to other rooms, one showing the garden at the other side. They make the house look somehow both open and private. It seems deserted too, but the poet – we have both met him before, though only casually – soon appears in response to our knock. He takes us into a sitting room, then goes off to make coffee. With its paintings, pottery, and books the room feels full of good taste, but again there is no sense of being shut in; the air is pleasantly cool, and through the windows the silvery light seems always to reflect the invisible sea.

The poet comes back with the coffee. He is tall and well-made, 'in the middle way' of his life, but looking younger; his grey-blue eyes are cool without being cold. His manner is oddly like his house – open yet private.

The talk soon turns to Katherine Mansfield, and when I ask him about his book, he says that he wrote it in London, that it's really all about his New Zealand childhood, and that in these respects at least it's like some of Mansfield's own stories.

Listening, I'm struck by the curious fancy, perhaps triggered by a sense of the world's-end seas beyond the hills, that he could be a Roman on the margins of the later Empire; cultured, sensitive, urbane, from a family settled here for generations, yet still with a thought for Rome, and with a sense now of an Empire ended. An odd fancy indeed in many ways. This ex-colony is independent and thriving, and there are no barbarians at the gates, only Japanese businessmen, wealthy and polite, or Chinese migrants, industrious and thrifty – and of course the Maori, the 'people of the land', seeking redress for old colonial wrongs not on the battlefield but in the law-courts. But though un-stormed, the gates are being knocked at quite insistently, and many 'European New Zealanders', even those little given to such thoughts, have lately felt more need to clarify their own 'identity'. In this exercise in cultural self-definition, sport still looms inordinately large, the fine scenery is much spoken of, and the arts are occasionally mentioned. Bill Manhire – witty, sceptical and ironic – is essentially in the line of T.S. Eliot, who of course is never mentioned at all. Does this matter?

In Manhire's poem 'An Outline' a couple look back on their life together:

> At home, away from home, but mostly
> nowhere special, we took our own advice.
> We got in the car and then just drove
> along the road past cliffs and river,
> and when we stopped
> we slept on the parchment floor,
> taking it for the real thing.

Their youthful trust – in themselves ('we took our own advice') and in life (they 'just drove') – has apparently given way to scepticism. Looking back, they see their lives as casual and illusory, made out of words. 'We are such stuff as dreams are made on…' Of their early trust in life they say,

> and then again there was always something
> coming next, though no particular direction.
> The baby lay in its cot and cooed
> or it lay afloat in water inside mother.

The casual reversal of the natural temporal order – the child lying first in its cot and then in its mother's womb – may prompt a deep thought about the uncertainties of memory and time; but even at its best a Prospero-wisdom seems rather one-sided – it needs 'O brave new world' to balance it – and the couple here seem to indulge it almost mechanically. Perhaps they've been hypnotised, like so many of their generation, by Heisenberg's uncertain particles and Saussure's arbitrary signs. Their anxiety, and their fear that any movement must be in 'no particular direction', is subtly and movingly conveyed, but the poem itself, suggesting no alternative, seems to share the fear.

Movement 'in no particular direction' is the most striking feature of *The Brain of Katherine Mansfield*. A game-style narrative, written with all the economy and verve one would expect of a poet, it proceeds in any number of directions, dictated by the reader's choice. At the beginning you meet an old man who says he's reading the unfinished book of your life, and wants to know how it will continue: 'If you decide to accompany him, go to 5. If you decide to go home and think it over, go to 11.' And so on. There are various conclusions and it's possible to arrive at one very quickly. At her first reading my younger daughter was dead from cyanide poisoning within a few real-time minutes.

The reader's decisions – like the opening choice between boldness and timidity – have often a moral cast, and the narrative has a clear pattern; the structure of each chapter is that of the moral tale – a choice followed by reward or punishment. But early on we must also choose one of three magic objects to help us on our way; this choice is purely arbitrary, and it determines the outcome at a number of later points, so any final conclusion is really a matter of chance. When I put this to the poet he confirms it, and adds with a smile that where the choice seems moral it's often subverted; courage is sometimes rewarded, timidity punished; sometimes vice-versa.

Such unions of formal symmetry and narrative randomness, as Christopher Nash has well observed, are common in recent 'experimental' fiction. One might also observe that if the experimenters actually lived by the same model, paying punctilious regard to formality but making life-decisions at random, they would soon find themselves arriving at conclusions of all too predictable kinds – incarceration, disease, or death, for example.

But of course they don't in fact live like that, and the discrepancy between theory and behaviour can smack of hypocrisy; we all know the professor whose radical scepticism about narrative is matched by a relentless cause-and-effect realism about career. Bill Manhire – no academic time-server but a fine poet and scholar – is subject to a more subtle tension. Even in this casual conversation, his words have the weight and edge that come from the poet's habit of pressing them hard against experience. But you feel their irony too – not just particular ironies, but an ironic habit.

Which brings us back to the line of Eliot. Donne's ironies, as Eliot remarked, imply that whatever he says might be said in another way. They're 'particular' ironies, I'd add, when specific other ways are made clear. When there's merely a suggestion that some other way is possible, the irony is habit, felt by the reader as an endemic cautiousness or hesitancy.

'The best lack all conviction...' – while those knocking at the gates have a certain passionate intensity about their own life-stories; 'a struggle to make a new life', in the case of the migrants; 'a fight to get back some of the life they have lost', in the case of the Maori. And their passion, so far from making them 'the worst', is surely admirable. But it sometimes makes their stories rather crude and sentimental. A country's official literati, one might think, are paid (by the government mostly, in one way or another) to raise the narrative level, not undermine belief in stories altogether. As Manhire sits sipping his coffee, there's a curious contrast between the cultivated diffidence of his manner and the muscular power of his forearms. It would be interesting to see him trying more muscular ironies, something more Swiftian, to clear away the neo-Saussurean morass rather than sink deeper into it.

The old modernists, I think, told better stories. The opening of *The Waste Land*, for instance, is a poignant tale about the narrator and Marie. Graham Hough once noticed this, but he left the insight undeveloped; a pity, for the whole poem is made up not of 'fragments', as is commonly said, but of narratives; some of them, like 'What the Thunder Said', are quite extensive; some, like the encounter with Mr Eugenides, very brief:

> Unreal city
> Under the brown fog of a winter noon
> Mr Eugenides, the Smyrna merchant
> Unshaven, with a pocket full of currants
> C.i.f. London: documents at sight,
> Asked me in demotic French
> To luncheon at the Cannon Street Hotel
> Followed by a weekend at the Metropole.

This combines two common sorts of story – 'the shabby vulgarian turns out to be well off', and 'the friendly overture turns out to be a sexual proposition'. But the cool irony of the narrator's voice, neither shocked nor indignant, gives us pause. Has his complex sexuality (he becomes Tiresias in the next episode, of course) been intuited by a man from a culture more at ease with it? Do the old gods still wander the world disguised as merchants, seeking out new prophet-poets? And is the narrator implying that – *autres temps, autres moeurs* – he might have accepted?

The resolution of the uncertainty is of course as clear as it's abrupt; we can see the narrator's ironic eyebrow raised at the very thought of such a 'weekend'. This is how the stories are resolved throughout the poem – with a gesture, and an inflection. The narrative style is elliptical and intimate. And it's in these movements of each episode that the poem's subtler unities are to be found, not in its overall theme – which, as Eliot frankly confessed, is rather loose.

Mansfield's 'At the Bay' is episodic in a similar way, each episode rising to a climax: Stanley departs for work in a temper over his lost walking-stick, and the women in the house are blissfully relieved; the

little boy at the beach shows the girls 'a nemeral' – a bit of green
bottle-glass – 'as big as a star and far more beautiful'; the love-starved
Beryl sees Mrs Kember's face as 'a horrible caricature' of Mr Kember;
Stanley's wife Linda, her maternal feelings long frozen by fear of
more child-bearing, has a sudden impulse of love for her baby boy;
and so on. There's an overall theme of course – of women and men
(and boys and girls) and the queasy pain of loving and being loved
– but it's in the smaller narrative rhythms that Mansfield's emotional
and imaginative power reveals itself.

Will the tall pale girl in the Mansfield house lose sight of all this,
and become one of those students who spend their days 'turning the
analysis of literature into a mode of cultural critique' (as the new
historicists put it), and their nights feeding their starved imaginations
on Mills and Boon? She might find it hard to resist. 'Cultural criticism' seems to have become *de rigueur* here in Wellington. Even the
mayor, a hearty, energetic woman, who looks like a hockey centre-
back, has embraced the cause of art as revolutionary agent. The
occasion was her recent defence of a local exhibition of Robert
Mapplethorpe's photographs. We're going to look at them after
lunch in fact; an essay about the photographer in the *New York
Review* has whetted my curiosity.

Over lunch, to confess the truth, I feel some resentment at
contributing my mite towards such a gross *succès de scandale*. The
café has fresh pizza, good coffee, and a panoramic view. Blue chasms
have opened between the luminous clouds, the city looks brighter
and newer than ever, and the sea is a magic carpet, one moment a
ruffled grey, the next a shifting pattern of brilliant blues and greens.
To leave all this for Mapplethorpe's world of sado-masochistic
homosexuality in pre-AIDS New York seems itself an act of
masochism. But at length we make our way to the town square, with
its citizens basking in the sunshine, and its staid, civic art gallery, a
cool cultural hall, with cool cultured ladies in floral dresses selling
tickets – which entitle us, for instance, to a rear view of a naked man
on all fours, leering, or snarling, over his shoulder at the camera,
while thrusting a bull-whip handle up his own anus.

One argument in defence of the exhibition is that in such a setting
such photographs cease to be 'dirty'. This has provoked some indignant mirth from the Christian Heritage Party, but is less simply
snobbish than might appear. Installed in a gallery, Duchamps'
legendary toilet-bowl became, albeit at a humble level, an art-work
– an object of the detached attentiveness that Coleridge, to adduce
a safe witness, saw as one of the two poles of aesthetic experience.

Duchamps, you might say, put the lavatory into the gallery, and
Mapplethorpe has taken pornography out of the lavatory.

But what of Coleridge's other pole – our emotional involvement,
paradoxically united with our detachment? The photographs in fact
seem devoid of feeling. 'Ice-cold' is the word used by the New York
reviewer; 'an ocular and cerebral vision of sex', he calls them, like
the pornography Mapplethorpe apparently enjoyed as a teenager.
The reviewer, although a Mapplethorpe admirer, then describes not
only the photographer's sexual 'shortcomings' (the reviewer's word),
but also his desire to shock the audience into condemnation.
Mapplethorpe, he suggests, would have been delighted – had he lived
long enough to see it – by the moral outrage of Senator Jesse Helms.
'Do it for Satan,' the wicked photographer was apparently wont to
say (apostate Catholic that he was), when urging his friends on to
deeper naughtiness. To be crucified for evil was evidently his Satanist
idea of apotheosis; he needed the Helmsian response. The reviewer's
cool view of him not as a fiend incarnate but as a man with sexual
'shortcomings' in fact subverts the bid for Satanic martyrdom.

A number of lessons could be drawn from all this. The one most
pertinent to 'theory' is an old one: art designed to manipulate the
audience, whether to flatter or to shock, has a limited shelf-life. The
artist's job, as they used to say in pre-Saussurean times, is rather to
keep his eye on the object. And implicitly the reviewer acknowledges
this. He notes for instance that of all Mapplethorpe's pictures, only
those of Patti Smith – 'punk priestess' and long-time friend of the
photographer – record a real awareness of another human being.
And this judgement is clearly sound – though one might want to add
some photos of the human penis, an object Mapplethorpe evidently
found no difficulty keeping his eye on. Even here, admittedly, he can
get carried away by desperate ideas, subjecting the unlucky member
to some painful-looking operations, and he gives, it seems to me, an
exaggerated impression of its size; but he can also convey its real
complexity – warm, vulnerable, and user-friendly, 'at times almost
ridiculous' (and frequently obtuse), but unpredictable too, and
dangerous. The shock he gives you here is at the level of experience.

But as a rule we get only the shocking idea. We see for instance a
man urinating into the mouth of a man kneeling in front of him. In
itself this might be an act of degradation, or an impulse of strange
love, or a literally in-your-face joke on the public; but it's impossible
to say which; the picture tells us nothing of the thoughts and feelings of the protagonists. It isn't pornography – the only desire it
seems remotely likely to arouse is to rinse out one's mouth. The

curious human act is simply a human void. In the bull-whip picture the man's face has more expression, but whether leer or snarl, all it clearly conveys is indeed the in-your-face (or up-your-anus) motive, which the reviewer so acutely analyses.

But unfortunately he sees the 'shortcomings' of both the artist and the art not only as the same, but also as inevitable. In the story of Mapplethorpe's life, as the reviewer tells it, there's no sense of choice or struggle. Given his genes and his social background, we are meant to feel, his life and work were simply what they had to be. He was born to shock and his art is shocking.

There is of course a long tradition – perhaps as old as art itself – of self-destructing shock-artists like Mapplethorpe. Figures as diverse as Lord Rochester and Sid Vicious spring readily to mind. The latter appears in pop-music commentator Nick Kent's *The Dark Stuff* as 'the exploding moron'; his suicidal deviance was evidently both encouraged and despised by some who watched him throw himself over the edge. Our reviewer's fatalistic 'tolerance' of Mapplethorpe isn't as dark as that of course, but it still strikes a patronising note. As words like 'ice-cold' indicate, he claims to enter fully into Mapplethorpe's world; he feels it and estimates its quality, as anyone must who sets up as a critic; yet he assumes that Mapplethorpe himself is incurably one-eyed.

This sort of contradiction is built-into neo-Saussurean thought. The 'theorists' tell us we're all locked into the sign-world of our particular culture, but in practice this is simply ignored. Translation of neo-Saussurean texts themselves, for instance, is a flourishing industry, and its success bears out its assumption that signs in different languages share a common reference to things in the world. Even Umberto Eco, having been much translated, has been driven to notice it. But, as translators have always been the first to acknowledge, an absolute fidelity of translation, a pure semantic identity, is clearly impossible, and the neo-Saussurean remnant still try to cover their nakedness – from themselves at least – with this absolutist rag.

The guide has now reached Mapplethorpe's photographic studies of flowers. They're extravagantly sexy flowers of course, and in a distinctly human style – all sinuous curve, dewy orifice, and thrusting stamen. I can't hear what the guide is saying, but the movements of her pointer suggest a continuing discourse on form. Her group don't look remotely like aesthetes. They give a general impression of being dumpy, drab, and middle-aged – you have to be eighteen to get into the exhibition at all. I think of the schoolgirls at Mansfield's house;

a rather different 'interpretive community'; if they could get in I suppose they'd giggle.

'Variant reader-response' has been the theme of a recent analysis of one of Mansfield's own stories – 'Bliss'. The heroine's intensities are seen first as a Freudian hysteria, and then as a female mode of creativity; then a third reading claims that the first two are 'deconstructed' by the text itself. The essayist evidently regards all three readings as acceptable, and adds that there will be others; the critical task is to understand their implications.

I.A. Richards once proposed a similar programme, but as a study of the pathology of reading; and in the end the Mansfield essayist, though inadvertently, takes the same view. Herself a very sensitive reader, she supports all three readings with subtle insights, and thus implicitly acknowledges that they must be brought together if we are to do the story justice. Her 'pluralist' tolerance thus patronises the one-eyed reader, just as the Mapplethorpe reviewer patronises the one-eyed artist; and they both do it at the expense of the art itself.

At the expense of the good reader too. To hide your brains for fear of frightening the unintelligent has been the traditional fate of clever women. It would be ironic if 'pluralism' drove the tall pale girl into the hypocrisy of pretending that her readings are no better than those of any chatterer at the window; or even worse into the belief that all texts and interpretations are after all simply word-games played for political ends – which may turn to commercial ends when you graduate from writing deconstructive essays and take a job in, say, 'public relations'.

My flight of fancy about Bill Manhire in an imperial twilight returns suddenly as a Lowe cartoon, of some far-flung Roman bathhouse asprawl with aesthete-hedonists and bloated politicians. They are listening languidly – their belief in any words at all destroyed by a century of wars and lies – to a be-laurelled bard whose own struggle to 'purify the language of the tribe' is slowly dissolving in irony. An exaggerated picture, yes, but with truth enough for a cartoon. Only the *fin-de-siècle* note is really false; wars and lies are a human constant – as are pedants who think that all words are as empty as their own. The constant task for criticism of course is stop pedantry from getting out of hand.

By now the gallery guide is confronting Mapplethorpe's dark stuff. Her pointer is tracing the curves of a plump penis garrotted by criss-cross wires – like a sausage-maker's nightmare. She's discoursing on the tension between the beautiful form and the shocking content. Her flock look doubtful; and they have my sympathy. The wires are no doubt nicely arranged, but this doesn't even begin to offset my own reaction to the poor penis; I simply feel weak at the groin. I should address myself here and now to the critic's task, and harangue them all about art and reality. But they'd just suspect me of being 'a Christian'. In any case it's time for us to start our journey back, before the roads are jammed with homeward-bound commuters. And – of course – I really haven't the nerve to cause such a stir in a temple of culture.

On the motorway, still thinking about historicism, I find myself telling the biographer about a professor, now deceased, who played a large part in shaping English studies in New Zealand. In his old age, he used fondly to recall his school-days back in Britain, when *The Waste Land* had just appeared, and other literary suns were rising – Pound and Joyce, not to mention Mansfield herself; ah, bliss was it in that dawn... It was all humbug of course. So far from being in the eager van, the old hypocrite had always trailed in the dusty rear, muttering darkly about the new-fangled notions of the leaders.

The whole idea of historic dawns and sun-sets seems to generate falsity of one sort or another. Modernist poetry may have moved, as Eliot said it should, to the rhythm of the internal combustion engine, and this was indeed a new sound on the face of the earth, but in both its mechanic and poetic guises, the engine was still propelling human nature on its eternal pursuits – of pleasure and plunder, love and war.

Human nature? Well, even Barthes in his heyday couldn't really deny its existence. He simply dismissed it as insignificant. What mattered, he cried, was not the universal fact of childbirth – to take an obvious instance – but whether the child was being born into a just (ie. Marxist) society. Even discounting the Marxism this was simply inane. Justice matters intensely, of course, but so does child-birth, to the mother – even, or perhaps especially, if the child dies of malnutrition.

But having been brushed aside for so long, 'human nature' now gets simply forgotten. How is it – the new historicists solemnly enquire – that the 'social energy' of a given historic moment can be 'textually structured' in such a way as to be available for 'refash-ioning' in terms of the 'social energy' of the reader's own historic moment? Are these devious locutions, one might enquire in turn, expressly contrived to avoid admitting that the answer is something as obvious as the continuities 'human nature'?

As we come off the motorway and into Porirua, a sea-side town with a conspicuous Polynesian population, I'm reminded of the controversy about the death of Captain Cook, currently raging amongst the anthropologists. The islanders killed him, so the structuralists claim, because they could see him only in terms of their own mythology, as a god. But this, the post-colonialists reply, is just another white-man's insult; the homicidal impulse was simply 'human' and 'pragmatic', and obviously sparked by Cook's own propensity to violence.

Given the current neglect of 'human nature', my own sympathies here are with the post-colonialists, but the truth of course must lie between the two sides. A story-teller would see it immediately – a volatile mix of universally human and culturally specific motives, proportioned variously in various individuals, and ignited in the end perhaps by some chance event. Of course the story-teller wouldn't get it all right – nobody ever will – but he'd surely be less wrong than the anthropologists, who in the cause of either 'social science' or 'political correctness', simply omit one half or the other of the essential ingredients.

I remember last year's Waitangi Day – the annual celebration of the 1840 Treaty of Waitangi as an instrument of New Zealand's national unity. Of late, with burgeoning land-claims and talk of 'Maori sovereignty', the Treaty's guarantees of Maori rights and possessions have turned rather into an instrument of division, but last year the dignitaries all lined up as usual, to face the usual ritual Maori challenge – always a dramatic display as a half-naked warrior advances, shaking his spear, contorting his features, and stampinging his feet. Then at the climax, confronting the Governor-General, the challenger – not at all as usual – spat, and pandemonium ensued.

Waiving the rights and wrongs of the gross breach of protocol, what struck me most was that the whole scene – the threatening figure, crouched like some great spider, malevolent and poisonous, in front of the gowned ladies and besuited gentlemen – brought out so vividly the significance of the challenge. A deterrent display, it shows the human face of war for what it is. No tight-lipped John Waynean calm. 'If you're thinking of a fight,' it seems to say, 'remember that this is what it's like.'

Modern images of warriors – especially 'our own' of course – don't as a rule display a face twisted with hate and rage, but rather an eye intent on a glowing screen and a finger pressing a button. And this muting of bodily reality, as many have remarked, seems to pervade technologised life. I find it there in Barthes on childbirth, and in the rest of the neo-Saussurean academicians, droning their windy abstractions high and oblivious over humble, often repellent, human nature.

Cook's crew, the reverse of the structural anthropologists, tended to see human nature and nothing else. When they first encountered the ritual challenge, they realised at once its warlike content, but failed to recognise its ritual form, and promptly shot the luckless challenger dead.

I have a daughter who learned the challenge while studying not anthropology but dance. She was a student at the polytechnic here in Porirua, as it happens, where the performance arts have a strong Polynesian base. I remember vividly all the winter evenings my wife and I drove down to their fund-raising concerts. No trace of south-sea paradise; only wind and rain in the deserted fluorescent streets. Inside the hall the audience would be mostly Polynesian: the adults, in baggy old overcoats and jerseys, huddled together on makeshift seating; the children sprawled or cross-legged in front of the dance floor.

The dancers, bright-eyed and bare-limbed, hips swaying and feet beating to the drums, seem to be of another world. And in a sense they are – a showbiz world of lime-light and grease-paint. The children at the front are starry-eyed with its glamour. But the dancing is still communal too. Always, as the evening progresses, some formidably-proportioned matron will emerge from the audience in the shadows, her body swaying to the music, and slowly advance across the floor, half-rapt, half-laughing, towards some young male dancer; and then, to whoops and cheers from the audience, she sticks a ten-dollar bill on his glistening chest. Fund-raising at its most fundamental. The atmosphere reminds me sometimes of the old working men's clubs on Saturday nights in the north of England – half music-hall, half ritual.

The money pays the dancers' fares to international festivals. It's all culturally very makeshift, and I have no 'master narrative' to tell me what it might portend. But traditional rules are still at work; and the school insists on some of them. About dancing well, for instance. I wouldn't claim – though the students occasionally do – that they drive themselves as hard as the Ballet Russe, but at the end of the course they're starting at least to move like dancers. When they perform, they share with the audience some of the pleasure in creative excellence that is the essence of art. And something more. The school's working motto is 'where there's art, there's self-respect' (the latter is in short supply amongst young Polynesians). Of course you'll find here too all the human failings endemic to artistic communities – affectation, envy, rampant egotism. Enough to make a pure-minded Walter Benjamin shudder. But the school remains for all that a model of the mutually sustaining relations between society and the arts.

In the Mapplethorpian world of academics busily 'critiquing' (how can they abuse words so?) both art and society, judgements of value of course are seen as merely political; 'good' means simply 'flouting social conventions' – a definition recently enshrined, at this end of the world, in a report on English studies commissioned by the Australian Vice Chancellors' Committee. A neo-Saussurean here in Porirua wouldn't ask whether a dance was performed well but how it 'gendered the body'. Of course such questions aren't without a point. And in fact the male students at the dance-school, especially after a war-dance, are wont to clown around in bras made out of coconut shells. But when the questions asked of it are only political, art quickly dies – as it did during China's Cultural Revolution, where pleasure and self-respect died along with it too. 'Cultural criticism' goes about its business of aestheticide more discreetly of course, but it's no less lethal.

As we drive through the town I think for a moment of calling in at the school to say hello. But my daughter and most of her friends have moved on, to the uncertain life of the arts – a prospect that sometimes makes her a little nervous (though not as nervous as it makes me on her behalf; I still sometimes think I should be urging her to walk down cemetery road with some old toad of a steady job).

When we emerge again onto the motorway, the thought of the uncertain future makes me feel for a moment like Baudrillard in America. Driving the long desert roads, it seemed to him that 'movement through space' was becoming 'absorption by space', like a jet engine 'creating a vacuum in front of it that sucks it forward'. And so he drove on, in 'an irreversible advance into the desert of time', his consciousness strung out between past and future, in existential *angst* or ecstasy.

But he was really being sucked – or suckered – forward by his own engine of historicist abstraction, fuelled by a potent mix of free-market frenzy and post-marxist gloom. Time, so far from being a 'desert', only exists through organism. No eternal abstract tick-tock, but the movement of the earth, the unfurling of a leaf, the weathering of a face with the years; body-time. The tick-tock, as so many eminent thinkers have so often said, is a useful idea, but deadly if you mistake it for a reality.

Of course the idea of unfolding body-time, where history is

growth and decay, death and rebirth, has its own limitations. It can make life feel enclosed and repetitive, an oppressive cycle of mere matter. Beyond Porirua, the road climbs up and round a hill, then suddenly drops again, to run for a few miles beside a rocky shoreline. As we come down the hill, the sea is shining in the late afternoon sun, with dim promontories and islands in the west, like a dream. A release for the earth-bound spirit into a place of wonder; 'there is a happy land somewhere' – in the 'bright blue yonder'. A universal impulse, evidently, but sharpened for modern westerners by Cartesian dualism and romantic poetry – and further sharpened for some earlier antipodean writers by a sense that 'the happy land' was London, the literary metropolis, far away from heavy agriculture.

The promontories in the west are in fact the northern tip of New Zealand's south island. If you fly from Wellington to Sydney, you pass directly over them, their ridged, ribbed hills stretched out on the opaline sea like great lizards asleep in the sun; through the aircraft-window, the sky darkens to a hard, blue monotone, then fades to a dull haze; down below – as you clear New Zealand – Cape Farewell and the foam-fringed curve of Farewell Spit are like a map come to life, or a view from a space-craft. The magic isn't in the heavens at all, but on the earth. The sod beneath your plane.

Coleridge implicitly rhymes the word with 'clod', dull and senseless. For Mansfield it implicitly rhymes with 'god' – 'the god in the middle', to recall a phrase of D.H. Lawrence's. The god in the sod. When Stanley feels the sand with the soles of his feet, the immediate and the universal come together, and so far from being heavy and commonplace, they renew the world.

Of course Stanley is a social and historical being too. The rude energy with which he runs across the beach – and with which he also runs his business – is that of 'the nineteenth century English middle-class male' let loose on a 'new' country. And Mansfield conveys this with sharp subtlety; she herself of course went back to the 'old country' and consorted with men of a very different kind. But the energy, rude though it is, is 'life' – to use Mansfield's own favourite word. It's in this, and in the art that records it, that her love and pleasure are invested. And it's here that she stands against Coleridge – and, implicitly, with Wordsworth. Unless grounded in this sense of universal life in an immediate place, a 'sense of national identity' soon turns to 'nationalism', a purely social affair, sterile and destructive.

Like dancing, Mansfield's art follows some elementary rules. It puts 'the best words in the best order', for instance. When Stanley presses 'his toes into the firm, wrinkled sand', the word 'wrinkled' gives a visual impression and has a wrinkled sound; and since it usually applies to skin, it also heightens the tactile effect – the soles of the feet on the sand are like skin touching skin. The 'best words' are always like this – 'effective in several ways at once'. The phrase is Empson's basic definition of 'ambiguity', but, as he himself acknowledged, he was simply reviving the old principle of 'propriety' – the principle of *le mot juste* at the highest level, keeping the language sharp-edged for the fashioning of life.

Compared with the political agenda of the 'cultural critics', the attentive reading of 'the best words' may seem an excessively modest or merely escapist practice. But an attentive reader can, for instance, see why a Baudrillard won't do; his theatrical gestures towards the immediate are a mere prelude to mental gyration away from any perceived reality. And to see this isn't a modest achievement at all. Good readers are never a numerous tribe, but they're the salt of the literary earth of course – and if the salt should lose its savour...

The Mapplethorpe and Mansfield essayists haven't lost theirs. They're sensitive critics, but misled by obtuse theories. Were they to read my account, they would evidently have a choice: they might agree with me, or disagree; or (a common strategy) they might disagree out loud and silently modify their position; or they might simply say that we belong to different 'interpretive communities'. That last option may seem a real closing of the mind, but it's usually no more than a refusal to argue in public, and is often a cover for silent modification. Critics inevitably enter each other's worlds, as they enter the worlds of Mapplethorpe or Mansfield, and some kind of exchange almost always takes place. But who knows what it might bring? Such junctures are 'chaotic' and of uncertain outcome. Or at least that's my story.

The 'theorists' of course tell a different tale – and in two variant forms. The first is darkly ironic: the human world is an ineluctable maze of words, which we are doomed forever to wander (for there is no way out), forever duped by the more adroit manoeuvrers. The second version has a heroic twist: the more adroit, it says, are in control of the maze, but there is, after all, an exit, and we can find it if we follow the directions of the hero-theorists.

The ironic and the heroic are evidently important genres. They tell selective tales for specific purposes – to sharpen our wits or raise our self-esteem. But they have their dangers. Sharpness can become mere cynicism, and self-esteem mere self-conceit – as the hero-theorists themselves bear ample witness; they've mistaken, as popular story-tellers often do, the ironic and the heroic for the real. Of course realism itself is also selective, but it's a more complex mode, by turns heroic and ironic, and many other things too; more adapted to life's diversities. We need an urgent injection of realism into our stories about stories.

In Search of My Hero

When the soldiers drinking at the bar ask me where I'm from, I hesitate for a moment. Here in the United States my dual nationality – New Zealand and British – serves as a minor instrument of social research.

'New Zealand,' I reply.

'You don't sound like a New Zealander.' This from someone wearing a sergeant's stripes.

I didn't think backwoods Americans were supposed to know so much about the outside world. I explain that I'm a migrant. The sergeant – lean-faced, with bushy eyebrows and hard brown eyes – laughs drily and launches into an account of a Kiwi (he gives the word an ironic emphasis) who passed through here about a year ago; he stayed long enough, it seems, to take on a fence-building contract, then left just after it was completed – and just before all the fences collapsed. I smile; the story rings half-true perhaps. The lean features sharpen, and their owner progresses, naturally enough, from fencing to sheep – New Zealand's fifty million sheep and its three million human beings. Another dry laugh. I'm surprised again by his knowledge (his figures are accurate enough), but not by his tone; citizens of great powers tend to find small countries amusing simply on principle. I almost wish I'd tested his reaction to 'Britain' instead; being a soldier he might have recalled 'our' Argentinian expedition. Old and *deraciné* as I think I am, I'm still prey to this sort of impulse.

A younger soldier, tall, slim, and square-shouldered, with dark eyes and a sensitive face, asks me what brings me here. He seems a little embarrassed that the sergeant is 'joshing' me, and evidently wants to change the subject. The thought that he might be feeling sorry for me is rather irritating. Exactly how offensive is the lean-faced man being? A common sort of cross-cultural uncertainty. Should I show resentment? I glance at the watching faces along the bar. Perhaps not. I say that I'm visiting an old man who lives up in the hills nearby. When I mention his name someone nods vaguely, and I cease to be an object of interest.

In fact I paid my visit earlier in the afternoon, and was greeted by the 'old man' – custodian of D.H. Lawrence's ranch, now owned by the University of Mew Mexico – with a degree of circumspection. I sensed a history of difficulties with previous Lawrence-seekers; and possible reasons for it were soon in evidence. His rambling wood-panelled living-room was pleasantly over-furnished – with local Indian paintings and carvings, and big old easy chairs – but its dominant image was a life-size black-and-white photograph, pinned to a cupboard door, of John Wayne in full cowboy rig, a shot-gun in his hand and a steely glint in his eye. I think of Lawrence's subtle meditation on violence and the struggle of life, after shooting a porcupine – just out there, it must have been, amongst the trees on the sunny hill-side. Does the custodian regard the 'Duke' of Hollywood as 'Lawrencian man'? He himself has a glint in his grey eye, not to mention a square brow beneath a stiff brush of white hair; and in a surprisingly short time – prompted by my tenderfoot question about the local fauna – he was denouncing President Clinton's attempts at gun-control. But he soon seemed reassured that I presented no threat to his person or prestige. In fact when he asked me where I planned to stay, I thought he might offer me a bed at the ranch. He didn't; he offered instead, as though making a rare gesture, to have dinner with me at my motel, in Questa, and to show me the ranch in the morning – the best time of day.

So here I am, late Saturday afternoon, in the bar next door to the motel, still thinking about 'American individualism' and the assertive will – and about Lawrence's own response to them. It varied of course, from apocalyptic visions of America as a continent of death to light-hearted remarks that 'in the United States it's either shove or be shoved'. I glance at the soldiers chatting and laughing at the bar; they seem human enough. Their totemic hero none the less is probably the same as the old custodian's – the 'lone wolf gunman'. And I could persuade myself that there's a hard dry undertone in the atmosphere – the friction of opposed wills. It might be just the dryness of the desert air, but Lawrence of course regarded place as a psychic power. I suddenly have an image of his face – or some vague composite of various pictures and descriptions – with its rugged features, rough reddish hair and beard, and intensely blue eyes. My own totemic hero, evidently. Is it a logo-centric delusion, a piece of bricolage? Or a 'real idea', Platonic and Polanyian? And why do I come so far to pay it homage?

I finish my beer and walk out into the street – there's only the one, the highway, and only one side of it is built-up; the other is just a straggle of wooden houses, with sparse scrub and pasture rising steeply up to a rocky ridge. The blue air above is beginning to darken as the afternoon wanes. The whole township, it seems to my English eye, could be scraped so easily off the face of the earth without leaving a trace. My New Zealand eye, more accustomed to land-scapes only lightly humanised, sees the one-story weatherboard motel (its signboard announcing, without conscious irony, both 'TV' and 'Vacancy') as ample cover against the approaching night, and not so heavy as to quite shut out the stars.

As I install myself in my 'unit' and enjoy a hot shower, it seems strange that only a few days ago I was pursuing my totem in Cornwall, my English eye enjoying the streets of St Ives, their cobbles and cottages so deeply integral with the bedrock beneath. In the evening I walked along the cliffs at nearby Tregarthen, where Lawrence spent most of the Great War, and where at night he used to call out for the other-world spirits – 'Tuatha De Danaan – come to me'. At dusk I had to cross a field grazed by a herd of black and white heifers, their whitenesses glowing in the twilight. As I drew near, one of them cast a rather absent eye on me, then began to grow restive at this alien presence traversing her field of vision. At length she gave a snort, kicked up her heels, put her head down, and made a sort of skipping run at me. I suppose I ought to have shouted and waved my arms, but knowing nothing of cattle I panicked and ran for the nearest wall. I scrambled over it unscathed – she evidently just wanted to see me off – and she stood there twitching her ears and glaring irritably. As I leaned against the wall to get my breath, her expression seemed so human, so comically easy to read, there was no feeling at all of the bovine 'other', unpredictable, and dangerous; and it was such a pleasant summer evening too, with the lights starting to twinkle in The Tinners Arms across the fields. Indeed Lawrence's own invocations of the other-world strike me as rather would-be; a willed recoil into the Druidical dawn, away from the modern war that was so abhorrent to him.

But when he came to Taos he found no need for conjuration: 'I think New Mexico was the greatest experience from the outside world that I have ever had. It was New Mexico that liberated me from the present era of civilisation, the great era of material and mechanical development. The moment I saw the brilliant, proud morning shine high up over the deserts of Santa Fe, something stood still in my soul and I started to attend.' The spirits here were already waiting for him.

As I walk back now, still warm from my shower, across the gritty asphalt carpark to the motel restaurant, the stars too look proud and brilliant, above the dark bulk of the ridge. The motel seems old, even a little run-down, but the dining-room is bright and spacious – some twenty tables, each laid for four, with linen tablecloths and napkins, sparkling cutlery and glasses. The old custodian – already seated at one of them, and the room's sole occupant – explains that the place is a scheduled meal-stop on the bus-route from Denver to Albuquerque. The Mexican dishes, he adds, are particularly good. I study the menu with interest. I know little of Mexican cooking, but I like 'hot' food, and I'm distinctly hungry. The prospect of a convivial dinner and a glass of wine with an authentic dweller in Lawrence-land beckons invitingly. But at the mention of wine, the old man stiffens. The bar's along the street, he says; the restaurant just serves food. When I suggest buying wine out there and bringing it in here, he stiffens further. That's not allowed, he says; and anyway he's a tee-totaller. Is all this some manifestation of American puritanism? Or is it just him – a man living alone in the hills and nervous of the demon drink?

In any case it's a slightly awkward start to our meal, and we don't seem to quite get over it, even though the food is as good as he predicted. In the rather desultory flow of conversation, I mention Lawrence's poem about the mountain lion, and ask him whether there are still any to be seen around here. He half-nods, half-shakes his head, as if to say, 'just occasionally'.

'What do you do if one appears at the ranch?' I ask.

'Feel honoured,' he replies with raised eyebrows, as though surprised that I need to ask. He still seems anxious to maintain the dignity of 'the custodian' against 'the professor'; and his claim of reverence for the lion seems more of a claim that he himself is of their kind. But having made a space for himself as 'mountain man', he grows more expansive, and starts telling me about his travels – he's even been to New Zealand (for the big-game fishing, naturally). This carries us through the rest of dinner, and coffee too. At length, after reminding me to come to the ranch about ten in the morning, he strides off to his car, with the air of having acquitted himself with social distinction.

Back in my box of a room, with its foam-rubber and plastic, and its blurred TV, my English eye peers through the window at the starry desolation, and I reflect a little wryly again on my Lawrencian excursions. The most recent was in the studious silences of the Harry Ransom Research Centre, at the University of Texas in Austin; so beautifully ordered and appointed, I found it rather suffocating – perhaps I really haven't the scholar's temperament. My most vivid experience there was the sudden howl of the fire alarm one somnolent afternoon, followed by a flat, metallic voice from the PA system instructing us all to 'proceed without hurry but without delay, and by the staircase, not the lifts, to the assembly area on the lawn in front of the building'. So off we marched in the wake of a pale and sombre librarian. In front of me a woman of tremendous girth, nego-tiating her way painfully down the narrow, winding fire-stairs, ensured an absence of hurry that soon grew nerve-wracking.

It turned out of course to be a fire-drill – albeit the most convincing I've ever seen. The more quiet events at the Centre were slow to assume their due significance. Lawrence's manuscripts, for instance – school exercise books filled with his neat, fluent handwriting – made little impression on me at first. But later, visiting places where he'd lived, I thought of his pen moving across their pages – at an Australian kitchen table, perhaps, or under a New Mexican pine – and they seemed emblems of the 'free lance', the writer living on talent, nerve, and tenacity; an image with a strong appeal for someone like myself – a salaried foot-soldier in the literary academy. And my first impressions of the originals of his paintings, laid rever-ently in tissues in the Centre's smooth-sliding mahogany art-drawers, slid just as smoothly to the bottom of my consciousness.

They lay dormant there until just this morning in fact, on the way to the ranch, when my attention was caught by a notice outside a hotel in Taos: 'D.H. Lawrence', it proclaimed. 'Author of Lady Chatterley's Lover. The Only Showing of his Controversial Paintings Since His Exhibition Was Permanently Banned By Scotland Yard in London in 1929.' 'Scotland Yard' strikes a rather dramatic note, as though a general moral collapse was narrowly averted by the 'flying squad'; but Lawrence's name of course means very little to the tourists here. As the custodian was to tell me later, the few who are tempted from the highway by the sign for the ranch, tend to assume that it refers to Lawrence of Arabia. The hotel foyer-cum-lounge was silent and deserted, but a bell-push on the desk soon evoked a power-fully built and middle-aged blonde, her rugged features plastered smooth with make-up. Apprised of my intent, she charged me two dollars, said the pictures were 'in the office', gestured off-handedly towards a door with frosted glass panels, then disappeared again.

Left to my own devices, I opened the door rather tentatively, to discover a room with a glass-topped wooden desk, and a row of filing cabinets; it really seemed an ordinary working office, except that the walls were literally covered with Lawrence's paintings, diversely framed and haphazardly hung. Perhaps it was the sense of incon-gruity, or perhaps I feel more alive in main-street hotels than university libraries, but my impression was suddenly very sharp. They are mostly nude-studies of course, and they all convey a vivid sense of light and dark united in the glow of flesh; the dark-sun radiance of some black women finding Moses in the bulrushes; a group of dancing 'Nymphs and Fauns' with the red-earth glow that Lawrence found so striking in the American Indians; the rosy bloom of an Amazon with orange pubic hair. In the delightful 'Bocaccio Story', a naked farm-labourer – sprawled asleep in the mid-day sun and subjected to the female gaze, amused and amazed, of some passing nuns – glows quite comprehensively; golden-limbed, but with a dove-grey light on the torso and flanks, he has a dark-sun head and genitals, the latter like a small volcanic mound between the rosy inner thighs. The impressionists, Lawrence remarks in his 'Introduction to These Paintings', 'escaped from the dark procreative body... into the open air, plein air and plein soleil: light and almost ecstasy.' His own sleeping labourer brings light and body back together.

Its opposite, it occurs to me, is Gerald's corpse at the end of *Women in Love*: when Birkin 'looked at the blue fingers, the inert mass, he remembered a dead stallion he had once seen: a dead mass of maleness, repugnant. He remembered also the beautiful face of one whom he had loved, who had died still having the faith to yield to the mystery. That dead face was beautiful, no one could call it cold, mute, material.'

It's a recurrent theme of course. 'Does the body correspond so immediately with the spirit?' Ursula Brangwen asks herself, earlier in the novel, after her thoughts of death have triggered a physical pang. And her answer is yes, 'the body is only one of the manifestations of the spirit'.

This glow of spirit as body is the heart of my totem. A few weeks ago I felt it through its absence, curiously enough, as I stood in the coal-town terrace-house where Lawrence grew up. The pale sunlight on the empty hearth and the museum-atmosphere of the whole place afflicted me with sense of emptiness and futility – an echo perhaps from my own childhood in a similar place. It seemed suddenly a dead house, in a dead neighbourhood of mean industrial streets. I fled the town, and was soon leaning over a five-barred gate, looking at the distant roofs, half-hidden amongst trees, of the fabulous farm of *Sons and Lovers*. It's still a working farm too, but there was nothing in sight that Paul and Miriam couldn't have seen – no other houses, no television aerials, no power-lines, not even a jet-trail in the deep blue sky. A corn-field slopes down towards the farm-house in the hollow, showing the contours of the land, the earth's living body, and it brought to mind of course the opening of *The Rainbow*, where the heavy midland soil clings to the Brangwens' feet 'with a weight that pulled like desire'. But then, just by the gate, between the pathway and a copse, my eye was caught by one of those inexplicable heaps of rubble – broken bricks in jagged lumps of concrete, half-buried in weeds – that sometimes appear in the midst of the English countryside; it seemed here a reminder of dead materiality.

In Thirroul, the coastal township south of Sydney, where Lawrence passed his few months in Australia, I'd felt an oddly similar counterpoint. The place has its own kind of unleavened lump – the stucco pub, for instance, though painted now lime green, still stands just as Lawrence described it, squat and four-square at the cross-roads, like a huge public convenience, or factory for the conversion of distilled sunshine into human waste. But in Australia too of course the earth itself feels alive – though it exerts a very different kind of pull. Like this whole stretch of coast, Lawrence's bungalow, still crouched amongst its trees at the tip of a headland, is sandwiched between the Pacific rollers and the scarp of the Illawarra. We came down the steep hill-side on the way to Thirroul, and at first we drove a little nervously, skirting the forested clefts, their green darknesses splashed with sunlight; but the narrow road, steep and winding though it is, soon seemed to be drawing us downwards with a curious ease, even a gentleness. And next day, as we drove through a fierce electrical storm to Sydney, on the highway north along the scarp-summit, even the lightning, each bolt a naked tree of blue fire, stood quivering in the wet grey world until it seemed almost literally to be earthing – striking root. This magnetism of the earth – you can feel it, Lawrence said, in the kangaroo's low centre of gravity – suggests no procreative urgency, but simply the inertia of the vast low land mass.

A few hours later we found ourselves in the sunshine of the Blue Mountains, at a 'scenic look-out' with a crowd of Asian tourists, watching two Aborigines, burly men in loin cloths, with white body-paint on their glistening black skins. One of them was dancing a soft-treading little dance, while the other played a didgeridoo, and they were both quite happy to stop on request, to be photographed with the giggling spectators. A pitiful display of cultural ruin, it might seem, and the didgeridoo, especially, a sad joke; but it still gives out the earth-vibration that Lawrence felt – though he never seems to have heard the instrument itself. The bluffs and canyons of the Blue Mountains are high and deep enough to possess a certain majesty and mystery, but the landscape is too broad for any sense of soaring; the deep noise – a brew of insect-murmur, air-currents, and whispering foliage (is it?) from the sun-soaked canyons – suggests no rumour of transcendence but the sheer life of the earth.

We heard the didgeridoo again in Sydney, at a lunch-time concert and lecture given by the artist-in-residence at the Museum of New South Wales. He too wore a loin-cloth and body-paint, but he was less heavy of build and less blunt of feature than the Blue Mountains buskers; and the audience here of course was seriously attentive, in pursuit of 'culture'; and so is the artist himself; brought up in the city – as he tells us with a strong Sydney accent – he's struggling to connect his modern self with his ethnic roots.

Great urban civilisations evidently tend to cut their citizens off from the earth. The new parliament building in Canberra, a long low structure built into the contours of a hill and surrounded by broad expanses of reddish gravel and sheets of water roughening over pale stone, makes a brave attempt to evoke the spirit of the land; but the interior of the building, though it 'makes full use of native materials' (the words of the brochure), seems more like The Grand Babylon Hotel, with an opulence expressing modern wealth and power.

'Only connect' – the ancient with the modern, the body with the spirit (for the body of course is always ancient, no matter how modern the spirit). Can this aboriginal artist-hero do it for his people – or even for himself? Does Lawrence really do it for me?

*　*　*

As I walk next morning across the gritty asphalt to the motel dining-room, the brilliant, proud morning is here again, but I can't say that my soul is standing still to attend. The iced-wine air is making me think chiefly of breakfast, and then of the drive up the mountain road to the ranch. I've been enjoying my racy red hire-car – after an unpromising start. In Albuquerque where I picked it up, a row of Indian-looking folk were sitting, for some unobvious reason, on a bench along one wall of the car-hire office; men, women and children, impassive and shabby, so out of key with the glittering, ready-to-go, cars out in the yard. My car was waiting for me at the door, but when I got in and switched on, there was no perceptible response from the engine, and the ignition seemed noisy; I tried again; and then, just as the anxious face of the hire-clerk appeared at the car-window, I realised that the engine was already running; its smooth purr had been too quiet for my hearing-aids to pick up –

a problem I don't encounter in the sort of car I own myself. And at the same moment I caught sight of the blankly inquisitive Indian faces staring through the open door of the office, my modern self exposed to their ancient gaze and found wanting.

The episode dampened but failed to extinguish my middle-aged-academic's thrill at being in America and on the road. It kindles again now as I leave the motel and turn onto the highway through the great foothills of the Rockies, and it's soon fuelled by the blue of the sky and the gold of the aspens. Only when I've left the asphalt and driven some way up the dirt side-road is my soul's attention caught, when I round a sharp bend and see the desert floor spread out below, with its endless vista of red-rock fortresses and ramparts, and the mountains of Colorado glittering faintly on the horizon.

I pull over onto the shoulder. This is the 'fierce, proud, inhuman' land that Lawrence saw. But my feeling for it, I must confess, remains somewhat notional. In part this seems a matter of temperament. Nature dealt me rather short in the fierce-proud-inhuman suit. In part a matter of experience. To my minimalist New Zealand eye, the iron roofs glittering here and there on the desert below, like specks of mica in the sunlight, are flashing strong signals of humanity.

For Lawrence, so vividly receptive to the spirit of place, and yet so incurably restless, the Nottinghamshire countryside always remained, as he said, 'the landscape of my heart'. The landscape of mine, though less vivid of course, is perhaps more various. It includes, for instance, the undulating line of antipodean hills beyond the fields I cross every day to work; a line running north to darker heights, brushed with snow in the winter, and south to the coastal plain, with a sense of the oceans beyond, curving down to the pole. And my feeling for this sky-line is largely a product of routine, of crossing the fields each day, in whatever mood or weather, letting the pathway through the fields deepen its pathway through my synapses. Lawrence, as he himself well knew, was too impatient of routine.

I look again at the desert. So beautiful – as everyone says. The reds, yellows, and purples; the distances. A visual feast – and turning, before my complacent gaze, into a visual cliché. Who am I to pass judgement on D.H. Lawrence? By nature too inclined to a 'quiet life', I ought to be working harder at the fierce-and-proud.

I start the car and, with a crunch of gravel and a roll of the springs, ease back off the shoulder. Better think of something less demanding, more cut-and-dried – of Baudrillard for instance driving through

these same desert landscapes. 'I knew all about this finished catastrophe when I was still in Paris of course,' he says at the start of
America. One doesn't – of course – expect great discoveries from
someone who knows everything already, but even so his 'catastrophe' is disappointingly familiar: the world as a waste-land, its
citizens trying to fill the emptiness with speed and money. The wise
men of old went into the desert to find the fullness of god. Baudrillard
– typical latter-day doom-sayer – finds merely a confirmation of the
world's emptiness. And he could feel it (of course) from the start;
'even the flight from London to Los Angeles, passing over the pole,
is, in its stratospheric abstraction and its hyperreality, already part
of California and the deserts'. A 'deterritorialisation', he calls it, a
disconnection from the earth.

But that particular flight – it's on a standard route from New
Zealand to England – can in fact vividly heighten your feeling for
the earth. As you fly into the approaching dawn, you grow aware of
the world in its 'diurnal course', down there beneath the cloud-cover,
as the place of life, and the brightening emptiness round the plane
as the place of death. And on such long flights of course the
passenger-seats become little lairs, with cushions, blankets, soft toys,
magazines, and food and drink, all the usual human clutter – touched
by pathos if you think of it scattered suddenly into space. I remember
seeing Concorde once, coming towards us and then hurrying silently
past, above a sea of cloud; nose down and wings stretched back, it
seemed like some great insect rigid with the effort of flight, an earth-
creature not meant for these desolate spaces.

Obviously, we each feel what we feel; no quarrelling with that;
but a phrase like 'stratospheric abstraction' describes for me not the
polar flight but Baudrillard's own style. His alleged insights into the
cultural depths claim to start from sensory impressions of the
surface, but the claim is empty. When he actually arrives in Los
Angeles for instance he sees, if that's the word for it, 'thousands of
cars, moving at the same speed, in both directions, headlights full on
in broad daylight, on the Ventura freeway, coming from nowhere,
going nowhere'. The waste-land clichés are clichés of thought, clichés
in any language, and they drive one irritably to reflect that while
Professor Baudrillard may have been there merely in order to pontif-
icate, most of the traffic would have been on business, going both
ways because that's what traffic does, at the same speed because of
the limit, and with lights switched on for safety.

I was once taken to my hotel from Los Angeles airport in a 'cheap'
shuttle-bus driven by an Iraqi. I had asked the friendly black woman

at the information kiosk to explain the difference between the cheap and expensive buses – for the price range was remarkable – and she had replied laconically that the latter were, well… they more expensive. She was, I suppose, in breach of the rule (displayed above her counter) forbidding her to recommend particular bus-companies, and indeed, as I made my way to the cheap end of the rank, a driver stuck his head out of an expensive bus and shouted angrily, 'What did she tell ya?'

What she didn't tell me was that the cheap buses have no fixed routes, and will take passengers virtually anywhere. Before I reached my hotel I had done a tour of the city that would have cost me a blood-vessel had I been in a hurry; but I wasn't, and I had the seat next to the driver, well placed both for the view and conversation.

It turned out that he had lived for a time in Leicester, before being drawn to the United States by the 'greater opportunities'. Opportunities mainly – I couldn't help reflecting – for perfecting his driving skills. He worked, he said, twelve hours a day, seven days a week, and was the longest-serving driver on the company. He drove, as one would expect, with brilliance – and, for much of the time in fact with his knees, his hands being variously occupied with a radio-phone and a street-directory, as he responded to calls from colleagues in distress – unsure of a destination, or simply lost. It was a rather conscious brilliance, and as he weaved from lane to lane, overtaking, shouting into his phone, and shuffling his maps, he made a point of still keeping our conversation going. His bright eyes and sharp features, street-wise talk and dramatic driving, made him seem like Sam Weller and his father rolled into one – and no doubt he hailed from a branch of the same human family in Baghdad.

There are different kinds and degrees of verbal emptiness, and Baudrillard's of course has a sociologising resonance. No individual appears in his 'America', only social beings – 'Americans', being 'American'. And since he fails to see the human individual, the universal inevitably eludes him too. My Lawrence totem suddenly reappears, at an Apache ceremony here in the New Mexican desert:

> the tepees and flickering fires, the neighing of horses unseen under the huge dark night, and the Apaches all abroad, in their silent moccasined feet; and in the khiva, beyond a little fire, the old man reciting, reciting in the unknown Apache speech, in the strange wild Indian voice that re-echoes away back to before the Flood, reciting apparently the traditions and legends of the tribe, going on and on, while the young men, the braves

of today, wandered in, listened, and wandered away again, overcome with the power and majesty of that utterly old tribal voice, yet uneasy with their half-adherence to the modern civilisation, the two things in contact. And one of these braves shoved his face under my hat, in the night, and stared with his glittering eyes close to mine. He'd have killed me then and there, had he dared. He didn't dare; and I knew it; and he knew it.

This is densely 'socio-historical' of course and its theme is the changing world; but the tension between 'the old tribal voice' and 'modern civilisation', is focused in the individual encounter, where the dramatic particulars are also human universals – of hostility and fear – and where the flash of mutual insight springs from the capacity for detachment, that bedrock of our humanity. The vision of change is held in the deeper perspective.

But Lawrence himself of course sometimes succumbs to the apocalyptic. It is, for obvious reasons, a twentieth-century weakness. These days the intellectual hucksters of the both left and right – the Baudrillards and the Bill Gates's – are equally strident about the imminence of a brave or bad new world. Apocalypse is news, and news is good for business.

* * *

At the ranch the custodian invites me in for coffee, and it soon becomes clear that he regards himself as the keeper not only of the Lawrence property but of the Lawrence story. He's particularly anxious to see Frieda as a womanly woman let down by unmanly men – first Lawrence, 'the artist', temperamental and effeminate, then Ravagli, 'the Italian', promiscuous and lazy. When at length he takes me into the historic ranch-house – little more than a shack amongst the trees – he points to a coat-peg with a faded blue linen jacket (I reach out of course and touch it) that allegedly belonged to Lawrence but looks small enough for a child. What a wretched specimen the man must have been, he remarks contemptuously, to have worn that.

There's a tribe in the Philippines, it's said, who habitually talk to dead or absent people as though they were present. I came across them in a case-study of a teenage American girl who was given to the same sort of communication with her pop-star idol. Her conversations – often conducted in the presence of her family and quite without embarrassment – covered matters of general or topical interest, it seems, and (discounting the star's non-presence) seemed perfectly rational. But in due course the girl sought the real man out and attacked him with a knife – for marrying a woman she considered beneath him.

I've no reason to suppose that the custodian actually talks to either Lawrence or Frieda, but his involvement with their ghosts is evidently close, and his role as Frieda's champion rather dear to him. But then my own exchanges with my totem are quite dear to me too. Sanity – or the loss of it – in these matters is clearly a question of Whiteheadian 'double location'. This slightly prickly custodian, for example, with his square brow, blue eyes, and grey hair, is not only out there beside me but also in my retina, nerves, and brain. To get a clearer sense of this dynamic, I could, for instance, touch the jacket on the peg not with my fingers but with the old walking stick that stands in the corner by the door. I could perhaps even feel the texture of the linen with it. It's extraordinary how sensitive such a 'probe' can be; an 'extension of the self', in McLuhan's phrase. You feel through it as if through your finger-tips, simultaneously taking the probe into yourself and projecting yourself out into it. And this is the inside-outside dynamic of all perception; Michael Polanyi called it 'indwelling'. In hallucination of course you only project, but mistake it for the full dynamic.

At the moment, I must confess, the custodian seems rather less real to me than the absent Lawrence. The house has a kind of fairy-tale simplicity; deal table and unvarnished chairs, stone hearth and adobe chimney; altogether an earthy place; but it's suffused with the wonderful New Mexican light, like an indwelling of spirit in matter. I recognise it at once of course as a manifestation of my totem – who like all good totems can adopt many guises. I remain aware, I hasten to add, that he isn't 'there' in the same sense as the custodian. Is he 'there' in any respectable sense at all?

I think of poor Poulet, leading literary-totemist of the sixties, flowering so late in his career then so ruthlessly cut down by the deconstructionists. His famous Tintoretto-totem first appeared to him in Venice. It was a 'common essence', he said, a 'subjective power at work in all Tintoretto's pictures, and yet never so clearly understood by my mind as when I had forgotten all their particular figurations'. His joy in naked communion with this 'essence', in all its 'ineffability and indeterminacy', exposed him to the derision of both the first wave of deconstructionist shock-troops and the re-grouped and re-armed Marxists. He was accused of 'logocentrism',

'idealism', 'withdrawal from History', and in general of conduct
unbecoming a true critic in the face of the enemy (art). Some erst-
while followers, like Hillis Miller and De Man, argued that the
master's emphasis on the 'indeterminacy' of his totem was in effect
a 'de-centring of the subject', and that he was thus no logo-centrist
after all, but since they themselves were among the first to defect,
their protestations seemed rather a cover for their desertion.

It's easy to see why Poulet had to be abandoned. He was (as who
wasn't?) an abler literary critic than Derrida, but he had the ill-luck
to set up as a phenomenologist while Derrida was a top anti-
Husserlian gun. What Derrida claimed chiefly to have shot down
was the Husserlian 'epoche', that 'moment' at which – to stay with
Poulet's case – the particular paintings were transcended, to reveal
the essential 'Tintoretto'. A 'concentrated purity of ex-pressiveness
just at the moment when the relation to a certain outside is
suspended', as Derrida put it – with a characteristic display of typo-
graphic pseudo-precision. And he went on of course to dismiss it as
a moment of hallucination, a variant of the delusion that signs are
like windows, through which we see their meaning.

But it depends what is meant by 'through'. When we perceive
anything whatever as a whole we can be said to be looking 'through'
its parts. I already feel quite familiar with the custodian's face, yet
I'm not at all sure about his nose. 'Snub', I should fancy. But when
I turn to look, I see that it's quite well-shaped. Moreover, as I bring
it (rather furtively) into focus, his face as a whole recedes into a vague
background. In Polanyian terms, we can either 'attend to' the nose
or 'attend from' it to the whole face. And in this context 'from' means
'through'.

I remember once having the temerity to preach Polanyi to a real
philosopher – a professional. A slim, brisk man of sixty-something,
blue-eyed and elegantly bald, his crisp, coolness seemed to suit his
Scottish-Canadian origins. Happily married to an ex-ballet dancer
addicted to fortune-tellers, he himself seemed the arch-rationalist.

'Polanyi's point,' I insisted, 'is that knowledge can never be exact.'

'What is it then?' he countered irritably. 'Vague?'

'Exactly,' I replied evasively – feeling ill-equipped to pursue the
argument.

Yet my reply was true enough. The custodian's face has the essential vagueness incident to all my perceptions; it's impossible to focus
on the parts and the whole at once; none the less I could identify it
now amongst thousands. 'Ideas' of course are even more vague than
faces. The definition of 'human being', for instance, is in endless

dispute, and yet we human beings recognise each other as such with uncanny accuracy – if sometimes with Gulliverian unease.

Why should my philosopher-friend wax irritable about this 'vague' knowledge that's yet precise enough for so many remarkable purposes? The answer, no doubt, is that it's knowledge as 'experience' and 'judgement', the knowledge of the 'expert' in a given field, and this rather cramps the philosophers' omniscient style. If you're buying a Tintoretto, or are having high blood-pressure, you consult art-dealers and heart-specialists rather than epistemologists who might tell you that both the painting and the pressure are 'linguistic constructs'. Am I myself an expert on Lawrence? Well, I know enough for my own purposes. But surely my totem really *is* a linguistic construct? What could it be but words?

At length the custodian – he's clearly finding me rather tediously preoccupied – says he has some chores to do, and will leave me to look round the place on my own; there's only the cabin that once belonged to Lawrence's most faithful acolyte, Dorothy Brett – and of course the Lawrence memorial itself.

The cabin is even smaller and more primitive than Lawrence's. Brett was a truly heroic hero-worshipper, especially since her 'Lawrence', so far from being a verbal phantom, was very definitely there – mocking, criticising, and 'improving' her paintings. An aspen like a great gold fountain arches over the cabin, throwing dappled light on the shingled roof, but there's little inside to detain the attention, and I'm soon making my way up the sunny hillside to the memorial.

It turns out to be at the top of a slope. The bright stony soil, and the steps leading up through a grove of conifers have a Mediterranean feel, almost classical. Yet as one reaches the summit, the word 'classical' has too much suggestion of 'finish'. The memorial vault, with its wooden eaves and plaster phoenix on the roof-tree, has more of a folk-art look. It recalls the window-panes that Lawrence painted in the bathroom of Mabel Dodge's house in Taos. A museum now, the house is in a gentrified *pueblo* style; with its cool tiled floors, the inside is full of subtly borrowed light, with always a sense of further spaces beyond, of patios, alcoves, stairways to different levels – a sense amongst other things of Mabel's money. Only the painted windows show Lawrence's spontaneous touch, where the work has gone into the conception rather than the finish.

Here now at the grave, the buried source, so to speak, of all my totemic imaginings, the thought of Mabel Dodge is disconcerting. When Lawrence's ashes were brought back from France, so the story goes, Frieda was seized by the idea that the indomitable Mabel planned to steal them – as she had earlier tried to steal the living man. And in a striking display of her own indomitable nature, she forestalled the attempt by mixing her husband's ashes with the cement for his memorial. The thought of my totem set in concrete here before me, turns the place into a lump as unleavened as the pub at Thirroul; even the New Mexican light seems suddenly to darken a little. I think of Ursula Brangwen's question again: 'Does the body correspond so immediately with the spirit?' And when I answer 'yes, of course', of course the light returns. Let there be light, and there was light. Is light then a purely 'linguistic construct'? Of course *not*. I've kept my sun-glasses in my pocket, so as to get a natural impression of the place. I put them on, and my whole world darkens again. It's a darkness determined purely physically, but it pervades my full consciousness. I can remove it by removing the glasses, but not by any force of thought or word. And it's a purely individual element of perception, on my retina, right here, right now.

I can safely say, then, that my meetings with my totem are neither a wordless communion of souls nor a phantom procession of signs, but a dynamic of my Lawrencian thoughts and my own perceptions. I take the sun-glasses off again, with the slight feeling of disappointment that always attends a tortuous arrival at an obvious conclusion. And the conclusion quickly prompts me to others, equally obvious. That Lawrence himself, for instance, had more original thoughts and perceptions than I myself. A genius, he left strong traces; and strength here is a strength of vision, not a mere will to slay some literary father.

The word 'trace' of course has become cocooned in Derridan 'theory'. I.A. Richards – did Derrida ever read him, I sometimes wonder? – used to call it 'delegated efficacy'. Whenever I see or say the word 'light', for instance, it 'means' all the 'traces' it calls up from all the times I've seen or said the word before. And this in turn brings in traces of traces from all the times almost anybody has ever used it. These endless vistas of semiosis filled Richards with uncertainty and delight. And, in the end, no doubt, the complexities of meaning are indeed ineffable. But viewed nearer at hand – as when I see the New Mexican light and recall what Lawrence said of it – his traces are as clear to me as the custodian's face. And I perceive them in essentially the same way. Any perception is evidently a hypothesis – as we realise when we grope our way to the bathroom in the dark, 'attending from' obscure details to some conjectured whole (a chair, or just a shadow?), or when our belief that we can overtake that bus seems suddenly ill-founded. My totem, in its various elusive forms, is a hypothesis that both tests and is tested by my experience.

'Very true,' I hear the totem say, 'but rather dry.' I look at the grave again – and I imagine his face flickering there, with its rugged features, reddish beard, and blue eyes. It speaks not of death but of life, looks forward rather than back; in a few moments I glance at my watch (I want to have time for a detour through Santa Fe), then make my way back down the steps.

When I knock at the custodian's door to say goodbye, he doesn't invite me in, and when I ask to take a photo he turns suddenly coy. Perhaps the John Wayne image hanging behind him is some Lacanian millstone around the neck of his 'self'. He succumbs however to a little persuasion (though it seems fitting in the end that for some reason or other the photo didn't take).

Is my own 'self' being suppressed by my Lawrence-hero, I wonder, as the car crunches its way back down the dirt-road? A hero-theorist like Carlyle would evidently have dismissed the idea with contempt – and would have regarded Lacan's Freudian hypothesis as pitifully unrobust. It depends no doubt on one's view of the 'self'. I glance at my face in the rear-view mirror. I must admit it strikes me as rather nondescript. Does this reflect a failure to make the transition from the 'imaginary' realm to the 'symbolic'?

Lawrence himself of course was an early critic of Freud. He acknowledged the chained monsters of repression but not as true natives of the unconscious. In fact he redefined the unconscious quite simply as the 'soul' – that unique individuality of which one's DNA is the bare blueprint. Such an 'unconscious' may seem too deeply buried to be of any observable use, but in fact everything we are, our whole style of being and doing, reveals it. Its actual nature of course is a mystery – 'more distant than stars and nearer than the eye' – but its function is quite obvious from the blueprint: it's what organ-ises the organism.

As Raymond Tallis has pointed out, this primary 'self', for all its mystery, must obviously precede the fragmented 'self' born from the Lacanian mirror; it's the prerequisite for any sense of 'things out there' at all, whether reflections, mirrors, or mothers. The Lacanian 'self', with its endless lack, seems to be essentially a projection of Lacan's own vain desire to nail the mystery-self down. He ought to have tried instead the old strategy of finding the self by losing it. This might at least have spared us his nightmare prose, that strange Dunciad apparition of lead and feathers, struggling ponderously and emptily across the page, like a dream in which your limbs feel immovable yet weightless. I glance again at the face in the driving-mirror; 'nondescript' implies 'easily forgettable'; so I forget him; and he soon finds himself admiring the scenery, or stopping occasionally to look inside the wayside churches, where painted Christs display their wounds in the sunlit silence.

Santa Fe is wonderful. With its adobe architecture, it's my childhood 'America' of film-star cowboys. But as I wander round and find that not only the public buildings and private houses, but the department stores and even the multi-story car-parks, are all in the *pueblo* style, it begins to feel too relentlessly in keeping, like a Cotswold village with thatch over the petrol pumps. I soon find myself once again in a bar (adobe, of course) and once again in conversation with two men – though this time they don't appear to be soldiers. The city, I remark at length, is architecturally much more harmonious than Taos. Is this the result of 'zoning'? (I'm quite pleased about using this word – I came across it in some local newspaper.) One of the men bristles. 'Taos!' he exclaims, with an apparently equal scorn for the town and my question; 'Santa Fe can look after itself without goddam zoning.' The closing cadence – as though building restrictions were a portent of Stalinism – seems to preclude any light-hearted debate. That tone again; I still can't gauge it. Is it really, as Lawrence said in his gloomier moments, some deathly hypertrophy of the will? Or is that itself just an outworn generalisation?

I don't know. No doubt I'll enquire again from time to time, in dialogue with my hypothesizing totem. But when I'm outside again, the town begins to seem like Mabel's house, altogether too finished. Am I just reacting against the men in the bar? At any rate, walking back to the car park along the warm Santa Fe pavements, I suddenly recall Lawrence in Taos at Christmas, at the ancestral Indian ritual:

> twilight, snow, the darkness coming over the great wintry mountains and the lonely pueblo, then suddenly, again, like dark calling to dark, the deep Indian cluster-singing at the drum, wild and awful, suddenly rousing on the last dusk as the procession starts. And then the bonfires leaping suddenly in pure spurts of high flame, columns of sudden flame forming an alley for the procession.

His impressions are so quick, yet so vividly there; light and dark, body and spirit, together. As I walk back to my car, I can feel 'the images dancing in my heart' – Dr Johnson's words about some lines by Theocritus. More of my ancestral heroes and their heroes are cluster-singing at the drum.

But what of the literary community of the living? The one in which I'm mainly involved is the academy, and I by no means feel I undividedly belong – having spent the last twenty years or so at public odds with the 'theorists'. But that in itself of course has given me a sense of engagement – and against a significant foe. The universities in which I've been in search of my hero are all conspicuous for impressive grounds and buildings, well-appointed offices and well-groomed secretaries; the outward and visible signs of academic empire; but not always of an inward academic grace; and the struggle against the enemy within gives me a role, however ambiguous, in the system, and thus a place, however modest, in the world at large. Of course the emptiness of a Baudrillard's prose will never rival, say, the depletion of the ozone layer, as a cause for alarm in the public breast, but to measure it carefully is none the less essential for a certain kind of health. These heroic thoughts carry me out of Santa Fe and onto the open road, beneath trees so golden and a sky so blue that I feel like singing; and predictably enough, the words that come out, to the beat of the drum, are about mental fight and the unsleeping sword. They're out-of-tune, I must confess, and Jerusalem, the city without dunces, seems a long way off; but perhaps that's just as well – a critical mind might find it a little dull.

Back to Nature

The little Cantonese girl sitting cross-legged in front of the TV is fascinated by an urgent discussion between a sheep-dog and a piglet. The animals are 'real', not 'toons', and they're speaking the girl's own language, but since she's less than two years old, she probably understands it little more than I do myself. The pig is in fact Australian – or at least is the star of an Australian film called *Babe* – but the videotape we're watching is from Hong Kong, and we're sitting in the girl's house in Vancouver. The rest of her family – mother, father, grandmother, great-grandmother and various aunts and uncles – are upstairs, playing mahjong. I don't play well enough for any serious encounter, and in any case I'm quite happy to mind the baby. I'm her great-uncle (a disconcerting title – it makes me feel older and of more extended family than I'm accustomed to seeing myself) and I'm also her only non-Chinese relative; when we met for the first time, a few days ago, there was some doubt as to how she would take to me; but we got on very well, and now, as we watch the film, she turns round from time to time and points imperiously (her default gesture) at the screen. I'm charmed, naturally, by her insistence that I share her involvement, and charmed also by her deep identification with the piglet; she even shares the name, as it happens, being Nathalie aka Bébé.

I seem to have been oddly aware of animals ever since my arrival in Vancouver. At a tourist-park the other day I saw, for the first time, some West Coast Indian totem poles. The brightly painted animal figures – red, blue, yellow, white and green – with their big eyes and prominent beaks and noses, looked gay in the old sense, with a suggestion here and there of mischief or of wickedness; Disneyesque, almost, but without the sentimental touch. They were highly stylised of course, but clustered together there at the edge of a clearing, they seemed curiously alive, as if peering out from their forest world at the restaurant and car-park – and at the two Indians in an open-fronted workshop carving yet another pole for the edification of the tourists. The chief totem creature seems to be the Raven, the prankster-hero of West Coast Indian myth, and the actual bird still dominates the city; to an outsider's eye it looks too formidable for the tame suburban streets, and quite worthy of its old and ominous reputation.

And then yesterday, chancing upon Vancouver's I-max cinema, I saw a nature-documentary about South Georgia, a stray fragment of the Falkland Islands flung out towards the Antarctic Circle. The dominant creatures here were the male sea-elephants, thirty-foot cinematic monsters, in hyper-definition and quadraphonic sound, rearing up against each other in the struggle for mating territory; overwhelming images of sex and violence, but filmed against a background of snow-capped peaks and pastoral violins. A crude mixture, it seemed, of Darwin and Wordsworth; a typically modern view of nature – and ultimately scientific of course. On a stretch of high bleak tussock above the sea-elephants' beach, for instance, we see two pale and sensitive-looking young European men gently easing an egg from beneath a female albatross – who remains remarkably unprotesting on the nest. They measure the egg with a pair of calipers (the mother emitting a single squawk when they nearly drop it) and intone the statistics into a tape-recorder. Meanwhile David Attenborough, in breathless voice-over, tells of the mysteries of the great bird's life, its pilgrimages and its home-comings, its long courtship and its conjugal fidelity – which may one day be all explained, he seems to suggest, by this meticulous measuring of its eggs.

The camera cuts to a long-shot of an albatross gliding effortlessly against a sweep of high cliffs, the white sliver of life in the blue immensity of the sea and sky so beautifully caught by the camera, while the voice-over descants on the aerodynamics of its wings. No doubt Attenborough really feels a sense of wonder, but he fails to express it; that's left to the pictures and the music; the words are all about 'survival' – and thus essentially about numbers. 'Twenty thousand on this stretch of sand alone,' he intones, as we return to the mating *mêlée* on the shore-line. One is driven to imagine sea-elephants uttering the same awed remark, as they surface off-shore from, say, Bondi Beach.

The mythic Raven can take on every face of nature – creative and destructive, ridiculous and great. The neo-Darwinians seem to see only one aspect, 'survival', and only one way of explaining it – in terms of accident and necessity: the genetic 'freak' that just happens to be a better survivor supplants in due course the entire 'normal' population; a process statistically inevitable and entirely empty of meaning. It turns our sense of wonder into mere surprise that nature's immense variety should spring from so simple a mechanism. But human-kind, including even the neo-Darwinians, can only bear a little emptiness; the Disneyesque comes creeping in. Richard Dawkins, for instance, casts as clinical an eye on nature as any Robbe-Grillet, yet his prose style displays a Dickensian anthropomorphism; a night-flying bat – to take a random and representative example – becomes a cold-war spy-plane, bristling with military technology; and Dawkins is one of a growing number of academics from various disciplines these days who like to see themselves as 'story-tellers'. But the gross discrepancy between thought and feeling, philosophy and style, though it might pass muster in science, where feelings don't much matter, is of course a radical flaw in a story.

Dawkins himself would call such an objection 'artsy-literary', but in fact they reveal an essential weakness in his work – his evasiveness about his own reductionism. It's quite acceptable, he argues, to reduce organisms to molecules in motion as long as you do it by way of intermediate entities. But even as he tries to describe this feat its impossibility becomes apparent. 'The body', he assures us, 'is a complex thing with many constituent parts, and to understand its behaviour you must apply the laws of physics to its parts, not to the whole. The behaviour of the body as a whole will then emerge as a consequence of interactions of the parts.' But the key words here – 'emerge' and 'interaction' – are slippery and misleading. A physical and chemical analysis of, say, the parts of a bicycle – its sprockets, chain, and cogs, and so on – will tell us absolutely nothing about how it works; any machine-like structure, whether organic or inorganic, is fitted together according to principles quite external to its parts. And the philosopher-chemist Michael Polanyi, who pointed out this salient feature of both organisms and machines, has no difficulty in showing that DNA itself has the same sort of structure and must likewise elude complete physico-chemical analysis.

If Dawkins really wants to be a story-teller, he should integrate his sensibilities along neo-Darwinian lines; and he might learn something here from Ted Hughes's *Crow*, where thought and feeling are all grimly survivalist – though both Hughes and Dawkins alike, would do even better, I think, to consider the West Coast stories of the Raven, where thought and feeling are more subtly various – grim, gay, epic, ironic, and tragic, in turn, and always full of wonder.

Perhaps my great-niece's sense of wonder at the piglet is merely childish. So Coleridge, at any rate, would have thought. But surely Wordsworth had the better of the argument; the philosopher's wonder is rooted in the child's. And the two poets would in any case have agreed about Bébé's current behaviour; being alive, she's identifying with all living things. Her namesake is at present trying in vain to join the sheep-dog work-force – the sort of desperate attempt to break into the grown-up world that Bébé herself knows only too well. She turns and points with a frown at the head sheep-dog. 'He's so mean,' I nod in agreement, though I can't help reflecting that before she's much older her affection for pigs will turn into a taste for pork – that great cornerstone of Cantonese cuisine.

Zoology failed to thrive in ancient China, so the old joke goes, because any new animal always provoked the question not 'What is it?' but 'How do you cook it?' The joke is of course unfair. The Chinese view of nature has often been full of wonderment – as witness the great story of the Monkey King, a prankster-hero like the Raven. I recall my own children, in Beijing many years ago, watching a Chinese-opera version of his adventures in the under-world. We were part of a privileged audience – cadres and 'foreign experts' – but the Cultural Revolution, with its rejection of tradi-tional opera, had only just ended, and everyone still wore blue Mao-jackets (though some of them were already beginning to look exquisitely tailored); and the actors, or so the old aficionados said, were quite woefully out of practice; none the less they were loudly applauded at the expected moments, and there was a sense of the faltering return of an ancient art (though Beijing's children now, just a generation later, are said to prefer Mickey Mouse).

I look at Bébé again. Already so domesticated, so un-wild, in one sense she seems very Chinese – or very Confucian. But there's a tradi-tional tension between Confucianism and Taoism – a local form of the universal tension between 'culture' and 'nature'. The Monkey-King, whether stealing the peaches of heaven, scourging demons in hell, or helping human pilgrims through the world, is an exuberant Taoist manifestation – all magical energy and spontaneity, and often obtuse about the Confucian social proprieties. The reader laughs *with* the magic and *at* the obtuseness, in a witty negotiation between 'nature' and 'culture'.

The spirit of the Monkey-king runs deep in the national psyche, and one of the mysteries of the occident is the western stereotype of the inscrutable, impassive Chinese – especially as applied to the southerners, the Cantonese, who are as volatile as southern Italians. Their stock phrase for 'a good time', for instance, is 'heat and noise', and our film-watching has been intermittently disturbed by erup-tions from upstairs, cries of triumph and despair at the progress of the game. But they've evidently finished, and here they come, though still with enough 'heat and noise' to draw Bébé away from the tele-vision set.

They've been brought to Vancouver of course by Beijing's imminent take-over of Hong Kong. The 'Tiananmen incident' increased their distrust of the Chinese government, and they see the harbingers of historic change already arriving in Hong Kong – *nouveaux riches* from the mainland, strutting the pavements with their coarse speech and proprietary airs, like communist colliers in Piccadilly after a Scargill revolution.

Bébé's family – diligent, clever, already well-off, and with their ingrained respect for education – will do well in Canada economically. As for 'becoming Canadian' in any significant way, that of course will vary. The older generation simply won't, Bébé's own generation largely will; in between are those like her uncle in Calgary; a Hong Kong trained doctor, twenty-something, intelligent and personable, and a fluent English-speaker, he's doing research at the university hospital. What further adjustments between nature and culture will the march of History make necessary, or desirable, for someone like him? Perhaps I'll find out tomorrow, when we visit him – and go to see the Calgary Stampede.

The heat and noise have gravitated to the kitchen, and a festive lunch (part of a celebration of my birthday) is soon on the table – a tray of 'sushi' from the local Japanese restaurant, an assortment of Chinese 'dim sum', and a cream cake piled with edible decoration. On the gustatory plane Bébé already negotiates well between nature and culture; she eats heartily but doesn't guzzle, is beginning to discriminate without being fastidious. And on the moral plane too she's learning quickly. Being much-praised for her skill in eating with a fork, for instance, she's taken to handling it with a conscious flourish. A harmless vanity perhaps, but she's already in the process of being laughed gently out of it. On her part it's a negotiation between self-conceit and self-doubt, and between self and other. You can see the adjustments in her eyes, the moment of anxiety and resentment at being mocked, and then the happy recognition that she's still nonetheless loved.

I think of the Indian carvers at the tourist-park. The two men were of distinctly different physical types. Both are young and handsome, with glossy black pony-tails, but one of them was square-faced and shouldered, with a sharp eye and aquiline nose, a military-looking figure; the other, though still powerfully built, had more the look of the artist, softer-featured, rounder-shouldered. But it was the 'soldier', working on a twenty-foot pole, who stopped carving and talked about their art to the watching tourists. He spoke in standard Canadian, easily, rather laconically – cedar is the best wood to work with, both for ease and durability, and so on. He'd evidently said it all before, and in his manner and voice the slight aloofness and irony of the artist speaking to non-artists seemed compounded with that of the proud colonised speaking to the colonisers. The other man, leaning nonchalantly against his work-bench, evidently had a similar attitude to the tourists, but when his own work-in-progress – a smaller and more highly finished bird-figure – was singled out for admiration, he looked mistrustful of his companion's volubility. I was reminded of the old saying, 'For myself against my brother, with my brother against the village, with my village against the nation, with my nation against the world.' Always the dynamic of self and society, of nature and culture, the former always keeping itself a little detached.

Bébé's house is as culturally diverse as the lunch. North American in style, with a pillared portico opening into a high vaulted entrance-hall and then a reception room with fitted carpets; but there are nests of Chinese occasional tables and blackwood cabinets full of lacquer-ware and porcelain figurines. A Hong Kong eclecticism, not at all post-modern. For one thing it's un-self-conscious, for another it speaks not of 'fragmentation' but of abundance, of 'doing well'; plump upholstery on the sofas and a plump Buddha on the mantel-piece. And this is the keynote of the whole district; porticoed mansions set in manicured gardens, mounting the hillside in serried ranks above the city, and at the summit stands the 'jewel in the crown' (as the developers' brochure calls it) – an eighteen hole golf course, on whose final hole you aim your drive at the distant snow-capped peak of Mt Baker. Nature socialised with a vengeance – the golf-course being above all the place to show yourself off to your social peers – the brochure again; and the Confucians would agree with it; when times are good, they say, it's disgraceful not to thrive.

Hong Kong is no doubt too Confucian, too apt to make social success the only measure. My in-laws tend, for instance, to humour with just perceptible patience my own interest in the West Coast Indians, who latterly haven't had much social success at all. And I sometimes sympathise with my in-laws' view. The other day I picked up from the 'Canada' shelves of a local book-store, a battered old volume called *An Eskimo Diary*. It records the daily life of the diarist amongst his people, and the introduction records the European editor's primary article of faith – that 'human influence on nature disturbs its rhythm' and that the great merit of the Esqimaux is to have disturbed it very little. There's an obvious and important truth in this. But in the diary itself we find, for instance, that when hunters return with their kill, they give food to 'the poor of the village'. So this isn't the 'rhythm' of nature red in tooth and claw. On the other hand, since both poverty and charity exist, it isn't a socialist utopia either.

We also hear the story of a boy called Kaassasuk. One of the diarist's own crude but expressive drawings shows the lad, his trousers round his ankles, held in a head-lock by a laughing boy, while other boys and girls grab at his genitals. Is this 'natural' behaviour? Clearly Kaassasuk isn't much enjoying it, and at length, attracted by his cries, his mother emerges from the house and drives his tormentors off with the stick she uses for softening leather. The story goes on to relate that Kaassasuk is given the 'spirit-force' by a magical arctic fox, then bare-handed slays three bears, and becomes the hero of the tribe. An 'ugly duckling' story evidently, and it confirms that in matters like bullying, no less than poverty, Kaassasuk's people exist uneasily, as do all other human beings, in between 'nature' and 'culture'. But the book's editor tends to sentimentalise them a little as 'primitives', the wonderful lost thing – as I sometimes do myself.

So too did Lévi-Strauss – the West Coast Indians are amongst his subjects – but in the world of 'theory' of course he is mainly known for contending that the whole 'binary opposition' of 'nature and culture' is a 'scandal' (one imagines the indignant scholars, the libraries in shock) – a scandal exposed, he said, by the prohibition against incest. 'Let us suppose,' he argues, 'that everything universal in man relates to the natural order, and is characterised by spontaneity, and that everything subject to a norm is cultural and is both relative and particular.' And having thus manoeuvred his neat ranks of signifiers into line-of-battle, he has no trouble at all in showing that the incest-prohibition can fight on either side; it's universal yet entails conformity with a rule.

Dismay. The antithesis that structures all anthropological enquiry breaks down in the crucial instance. Lévi-Strauss's solution was pragmatic; he confessed that the opposition was unsustainable but kept on using it. Derrida of course saw this as an attempt to eat your cake and have it, to be both a structuralist reconstructing a 'total system' and an empiricist 'bricoleur'. And this is a version, he added, of the ultimate 'binary opposition' – between two radically different approaches to interpretation itself: 'The one seeks to decipher, dreams of deciphering a truth or an origin which escapes play and the order of the sign, and which lives the necessity of interpretation

as an exile.' The other is 'the Nietzschean affirmation, that is the
joyous affirmation of the play of the world and of the innocence of
becoming, the affirmation of a world of signs without fault, without
truth, and without origin which is offered to an active interpretation'. (If Nietszche could have seen the kinds of 'active interpretation'
that have gone on lately, he might have felt less joyous.)

Having shown us the fearsome horns of this mother of all bina-
ries, Derrida gestures, albeit vaguely, towards an escape route –
indeed two. First, though the two modes of interpretation are
'absolutely irreconcilable', we none the less 'live them simultaneously and reconcile them in an obscure economy'. Second (the
deconstructive route) we can at least attempt to conceive 'the
différance of this irreducible difference' between 'truth' and 'play'.
Though this latter is the route he evidently prefers, he makes no
further attempt to conceive it. As for the 'obscure economy', he
ignores it altogether, and this is sad, since it's crucial for any effective *literary* theory and it isn't very difficult to describe.

I think of the 'lived economy' by which Bébé reconciles the sense
that she is being mocked with the sense that she is being loved;
'mockery', she sees, can be a kind of 'love', yet she also retains a
sense of them as opposites. Remaining thus stable the opposition is
'true', yet it's also subject to the 'play' of the living moment. And
this 'obscure economy' is already using words – 'the growing tips
and buds' of the human organism, as Coleridge called them; and his
metaphor clearly highlights the integration of word and experience,
mind and body, thinking and living, whereas Derrida's two escape
routes, one lived and the other thought-out, betray the dualism of
all neo-Saussurean theory.

The modern critic who did as much as anyone to heighten our
awareness of the tips and buds was William Empson. In *The
Structure of Complex Words* especially, he takes words like 'sense'
and 'sensibility' (a pair related to 'nature and culture'), and shows
how the shifting equations of thought and feeling within them – their
'obscure economy' – can turn them on occasion into virtual
synonyms or even reverse their usual opposition of meaning. To
compare his semantic lock-picking with the smash-and-grab techniques of deconstruction is to wonder what happened to English
literary criticism between the 1950s and the 1970s. Was there some
fit of collective amnesia?

The 'obscure economy', the workshop of our opposition-recon-
ciling powers, is what Coleridge himself of course called the
'imagination': 'Who has not a thousand times seem snow fall on

water? Who has not watched it with a new feeling, from the time
that he has read Burns' comparison of sensual pleasure

> To snow that falls upon a river
> A moment white – then gone forever!'

Coleridge descants eloquently on all the usual reconciliations – image
and idea, feeling and thought, enthusiasm and judgement – and the
series culminates in the remark that Burns's lines produce 'the
strongest impressions of novelty, while rescuing the most admitted
truths from the impotence caused by the very circumstance of their
universal admission.' It's the imagination, in short, our chief weapon
in the eternal struggle against the 'the film of familiarity and selfish
solicitude', that keeps a received culture from stiffening into cliché.

In its primary form it's obviously a universal faculty, at the heart
of all learning, all adjustments of the self to the novel 'other'. I recall
Bébé's face at our first meeting, as her 'obscure ecomony' worked to
reconcile the contradictions between her idea of 'uncle' and the
image of this strange old European man. It's clearly a more than
human power too. I once saw a film about an American policeman
who became friendly with some sting-rays in the Caribbean. The key
to it was food of course. Whenever he swam into view with his plastic
bag, they came undulating round him, almost caressing his head in
a weightless embrace, while he popped his bits of fish into their
mouths – awful shark-toothed apertures on their undersides – then
gave their stings an affectionate tug as they shimmied away. We
weren't told how long it had taken them to get used to this strange,
new creature, but it clearly couldn't have been 'spontaneous', to use
Lévi-Strauss's word; it was a learned response, and therefore
'cultural'. The fact is of course that the act of learning is itself a
natural process. But it still makes sense to say that the sting-ray's
gills are 'natural' while the swimmer's oxygen cylinder and mask are
products of 'culture'.

At the Vancouver city art gallery the other day I saw an exhibition of work by the 'Group of Seven', the 1920s painters who
created, so it's said, the first 'Canadian style'. Like the sting-rays they
were adjusting imaginatively to their new perceptions – though,
being human ourselves, we find their achievement more impressive.
I was delighted by the energy and colour of the paintings in the first
room, and yet the Group's vision of 'nature' – they mostly painted
landscapes – has often none the less a 'big and empty' quality. J.E.H.
MacDonald's famous *The Solemn Land*, for instance, is said to show

an 'Oriental influence', and with regard to the composition – the harmony of mountains, trees, and lake – this may be true; but it lacks the human touch – no little pavilion, no lute-playing servant, no sage with gay and glittering eyes. It's 'solemnity' is distinctly unpeopled, too 'sublime', or too purely Taoist. It reminds me of Sylvia Plath's Canadian poems, where the sense of emptiness is overwhelming. 'We'll wake blank-brained as water in the dawn,' she says at nightfall in 'Two Campers in Cloud Country', and she seems half-attracted by the idea, yet the 'nature' that might dissolve her is felt as hostile of course:

> The colours assert themselves with a sort of vengeance.
> Each day concludes in a huge splurge of vermilion.

Tom Thomson, who seems to have been the Group of Seven's prime mover, liked to use a vermilion undercoat, as in *Jack Pine* – a gaunt tree against a luminous lake and dark hills in the evening light, with reddish earth in the foreground suggesting blood. And curiously enough he died by drowning in Canoe Lake, dissolved back while still young.

All cultures evidently need to tell a story about nature that will account for both its beauty and its danger, for the sting-ray's fearsome jaws and friendly manner, for the fact above all that nature creates each individual being and in the end destroys it. The younger of my sisters-in-law lives just outside Vancouver. Her front garden looks out on great forest- covered hills, beneath the 'Canadian light', or a cousin of it, that the Group was intent on capturing – a product (is it?) of the high latitude and the sunlight on the firs and cedars, their matt green foliage stirring stiffly when it stirs at all, and giving back no play of reflection to the sky. Her back-garden however slopes gently down to a stream, that slides and ripples over smooth round stones, and on the other bank are rose-covered trellis-fences, and weatherboard gables peeping out from amongst the fruit-trees. A calendar-cottage world, much more human and kindly. Old Mrs Moore, in Forster's great novel, finds in the end a passage not to India but to 'a hundred Indias'. Here at my sister-in-law's – quite apart from the Hong Kong-Canada inside the house – two Canadas co-exist even in the garden.

It's obvious why the Group of Seven had to ignore cottage-Canada; it didn't suit the needs of their time or their temperament. But of course the whirligig of criticism brings in its revenges. A book on sale in the gallery shop describes the Group as both technically 'unplayful' (nothing but 'oil on canvas') and politically primitive ('bloke-ish' and 'empiricist', they looked outwards at the 'untamed wild' not inwards to the Lacanian unconscious). The critic herself is 'post-feminist' and 'progressive', her prose a little tight-lipped and condescending, and her 1990s account of the 1920s reminds one that culture changes with time of course as well as place. And aware again of the 'obscure economy' – or rather of its failure, for her critique is based on the familiar and contradictory coalition between the 'play' of deconstruction and the 'truth' of progressive politics. A coalition that insists we tolerate all human behaviour (since there's no common human standard by which to judge it), yet insists also on *the truth* that salvation lies in the pursuit of 'freedom' and 'equality'. Faced with old cultures from which 'freedom' and 'equality' seem conspicuously absent, the coalition's 'economy' tends to grind its gears, and either shriek with missionary zeal or lapse into uneasy silence – depending on the other political variables.

Is there a better 'economy' for describing cultural collision and change? The post-Lévi-Straussian anthropologists themselves have joined the ranks of the academic 'story-tellers' of course. Anthropology – or so says the eminent practitioner Clifford Geertz – is like 'myth'; it 'describes not what happened, but what happens'; it looks not just at events but at their deeper pattern. This Aristotelian insight into narrative (Geertz seems to think it originates with Northrop Frye) indeed remains valid, but clearly there are different kinds of 'pattern'. One of the stories told by Geertz himself is about a recent civic decree in the town of Sefrou, in Morocco, requiring the owners of houses with extravagantly decorated façades to paint them over with a modest and government-subsidised beige. It's a story about 'old inhabitants against showy newcomers' and, beyond that, about 'the Islamic city in tension with the modern world'. In fact the 'pattern' Geertz is seeking is 'the track of modernity', as he calls it. 'We can't trace this track before it is laid down,' he concedes, 'but once it is, we shall have explanations enough for the course it has taken.'

A trend-hound in pursuit of 'modernity', yet doomed to be eternally looking back, Geertz fortifies himself with Kierkegaard's dictum that 'Life is lived forward but it is understood backward'. In some ways – either deep or obvious – this is no doubt true, but one can also say, and with equal truth, 'If I finish this bottle tonight I'll wake up with a headache'. This is clearly 'understanding forward', and in stories of this kind – they are of course the stories by which we conduct much of our lives – the patterns are far more simple. And indeed there's a simple moral in Geertz's own story of Sefrou: in a confrontation between 'traditionalists' and 'progressives' a peaceful outcome entails some compromise – as was in fact achieved in that particular case, though Professor Geertz, professionally interested in 'modernity' rather than peace, mentions it only in passing.

If cultural analysis comes down to 'telling stories' and the 'master narratives' have all gone, perhaps there's something at least to be learned from the narrative masters. Robert Louis Stevenson was precisely that – not a genius so original as to be unrepresentative – and his historic account of cultural collision in nineteenth-century Samoa shows his mastery – as in the episode where indigenous feeling against the German colonists and their Samoan puppet-king comes finally to a head:

> Both sides were arming. It was a brave day for the traders, though not so brave as some that followed, when a single cartridge is said to have been sold for twelve cents currency – between nine and ten cents gold. Yet even among the traders a strong party feeling reigned, and it was the common practice to ask a purchaser upon which side he meant to fight.

The imminent battle makes the irony sharp and clear (as Stevenson always is about the arms traders); but the monetary details also make us weigh, Robinson Crusoe-fashion, the whole question of bullets and gold, and their relative 'value'; and this more meditative irony colours our response to the traders' 'party feeling', and then sharpens again into the suspicion that they may well ask the question, then sell the bullets regardless.

After the first skirmish, Brandeis, the German commander emerges with his 'loyal natives' from the forest, 'smoking a cigar, and deadly pale, and with perhaps an increase of his usual nervous manner'. A suggestion here of 'the white man in moral distress', and indeed it turns out that the encounter has been the occasion of some head-hunting by his Samoan troops. But in a moment Brandeis himself is sending orders to a German warship, to bombard a village occupied only by women and children – a tactic used, according to Stevenson, by Germans and British alike, and sometimes 'on very trifling grounds'. On this particular occasion, however, the villagers emerge unscathed by simply walking off a little way into the forest. 'Conradian' is the word that might spring to mind – though Stevenson hasn't Conrad's brooding sense of human darkness.

Brandeis the morally susceptible also forbids the severed heads to be carried off by his victorious 'loyals'. One of Stevenson's eventual informants, riding off to investigate,

> was attracted by the sound of wailing, and saw in a house the two heads washed and combed, and the sister of one of the dead lamenting in the island fashion and kissing the cold face. Soon after a small grave was dug, the heads were buried in a beef box, and the pastor read the service.

That the head is disembodied makes this a strangely moving mixture of grotesquerie and grief; this isn't the sort of irony that subverts all feeling with a knowing attitude, but rather the sort defined by I.A. Richards, in which contradictory feelings *co-exist*. And this is the 'obscure economy' we find throughout Stevenson's story. This particular episode, for instance, concludes:

> through an ill-timed skirmish, two severed heads, and a dead body, the rule of Brandeis came to a sudden end. We shall see him a while longer fighting for existence in a losing battle but his government – take it for all in all, the most promising that has ever been in these unlucky islands – was from that hour a piece of history.

Poor Brandeis, we feel, ensnared by chance and necessity, that bleak Darwinian pair, but we remain aware that the ill-timing was in part his own choice. We feel sorry for him, or we smile at him, or with him, or disapprove, or admire. And it is this play of attitude, felt in the artist's subtly-varying voice, that persuades us of his 'impersonality' – not a suppression but a complexity of passion, its focus on the individual protagonist.

This kind of impersonality is beyond Professor Geertz. He aspires, he tells us, to a 'certain dispassion', but, in his pursuit of the unfolding pattern of History, he must perforce neglect the individual. His 'dispassion' is thus more simply a detachment, and his characteristic voice a rather academic monotone, attaining sometimes to a neat antithesis, occasionally trailing off in qualifications and asides. To charge an anthropologist with such deficiencies in the storyteller's art may seem unfair; but like other scholars who feel driven by 'post-structuralism' from the kingdom of Reason into the more modest realms of story, he remains rather irritatingly innocent about the requirements for full citizenship. An interestingly similar and equally sanguine migrant is the half-Derridan Richard Rorty. He seems to feel that story-telling is entirely personal, a matter of 'play', and to believe that philosophy ought frankly to follow suit, abandoning any general claim to 'truth'; but, as his own writing makes abundantly clear, mere abandonment in itself isn't quite enough. He writes acceptable prose of an academic kind but has none of the living voice of a Stevenson, nor any awareness of the way in which it reconciles the impersonal and the personal, 'truth' and 'play'.

Of course the storyteller's voice isn't the voice of god; it may charmingly mislead (the critic's task is not to be misled) or acquire a period timbre (like Stevenson's late Victorian mellowness). Nor is story-telling the only way to speak of the world; no one minds the monotone of a technical paper. But if you choose the narrative mode, you should be aware of its procedures.

You can choose of course not to tell any story at all – like Robbe-Grillet, again, who would have regarded Sylvia Plath's sense of 'emptiness' as just another story, told in reaction against stories about 'mother nature'; the hangover after the romantic excess. But Robbe-Grillet's attempt to achieve a purely neutral view exacts a high price; it requires us for instance – as did the Royal Society in its early days – to expunge all personification from our language. And this price, too much even for a reductionist like Dawkins, was evidently a factor in the collapse into post-modernism, where any story at all about nature is acceptable currency – provided that it's only proffered as 'play-money'.

Of course many variant stories about nature can indeed be told. From the point of view of grass, for instance, the story is all about the triumph of grass, with human beings evolving merely in order to assist. Cats obviously believe the same tale about cats, and Stephen Jay Gould has written in a similar vein about microbes. But these attempts to get outside the merely human point of view are in fact moral tales designed to puncture our self-importance. That is, they're told from a human point of view. And this, one recalls, is the final moral of Lemuel Gulliver's story: we can't escape the human point of view (even his madness is of an all-too-human kind) because we can't escape the human body, where the 'obscure economy' of all our thought begins. Culture is rooted in nature.

*   *   *

On the eastward flight to Calgary across the Rockies, the mountains to the north, even in July, look completely snow-covered. Stretching endlessly away, they seem emblematic of enormous difficulty, like the 'Alps upon Alps' of accumulated learning in Pope's classic simile, or of deathly sterility, like his Nova Zembla, 'where scarcely flows/The freezing Tanais through a waste of snows'. Pre-romantic mountain images. And approaching Calgary, one can see, in brilliant clarity far below, the catastrophic edge, where the mountain mass, inexorably driven against the immensity of the plain, tilts violently up in great jagged strata. It vividly suggests a blind, dangerous force, but our own higher altitude blunts one's sense of its scale – until, that is, the plane turns and banks into a descent, and we catch a glimpse of the city. The gleaming tower-blocks – tucked in between the mountains that stretch two thousand miles from north to south and the plain that extends almost as far from west to east – make scarcely any mark at all; you might simply fail to notice them. The inhabitants of landscapes like this perhaps need their glass and steel monoliths to maintain even a minimal sense of human importance.

At the airport our nephew is there to meet us with all the attentiveness of a Confucian 'eldest son', but when he takes us downtown, we're none the less surprised to find at the city's heart – and dwarfed by the surrounding sky-scrapers – a full-scale replica of Beijing's most illustrious building, the Temple of Heaven, where the Emperors used to offer prayers for abundant harvests. The round blue-tiled roof and crimson wooden pillars of the replica – built as a 'cultural facility' by a Hong Kong billionaire – offer sanctuary, it almost goes without saying, to a shopping arcade. Modern culture having conquered nature, prayers for good harvests are only rarely in demand.

'Modernity', Professor Geertz observes, is extremely difficult to define. Perhaps so; but the piquant contrast here between scraping the sky and praying to it, highlights one central and simple meaning: 'wealth and power'. It's an especially vivid meaning of course for the poor and powerless. Across the street, and dwarfed even by the Temple of Heaven, stands a shabby, two-storey, red-brick building with a faded wooden sign: The Indian Friendship Centre. In the deserted foyer we find the usual sad notices about alcoholism and drugs, and then a glossy poster showing a 'happy American-Indian family' in a sun-dappled woodland glade – a man and a woman, a girl and a boy, all in stylish sports dress, with a dog-show dog and a shining jeep. The ideal, one might almost say, and the reality.

Next day we see further versions of the ideal, when our nephew takes us out to Banff, the resort town in the Rockies. We lunch in the old 'grand hotel', whose dining-room windows look out on snow-capped peaks and a pine-clad valley with a mountain-stream, and, yes, a manicured golf-course. Nature as backdrop to the enjoy-ment of wealth and power. My in-laws love it; Alpine scenery appeals to the Chinese as irresistibly as the sugar-loaf mountains of Kweilin appeal to Europeans. There are no Indians to be seen of course. The only picture of them, even, is a post-card in a high-street gift-shop; the 'happy Indian family' but in pioneer-days – man, woman, boy, girl, all smiling at the door of a rustic cottage.

'Modernity' has clearly always been a story of wealth and power, tradition and technology, the dynamic of nature and culture at the leading edge. In its current version the story is fast-moving, and the Indians, their old ways shattered by new technologies, may almost have lost the plot. But as always it's essentially a moral tale, and the moral Scylla and Charybdis that confront the Indians are those made clear by the notices and the poster in The Indian Centre – delusion on the one hand, on the other despair. But if you can keep them in clear view, you can steer a course between.

Back in Calgary in the evening, some distant relatives from Hong Kong take us out to dinner, and afterwards to admire their new house. As we drive along the elevated freeway out of the city, the whole urban scene – the glass tower-blocks darkly gleaming, the pulse of downtown neon, the mid-night blue of the zenith, the sunset afterglow above the dark mountains – gives out the sense of electric evening promise that always recalls *The Great Gatsby;* wealth, power, and romantic yearning – and then the disappointment as you enter the suburbs, the dull common streets.

The house has a creditable quota of portico and vaulted foyer, and inside we find an elder daughter (the younger has been with us to the restaurant) watching TV with her Canadian boyfriend. She seems a rather difficult, restless young woman, but her interest is faintly stirred by my (to her) exotic provenance, and she soon confides that her great ambition is to live in Toronto. This news – clearly by no means new – is received in silence by both boyfriend and parents; and in a moment her sister, a lively eleven-year-old with big dark eyes and a beautiful brown complexion, seizes the opportunity to drag us off to to meet her dog. We discover the unhappy creature not only confined to the kitchen, but also muzzled, having recently bitten the girl's finger. Quite small and fine-boned, with pointed ears and nose, and a thick white coat, he looks at us rather dolefully. 'He's really wild,' says the girl, a wild gleam in her own dark eye; 'he's part Arctic Fox.' For her the wonder of life is here and now, not in Toronto, or the future. The child-philosopher again. The gleam fades as you grow up, said Wordsworth; but the girl's dog, and her words, and her kindled expression, remind me of March, the troubled heroine in D.H. Lawrence's 'The Fox', and of the fox itself, that looks up at her so disconcertingly. Making her usual rounds of the chicken-farm at sunset, her gun at the ready but her soul elsewhere, she becomes aware of him suddenly close at hand: 'His chin was pressed down, and his eyes were looking up. They met her eyes. And he knew her. She was spell-bound – she knew he knew her.' A grown woman's wonder.

Lawrence's fox could come straight from the totem world, where animals and humans share a common mystery, a common source; yet it's also a convincing presence in the modern story. In the past few days I've seen many attempts, intriguing and moving, to bring ancient and modern art together. Some, like the Indian artist Bill Reid's carvings and stories, seem primarily ancient; others, like rock-and-roll with an Indian catch in the beat, seem primarily modern. Museum-art and pop-art; and shop-art too of course – the myriad 'native' artefacts sold to the tourists. Perhaps great imaginative work like Lawrence's will appear; indeed it may have appeared already, for all I know, for I know so little.

What I do know of course, like everyone else, is that in the world of big publicity the current prophets of the North-West Coast are William Gibson, author of the cyberpunk novel, *Neuromancer*, and Bill Gates, creator of Microsoft. Computers, says Gates, will turn human beings into gods; no, Gibson replies, into machines. But it's their own visions, progressive or surreal, that have lost touch with humanity. In pursuit of 'modernity' they attend only to the future. We need to attend rather, as Blake advised, to the voice of the bard, who present, past and future sees. And the baby in 'Infant Sorrow', for example, shows quite clearly what he means. 'Helpless, naked, piping loud, like a fiend hid in a cloud', it tells us something essential about any parent's experience of babies, in any place and at any time. The 'holy word' from amongst the 'ancient trees', is always now, as the reader hears the bard's living voice. And this 'now' of course is Pound's 'making it new'. It may take unobtrusive forms. In even the most formal tribal dance for instance, when each individual dancer's nuances of movement and gesture are caught up in the common pattern, the dance comes to life.

'Are you Stampeding?' enquires a well-appointed middle-aged lady next morning in the lift of the well-appointed modern building where our nephew has a serviced apartment. Her affably ironic inflection seems to suggest that though all the hype about The Stampede is no doubt excessive, the event is still probably worth a visit. Our group replies 'Yes' in a happy chorus that drowns her little irony. Next floor down, the lift stops to admit another middle-aged woman, with a child. Or is he? He has the eager manner and bright eye of an eight-year-old but the wizened face and skinny dewlap of a nonogenarian. There's almost a frisson in the lift, as at something 'unnatural'.

Some words are capable of what Empson used to call a 'pregnancy' – as when Hamlet says of his father 'He was a man', meaning 'all that a man ought to be'. 'Natural' is a word of the same kind. As Michael Polanyi used to point out – and as the Greek sculptors would have agreed – our perception of any particular thing implies a general idea and this in turn implies a norm or ideal. In this sense a 'prejudice' against a deviation from a norm is itself a natural thing, not easy to remove. The wizened boy, our nephew tells us when we've left the building, has a syndrome that accelerates the metabolism and thus the whole aging process; and this information makes us think of him as more 'natural', but it would clearly take a longer familiarity to feel at ease with him. Prejudice isn't to be condoned of course, but it ought to be understood – as it customarily isn't by radical theorists; unable to see it as rooted in natural experience – which they reject as a 'humanist illusion' – they tend to veer wildly between rage against what they can only see as its wilful wickedness and despair at its strange recalcitrance. A more ineffectual rhetoric would be hard to imagine.

The Stampede – really just an agricultural show – looks at nature from a utilitarian point of view. In one of the first marquees a display featuring chefs and dieticians, agrarian economists and Famous Footballers, is devoted to the praise of beef, and the Stampede's centrepiece – the rodeo – is devoted to its subjugation. My food-loving and unviolent in-laws are engrossed by the former and repelled by the latter, so we give it a miss; but near the entrance to the grandstand we come upon a curious echo of it in the shape of a weedy urchin hanging onto the rail of a movable cattle-pen and stroking the rosetted foreheads of a pair of yoked draught-oxen. He leans suddenly forward, no doubt inspired by recently witnessed deeds of rodeo derring-do, grasps one of them by its horns and gives a steer-throwing wrench. The beast slowly shakes its huge head and blinks, as though in mild remonstrance at these juvenile liberties. The boy, apparently seeing this as a token of submission, jumps down from the rail with a cowboy whoop. 'Mongrel beef-witted lord,' is my first thought; but of course Thersites' vision is always one-eyed; a sense of pride and power, though always in need of restraint, is obviously essential to the story of human-kind. The critic of the Group of Seven or the commentator at the pioneer-museum might simply find the macho lad ridiculous, but they too of course have their own version of pioneer-pride – the academic's self-image as a 'ground-breaker', as the 'herald of a new age' of manners, morals, or ideas.

The Stampede's main thoroughfare has all the usual fun-fair side-shows with all the usual variety of targets, missiles, and prizes, but the biggest crowd by far is at a tent full of electronics and bearing the legend 'Battlestation Seven', where the missiles and targets are evidently ultra-modern. But only virtually real. The real game – going on not in the tent but in the queue – is the teenage mating ritual perennially renewed; the fat and giggly, the cool and witty, the blankly beautiful, the hard and calculating, the pale and furtive, the loudly excited, they're all still here, as bright-eyed as ever.

At the end of the thoroughfare we find an 'Indian village' – a scatter of tepees, inscribed with names like Maggie Black-kettle, Eric Runner, and Louise Big-plume, and an outdoor stage on which a stout, middle-aged man in a full feathered head-dress is introducing a traditional belt-dance. This particular renewal of the perennial no doubt leaves much to be desired; the dance turns out to be half-hearted and disorganised; the dancers, dressed in Indian and European motley, seem unsure of the steps, and the music booming and crackling from the loudspeakers is just a record. Art and nature, past and present, are dislocated and the performance inert.

I find myself thinking of it again in the evening, as we sit after dinner listening to our nephew playing a Mozart violin sonata accompanied on the piano by our hostess, a Chinese migrant married to a 'white' Canadian. She has a remarkable house – hi-tech American kitchen, French dining-room with a curious table of cloisonné and wrought iron, and in the drawing-room a blend of old Siam, post-modern Hong Kong, and imperial China. And the musical renewal here is very accomplished. I must confess I find the whole scene somewhat contrived, a self-consciously multi-cultural display. But then my own tastes don't run at all to the highly wrought; 'give me a smile, give a face, that make simplicity a grace'; and in both food and music I'm more hearty than discriminating. Our hostess doubtless finds me rather uncivilised. And after all, there's a touch of nature still in her bright eyes and the slight flush of her cheeks, as she plays for us. Is it nature totally geared to display? Is she a Rosamond Vincey? Or is she simply taking pleasure in giving pleasure through art, a capacity highly developed in Chinese culture?

Something of both perhaps. But in what proportion? A real story-teller would want to know, of course; it might be a moral crux in the story.

In any case I myself, half-Sinified scion of the British working-class, and long-settled in the Antipodes, am essentially no different from our hostess – or from the Indians, or the perennial teenagers, or all the rest – a bricoleur, constructing my life out of what comes to hand. 'These fragments I have shored against my ruins'. The modern notion of 'bricolage' evidently derives in part from Eliot, and it still bears the marks of his own sad lack of faith in the natural creativity of perception – in the 'primary imagination', that we all take for granted until we see it's loss in the sad cases described by an Oliver Sacks. In fact the 'fragments' that come to the bricoleur's hand are always already *shaped* by nature. A poet, for instance, may find an image simply springing to mind; a white horse galloping away across a meadow was Eliot's own favourite example, a stored *unit* – not fragment – of perception lying dormant till awakened by the poetic impulse. To find words that will fix the natural image in the poem is clearly an exploratory process; words and image react upon each other, and with results the poet doesn't always quite expect. Without this interaction of experience and word, of nature and art, bricolage becomes mere cliché-mongering, an assembling of prefab-ricated verbal chicken-coops, so memorably mocked by Orwell, in 'Politics and the English Language'. His point of course was that when words go dead, propaganda thrives, giving us 'the Aryan superman' and 'the sub-human jew'. A recent irony here is that the 'theorists' who have most vehemently denounced prejudice, have at the same time ardently espoused the neo-Saussurean dogma of the linguistic prison-house or ghetto; since their theory of meaning severs language from perception, they can conceive of nothing but chicken-coops.

My sister-in-law's house by the stream back in Vancouver is one of a dozen in a quiet cul-de-sac. Strolling the neighbourhood one summer evening after dinner, we chatted with an old married couple, here visiting their daughter. The woman is in a wheel-chair, a capa-cious hand-bag on her lap, and in a moment she was fishing into it for a photograph-album. She carries it always with her it seems, and has already shown it to my sister-in-law. The photographs are comprehensively banal – house, décor, garden, cats, in rural Alberta – but the old woman, her blue eyes naive and eager as a girl's and her face remarkably unwrinkled beneath her thinning white hair, displays them with a disarming simplicity. Her husband makes an

occasional mildly ironic comment, but this seems only a veneer, a
protective device, in case we fail to appreciate, as he himself so clearly
does, his wife's remarkable innocence. The old couple perhaps patro-
nise my sister-in-law a little as a 'new Canadian', and, being from
Hong Kong, she patronises them a little in return as 'country-folk'.
But only a little. They're also seeing each other, I can plainly see, as
individuals and as human beings, adjusting their old ideas – a little
– to accommodate the new image, just like the sting-rays.

A century ago, just down the coast from here, in San Francisco,
Robert Louis Stevenson noted that Europeans were wont to regard
the Chinese as 'a hideous vermin, and to affect a kind of choking in
the throat when they beheld them'. This, together with an even more
contemptible attitude towards American Indians, made Stevenson
feel 'ashamed of European civilisation', and we in turn may feel
grateful that our attitudes have changed. In Australia only a few
months ago, none the less, a populist MP made a speech against
Asian immigration and struck a nation-wide racist chord – with
small-town mayors expressing their revulsion against 'half-breeds' –
that took 'liberal opinion' completely by surprise. But why should
it? Politicians of course – in increasingly messianic mode as we
approach the millennium – like to talk as though we leave our vices
behind in the march of History. Newt Gingrich has just announced
the Republican 'mission for the twenty-first century' – 'to heal
America, then help America to heal the world'. But who will heal
the physician? – for Gingrich himself has just been revealed as the
eternal politician, not remotely to be trusted; and politicians aren't
uniquely wicked of course; we're all still brothers and sisters of the
fox and the raven.

I think of Professor Geertz again. A humane and learned scholar
he's no Gingrich of course, but his 'modernity' seems almost as
chimerical as the politician's 'twenty-first century' – and for the same
reasons. A Maori activist of my acquaintance called Dun Mihaka
moves in the post-colonial currents of History that particularly
interest Geertz. During a royal tour of New Zealand some years ago
he caused a media stir by baring his buttocks at the Queen. And his
interest in the media remains exploitative and acute – it was as a
teacher of 'media studies' that I first met him – and I suppose this
makes him 'modern'; but he seems just as comfortable with older
political methods – such as punching your opponent on the nose.
'War is diplomacy carried on by other means', said Clausewitz, who
is more 'modern' than Mihaka only in that he didn't envisage
fisticuffs at the conference table. Mihaka's forthrightness reminds

me of some of the working-class men of my father's generation, and in general we get on very well, though I'm sure he finds me rather tame and bookish. As indeed I sometimes find myself. And no doubt his own 'obscure economy' has its contradictions too. Shrewd yet impulsive, with the conflict sometimes written all over his face, and large and sudden of movement, as if he might burst out of his modern clothes, he divides his attention, when he comes to town, between the university and the gaol, where he visits his friends and where he himself has often spent involuntary time – for buttock-baring acts (metaphorical, as a rule) against various dignitaries. An unregenerate socialist, more concerned, he says, with class than race, he's also at odds with other Maori activists. Altogether, with his square jaw and powerful frame, stiff shock of grey-black hair and restless eye, he clearly belongs to one of the less ruly branches of the clan of the Monkey King; and our occasional meetings are always memorable – to me at least – not because of his place in the pattern of History but because of him.

But what of the relation between the two? We might, with the chaos theorists, think of History as a pattern of events always teetering on the edge of other patterns, to be tilted one way or the other by some particular event of apparently minuscule significance. But theory is one thing, practice another. What small events in the life of Mihaka – or of Bébé, or the girls in Calgary, or anyone else – are impacting on what larger patterns and with what effect, could be told only by an omniscient deity. Human beings, as Aristotle and Professor Geertz agree, can only describe the *sorts* of things that tend to happen. My sketch of Mihaka might, if I had the story-teller's power, be expanded into a tale about shrewdness and impulsiveness – which factor was decisive at some critical point, and what larger effect this had. 'Sorts of story' evidently tend to be moral tales. As the modernist Basil Bunting said, creative writers are 'wise to do as they usually do and stick to the commonplace'. But they make the commonplace new, make it now, and this is the kind of story-telling that really matters – and by the same token it's also the kind of 'modernity' that really matters. The balance of pattern and 'now-ness' is the poetic movement that Coleridge figured by the snake, that gathers itself together in order to advance, just as the reader's attention is both gathered at each rich moment in the story and also drawn to the future; an ideal balance between aimlessness and hurry, and a model for living in a world of time. Needless to say, it's yet another achievement of the imagination's 'obscure economy', and yet another commonplace that needs making new.

My sketch is also a '*kind*' in another sense; it's a 'version of pastoral', with myself as the over-civilised author half-admiring, half-patronising the more natural man. The genre is capable of great subtlety, as Empson's book about it long ago made clear. To imagine Clausewitz fighting at the conference table is an 'ironic pastoral' fancy; you might judge him merely barbarous or you might think it's a more honest and natural course than to despatch thousands to do your fighting for you. The pastoral mode can keep both attitudes in view – as Stevenson always does when he writes about Samoa. It's eternal theme of course is nature and culture, the 'primitive' and the modern – for though 'modern' is a rather modern word, the idea is evidently as old as culture itself; it arises wherever different levels of wealth and power collide, and if aliens ever do arrive on earth, cosmic pastoral attitudes will simultaneously appear.

The old human animal and the new human individual, old stories and new circumstances of their telling; these informing principles of the stories told by 'the bard' are clearly important in a shrinking and changing world. They keep the imagination alive to both community and difference, continuity and change, in both time and place. They prevent us from losing life in mere pattern or losing pattern in mere detail. A better basis for stories, surely, than that by which Geertz, Gibson and Gates are in their various ways sustained – the eternal march of 'modernity' into the ineluctable future. And immeasurably better, of course, than the one that sustains the 'theorists' – the eternal march of words into further words.

A Quick Trip to China

At the top of the steps we lean against the cool stone of the battlements and look back. The Great Wall tumbles and climbs its way over the mountain ridges, just as it does in all the pictures, disappearing at last into the blue distance. Down on the plain to the south we can make out a tiny patchwork of fields and the dots of houses. The plain to the north is just a silvery-green blur glimpsed here and there beyond further hills. The breeze is cool but the sun is warm, and on the slopes below us the plum trees are white with blossom. And of course the real lines of defence are now elsewhere – in remote compounds, with high perimeter fences and missiles in buried silos. The amiable clown who wanders the battlements in Manchu warrior garb, crying 'boo' and waving his sword to startle the tourists, is theme-park 'tradition' at its emptiest.

But the Wall remains none the less a potent image of war. We can still imagine the ancient stir of fear and excitement here on the steps when puffs of smoke from some distant watchtower signalled the approach of the enemy – Tamburlaine, perhaps, or Genghis. My son – his mother is Chinese – has just recalled that this is the only human construct visible from the moon. Sad mark of a divided world. One's particular perception – of these stones, these blossoms, these jagged mountains – seems to figure the whole history of humankind.

But thoughts about this unfashionable cluster of terms – the idea and the image, the general and the particular, the natural and the new; all those pairs that Coleridge saw as unified by the imagination – have been flitting in and out of my mind for some time. Yesterday was my elder daughter's wedding – the reason for my being in Beijing – and it was of course a very particular occasion, an affair of family and friends. In the garden of the embassy where she works, we danced till morning with no historic consequence at all, but tomorrow I shall be meeting some Chinese writers whose lives seem inextricable from great events – Mao's victory, the persecution of the Rightists, the terrors of the Cultural Revolution, Deng's economic reforms.

Since I'm standing on one of the world's few surviving tracts of socialist soil, I naturally think of those like Professor Eagleton who reject the whole idea of 'individual consciousness, set in its small circle of relationships'; for them we are all locked into the march of history; 'particularity' is a 'humanist illusion'.

I remember my first visit to China, in 1978. The Cultural Revolution was over, and Mao's widow, Chiang Ching, was cooling her radical zeal in prison, but she was still admired by the feminists of Paris, and Beijing's Friendship Hotel still housed not only innocuous persons like myself (I was looking into I.A.Richards's use of Basic English in China) but diverse Arabs, Africans and Latin Americans whose activities were of interest to 'western' governments. It was in short still the heyday of revolution regarded as an intrinsic good, and Beijing was its powerhouse.

It was a drab, polluted city. It often reminded me of Sheffield in the 1940s, though it was of course much sunnier. It's just as sunny now, and the pollution is unabated, but history has marched vigorously on, and all else – one might think – will have changed accordingly. Or has it? One of the writers I am going to meet spent ten years of the Cultural Revolution down a coal-mine, and started university in Beijing in the year I first arrived in the city. I'll talk about history with him tomorrow; today is for the present.

After running the gauntlet of laughing, red-cheeked countrywomen hawking embroidered table-cloths and Great Wall tee-shirts at the bottom of the slope, we board our mini-bus, and drive off for a picnic lunch at the Ming Tombs.

And here of course history soon returns, though not quite on the march; history as tradition rather than development. The great artificial hills of the tombs, set in the middle of a plain encircled in turn by distant mountains, are a reminder that China is Zhong Guo, The Middle Kingdom. How different from my home in New Zealand, where, so far from being centred in space and time, you readily feel yourself on their outer edge; almost any day at all the dawn coming out of the Pacific can seem like the world's first morning, and you feel a lightness of being either unbearable or exhilarating – it's up to you.

But even a history as long as China's can rest on one lightly enough. Our particular tomb, being unrestored, is deserted, and as we spread our picnic-lunch in a sunny corner of the forecourt, with wild violets darkening the grass, and dwarf pine-trees twisting out from cracks in the high enclosing walls, history is felt only as a deeper sense of quiet.

But it is, I am conscious, a history not my own; and this seems to increase its value. After eating, we clamber up a steep and crumbling staircase onto a platform where we find a vault containing an inscribed stone tablet. We look at it with the special respect reserved for an unknown script, then disperse and wander, singly or in groups, about the tumulus – a grassy knoll perhaps a hundred and fifty yards in diameter and completely encircled by the pine-studded retaining wall. It rises up through a grove of conifers, and at its summit is a dome of small stone blocks. The dome, about twenty feet high, with no inscription or any other distinguishing feature, takes you rather by surprise, and in this, as in its suggestion of the unknown, it speaks vividly of death. Half-hidden amongst the trees and almost a continuation of the curve of the hill, its unobtrusive symmetry seems a rather Augustan 'blend of art and nature'. The particular quality of the place, the full image it presents to the senses, is unlike anything I've seen from eighteenth-century England, but Pope would have responded readily to the idea. In Confucian China, nature was thought of neither as 'fallen' nor 'unfallen', but simply as something there, to be improved by art. In morals too the aim was to attain neither sainthood nor noble savagery, but to develop 'human heart-edness', or 'jen'. And the Augustans too of course were intent on moderating the old Christian conflict between nature and art.

On a sunny May Day some ten years ago, I remember cycling with my wife and a group of students to a Roman Catholic Church outside Shanghai. 'Socialist Revolution' was already a thing of the past, but the May holiday was still kept and the countryside was full of people, eating at roadside food-stalls, shopping at the village markets, or just wandering about. The church – an undistinguished pile but impressively large and perched on the brow of a hill commanding the Yangtze plain – was back in use again and a natural focus for the holiday crowd.

On the hillside just below ran a gravelled walk, winding its way amongst rhododendrons and azaleas, and lined with the Stations of the Cross. Our students were all interested in these exotic spiritual forms, and one of them – Liu, a clever, rather dreamy fellow from Sinkiang – was really fascinated. We left him gazing, and when at length he joined us again he announced that he was going to become a Christian. His classmates generally saw him as a country boy and they mostly responded now with sidelong smiles. But one of them, called Shao, fell into a rage. We all knew why. The Cultural Revolution safely over, Shao's wife and in-laws had reverted to their former religion – some form of Protestantism, I gathered. But Shao – himself religious by temperament and patriotic to boot – had become a Taoist. He had found a teacher and was practising 'chi gung', a discipline for the mastery of 'spirit'. (On the one occasion when I met him, the teacher displayed his power by apparently causing distant objects to move about, and by mastering a remarkable quantity of spirit of the alcoholic variety.) For Shao of course Christianity was both an alien creed and a source of domestic strife.

Liu seemed to ignore his angry scorn, but later, when we started out for home, they began to play the bicycle game. The rules are simple. You overtake your opponent then suddenly brake. If you force him to stop, while you yourself keep balance and pedal on, you win. But if your opponent can swerve aside and throw you off balance, then you're the loser. There are various forms of draw, and every result is disputed. When played in the middle of a cycling crowd the game occasions a general release of high spirits. Conviviality was soon restored, and Liu's impulsiveness shortly found a new outlet – in exhortations not to return tamely to Shanghai, but to keep on riding west, like the scholar-gypsies of old, trusting to the peasants for food and shelter. A nice idea, but of course we cycled home, where Liu at last achieved some degree of self-expression by plunging into the university pool at midnight, singing wild Sinkiang songs. Swimming after dark being an offence against regulations, he was duly fined, but this penance too was obviously part of his plan; perhaps he was one of nature's Catholics after all.

Here at the Ming tombs I'm not quite so carried away as Liu by the exotic religious forms. I have more to compare them with – starting from summer holidays in childhood, when I was dragged round hot London pavements to admire the nation's memorials to its great and good; this engrained a deep dislike of obituary pomp into my aching feet. The graves that mean most to me now are those of my parents, in a Yorkshire village, with headstones straggling amongst the tussocky grass and rooks cawing in the church-yard elms. But this Chinese tomb suggests not so much an exalted assertion against death, as the greatness of death itself, and I can feel my idea of memorial grandeur take a more affirmative shape.

To suggest that an individual soul can thus alight on a congenial idea, will seem a double affront to those who believe in nothing but history. But their view of history just seems absurdly limited. They shut out the whole perspective of biology. A genetic code, to take the obvious instance, is without doubt a product of history – of evolution – but it is none the less unique and its elements are none the less universal to all humankind.

The day before the wedding I went out cycling with some family friends. We followed the old tow-path along the Grand Canal – its handsome stone embankments in good repair, though its channel is a foul industrial sink – until we came at length to a public park. Feeling hungry we left our bikes locked at the gates, and went inside to look for a noodle stall. But, unusually for China, it seemed pure park; just grass and trees and flowers and strolling citizens. Our needs being gastronomic not bucolic we strode purposefully about until at last we came upon a red-striped tent by a lake. There was a fence and a box for the sale of tickets, but this was no deterrent to the hungry. Having paid our fee, we discovered that the tent had an open front looking onto the water, and inside there was a long counter with a plastic top; they were dispensing, however, not bowls of noodles but cans of worms and fishing rods. It seemed like a surreal joke about fast food.

Then we saw the anglers. They lined the shore of the lake, almost side by side, but being Chinese they looked at ease in a crowd, and they were plainly catching fish – we could see them being hauled out. The lake, one supposes, is replenished every night with plate-sized carp.

The New Zealand angler is a more elusive soul. You might catch sight of him at evening, waist-deep in the mouth of some stream where the currents run cold and strong into a roughened iron-grey lake. So different from this sociable Beijing pond. But these Chinese men, eyes fixed on their bobbing quills, poised to strike and feel the struggle of the unseen prey, embody the same idea, the same predatory impulse, and its history far transcends the human scale.

So does the history of death. I take a last look at the discreet Ming dome amongst the trees on top of the tumulus, then turn and make my way back down to the courtyard.

As we clear away our picnic, an embodiment of the idea of a caretaker appears and hovers in the courtyard-entrance, giving the imperial dust an occasional stir with his broom. A tall, pale, slow old man, his baggy trousers, cloth cap and faded blue Chinese jacket, seem symbolic of the old socialist days. He is pleased, we find, to take our empty bottles, from which he can make a few cents, but he accepts them with a gravity befitting the custodian of a royal tomb, and he himself seems almost as remote as the emperors.

The drive back to Beijing seems rather long. We are all too tired to take much interest in the landscape drifting past the bus windows. It seems the neutral sort of ground one finds around any metropolis; neither countryside nor suburb, just a straggle of buildings, fields, and hoardings.

Then the evening brings the sort of 'surprising' cultural shift that is in fact routine in the modern world – from the Great Wall to the new Great Wall Hotel, which houses the Beijing Hard Rock Café. As we make our way to it through the spring twilight, the streets are still 'teeming with humanity' – the stock phrase about 'the East' still sometimes rises to the lips of tourists, though in fact neither roads nor pavements are as crowded as, say, London's Oxford Street; and the cyclists, slipping silently by in their tree-covered lanes, are scarcely felt at all.

The dusk is starting to glow with the neon of Karaoke bars and restaurants. Fairy lights are in great vogue, falling in white cascades down the fronts of the shops, or strung through the greenery of the roadside trees. And even neon loses its crudeness when shaped to the complexities of Chinese script. The setting seems more attuned to romantic violins than rock guitars, and when we file at length past the motley of porters and security men at the entrance to the hotel, I wonder what Dionysian manifestations we could possibly find inside.

The café is big and semi-circular, with a bar along the straight side. It's already crowded, and music throbs from big black speakers hung on the walls; it's undoubtedly rock, but not very loud and not, I think, very 'hard'. In fact the gods of the place, I quickly find, are the heroes of my youth. There they are, all painted on the ceiling, the Beatles, and the Rolling Stones, reclined in a *trompe l'oeil* dome, with Michaelangelesque fingers reaching out. And from a high-arched 'window' in the wall, The King himself, in painted glass lit brilliantly from behind, advances his pelvis towards the gathered congregation.

You feel a conscious absence of irony in these effects. 'Can you deny,' they seem to say, 'that, for mythic fame and adulation, these figures indeed befit a pantheon?' The walls are covered with relics – historic guitars and posters of legendary concerts. Above our table is a glass case displaying a jacket 'Worn by Keith Richards on-stage in 1967'. The jacket is off-white and slightly crumpled; the case looks elegant and solid, all brass, mahogany, and plate-glass. And this is the key-note everywhere – costly materials, highly wrought, conferring value and respect, as in a church. And the worshippers all look solid people too, well-dressed and well-mannered as they eat expensive American food served by elegant Chinese wait-resses.

An unbeliever might remark an ironic fitness here; the music of the young and poor in Tennessee or Liverpool, like the religion that began in Galilee, has sold its soul; money always kills. And of course it's true that to be a paid entertainer is in many ways an unenviable fate. He who pays the piper will often call a tune the piper doesn't really want to play; Homer must have sometimes tired of sex and violence, but he had to earn his wine and mutton.

In this context of course money is simply a measure of popularity. What is it that popularity is supposed to kill? A really creative work, in Dr Johnson's succinct definition, is both 'natural and new'. 'Natural' here has its usual neo-classic range, referring both to 'human nature' and the 'nature' of the genre; it acknowledges, that is, the same continuum between nature and art that I was conscious of at the Ming tombs.

Rock music is clearly 'natural' in both senses. Like most ethnic dance music it has the desired effect on almost anybody's feet; and it seems a natural – almost inevitable – development out of earlier forms. As for the 'new', there might seem very little of it here. The rock classics emanating from the big black boxes make a very familiar appeal to the middle-aged, mainstream Western ears at our table. The woman on my left is exchanging glances with her husband, no doubt remembering the music of their youth, and her bright blue eyes are already dancing. But most of the songs are in fact more than mere exercises in the genre; they are still distinctively memorable, and this is Johnson's 'new'.

There isn't too much of it; not enough to distract the clientele from the essential business of the place – conviviality, sex, and social display; the Dionysian geared to the Darwinian. And one may feel that a genre so greased with social lubricant must slip very low in the hierarchy of musical forms – if such a thing is still allowed to exist. But at its own level it still meets the Johnsonian criteria; and they aren't of course just Johnson's; they reappear as Coleridgean indicators for the imagination – 'the sense of novelty and freshness, with old and familiar objects' – or in the formalist doctrine of 'defamiliarisation'.

As well as being natural and new, the music is growing steadily louder, but as the approach of Terpsichore is more nearly felt, my son informs me that it's time for us to go. He and my younger daughter and myself have tickets for a jazz concert that starts at half-past nine. I feel a momentary disappointment, but the concert is at a club and will surely afford further scope for cultural analysis and mild abandon.

The club turns out to be in a dimly-lit side-street, and shadowy figures can be seen, or rather sensed, standing about in the forecourt. It makes one think of old films about Prohibition, but a wooden signboard, its gothic script illuminated by a forty watt bulb, bears the legend 'The Poachers Inn'. As we stand discussing what time our car should come back for us, one of the shadows glides forward to say there'll be taxis after the concert. Convinced by his friendly Liverpool voice we deliver up our tickets and climb a rickety wooden staircase to the first floor.

The club's décor is a brave attempt to live up to its name, with exposed beams and horsey brassware and pheasants in glass cases. But the whole space – perhaps a hundred feet by forty, with a bar on one long side and a low stage on the other – is far too big for the village-inn effect. The beams look starkly structural and they make the stuffed birds seem more like *memento mori* than trophies of the chase.

The audience provides no more clue than the décor as to what sort of jazz we might be in for (all we know is that there is to be a saxo-phonist called John Zorn). They are Chinese and European in about equal number. The former are mainly young of course; avant-gardish women with startling make-up, and earnest youths in beautifully-tailored jackets. A crowd of men lounging at the bar with flushed faces, sharp suits and dazzling white open-necked shirts, could be a local species of lager lout. Sitting in a corner there are a couple of older men with long hair, refined features, and hollow eyes, who look unnervingly like the 'stinking intellectuals' of the old socialist propaganda films.

The Europeans seem mainly diplomats and business-people, full of the heady wine of life; but right in front of the stage, at a table by himself, is a man of forty-something with a strikingly bleak and stony face. And sitting near to us, with a young Chinese woman, is a silvery-haired old lady in a woollen cardigan who might have just come from baking scones at the Women's Institute. Would a Professor Fish regard all these as different 'interpretive communi-ties', I wonder?

At length the owner of the Liverpudlian voice steps onto the stage, which holds nothing but a set of drums and a microphone, and starts fiddling with the latter. In a while two other figures appear from the wings. One of them is a large young Chinese man with a loose build and an amiable face. He looks more like an athlete than a musician, but settles himself at the drums. The other – evidently John Zorn, though there are no introductions and no applause – is thirty-some-thing and slightly-built, with a white face, a stiff brush of blonde hair, and exhausted blue eyes. He wears a pale sports shirt and jungle combat trousers, and is armed with a dull green gun-metal alto sax.

After a brief conference, punctuated by taps and murmurs on their respective instruments, the pair launch into a fast blues. Though staccato and aggressive in the extreme, it is undeniably jazz even to ears like mine, weaned so long ago on Charlie Parker. But after the first number, Zorn abandons any conventions known to myself and starts making an altogether different range of sounds – somewhere, it seems, between whale-song and the howls of the damned. And since his rhythms seem determined simply by the physical adjustments required for the production of his noise – wedging his instrument between elbow and thigh, for instance, or jamming it against his midriff – they increasingly baffle the drummer, who eventually departs, leaving Zorn in command of the stage.

But what of the audience? The earnest souls in beautiful jackets have become steadily more intense. The stone face has cracked into an expression of grim delight, as if at the confirmation of some dark vision of things. And at Zorn's most startling acts of musical effrontery, the leading lager lout breaks into an appreciative whoop that sounds quite spontaneous though half-ironic. The 'stinking intellectuals' remain inscrutable, perhaps contemplating the whole scene, myself included, with a depth and subtlety I couldn't begin to fathom. A few of course – especially the glamorous Chinese consorts of some of the European men – have retreated behind glazed eyes and fixed smiles.

My daughter – who says that the music is hurting her ears – has picked up from the bar a type-written sheet presenting Zorn's credentials. It praises his range (said to include 'cartoon music', 'noise', and, surprisingly, 'country') but is chiefly a stock rehearsal of modernist orthodoxy, with the emphasis on 'fragmentation' – of the conventions, of unity, of the self.

But is Zorn's noise itself just a collage of conventional fragments? Or is it meant to be a fragmentation bomb, blasting through to some some anarchic substrate beneath all convention? At this point he is joined by a young Japanese whose instrument turns out to be the microphone itself, from which – by dint of licking, biting, chewing, sucking, and other kinds of mouthing for which a critical vocabulary has yet to be evolved – he elicits an order of sounds even more striking than Zorn's. The sounds, I suppose, of that 'poor, bare, forked animal', 'unaccommodated man'.

My daughter however – she is a student of dance at a college of performing arts – has taken her fingers out of her ears and is suddenly displaying symptoms of interest, even pleasure. At length she remarks that the microphone-sucker has a great dramatic talent. And it is, I realise, true. Quite apart from the noises, his face and gestures are vivid pictures of emotion – anger, fear, anxiety, bewilderment.

Gestures, being part natural and part cultural, again exemplify the continuum between art and nature. It's the same with sensory perception itself. The stone-faced man and the silvery-haired lady may be differently conscious of Zorn's noise, but it begins for both of them in similar sensory impacts. The neural transformations between impact and consciousness remain of course mysterious; they constitute that bodily 'mind', between the purely automatic and the purely conscious, that Jonathan Miller has recently described as the true unconscious, and that Michael Polanyi long ago defined as the realm of 'tacit' thought.

But inscrutable though the transformations are in detail, the continuum is apparent. Being rather deaf I wear hearing aids in both ears. I switch them off – so. The volume plummets, and this, though determined physically at the point of impact in my ear, remains of course as a feature of my consciousness – where Zorn's noise now sounds like the squeaking of distant mice.

To lose sight of this continuum is inevitably to lapse into the old routine – revived most recently by Lévi-Strauss and Derrida – in which 'nature' and 'art' rotate in increasingly giddy opposition, until nature simply disappears up its own Cartesian dualism.

The natural origins of Zorn's noise are easy enough to locate – in the urge to strip away comforting façades that was always a keynote of modernism. It's a keynote capable of varied resonance, from disturbing power to gross self-pity – sometimes both together, as in the poetry of Sylvia Plath – and no doubt it is now striking different chords in the lager louts, in stone-face, in the intense young men and the cosmetically iconoclastic young women; but they're all in the same key.

Where does this leave Professor Fish and his 'interpretive communities'? It leaves them where they've always been – in the apartheid fantasy-world of 'theory', where people of different cultural colour are forced to live strictly apart. It's a Professor Channing-Cheetah sort of world; the human animal beneath the social surface is kept carefully out of sight, and of course a multiplicity of interpretive communities does wonders for your publications output.

I look again at the silvery-haired old lady. Scone-bakers at the Women's Institute, as we all know, can have a cold grey eye, and hers, now fixed intently on the stage, has a glint that could be icy. She and stone-face, for all their difference in age, in class, and in gender, might well be children of the same idea.

But microphone-man is departing, and as Zorn prepares his gun-metal instrument for another raid on the inarticulate, we decide that it's time to go. His noise is interesting, but we've had enough. And some others in the audience seem to be flagging too – though stone-face still emits a grim glow.

Outside, we decide to ignore the row of waiting taxis and walk back to my elder daughter's place on Chang'an Avenue, the old imperial way that runs westward into Tienanmen Square. It's a clear spring night with just enough chill in the air to make one conscious of being well-clothed and fed. The streets are feebly lit, but night-time in Beijing – for a foreigner at least – still feels unthreatening, even comfortable in some curious way. Perhaps it's a sensation from my childhood in post-war England, playing pavement games in the pool of light from a street-lamp in the enfolding darkness. As we make our way now through the deserted streets, chatting about the concert, it seems to bring me nearer to my son and daughter.

My son – himself a pianist – seems to have mixed feelings about the concert. He grew up around a provincial university blessed with its full share of preciosity, and is still rather suspicious of 'minority tastes'. But he also feels, I think, a musician's solidarity with Zorn against 'the critics' (such as me). And since I myself am in sympathy with both his attitudes, our discussion meanders very mildly along, bringing us at length to the street the tourists call 'Silk Alley'.

Its narrow length is deserted and dark, except for the distant glare of Chang'an Avenue at the other end. We walk along between the booths, their shuttered silence a piquant contrast with the daytime jostle of shoppers haggling for cashmere and silk. But just as we reach the light of the Avenue, some figures emerge from the shadow of a wall.

We are startled, naturally, but before we have time to be alarmed, we see that they are in fact two women, each clutching a child by the hand. Beggars; still a rare sight in Beijing; rarer, I think, than in London; but as the women push their children forward in display, their pathetic gestures and insistent whine have a practised air; in China begging is an ancient art. On the other hand the night is really turning cold, and the children are only toddlers. My daughter – I can sense her distress, even fear – suddenly turns and strides away. My son and I follow her, but the women of course persist, whining in chorus and dragging the children along. And I am suddenly over-come by a terrible attack of Podsnappery. How dare they spoil our evening with their wretched display? Clear off, I tell them, clear off. They still persist of course, until I find myself virtually shouting. At last they drop away, and I walk on, full of rage and shame; I wouldn't, I already suspect, have shouted thus at a white male beggar, for fear of a punch on the nose.

My own children say nothing. In a while we start a desultory conversation about the day's events, and my feelings soon subside. But later, ready for bed, I stand in the dark at my fourth-floor window, the incident still on my mind. What was it? Women and children exposed to cold and want? Or a calculated exploitation of deep human bonds? Or both? And how did I appear in the eyes of the beggar children? Frightening, or ridiculous? The latter, I devoutly hope.

But in any case my ambivalent image of them turned quickly into the simple Podsnappian idea. I could and should have resisted it, but I didn't. I acted on it. Will there be consequences? Perhaps for the beggars I was some final straw to break their backs? But no, I'm over-dramatising. They no doubt found the episode commonplace enough, filing the image away in their minds amongst their ideas of the sorts of thing that can happen when you go out begging; hard-earned experience of their world.

But even so, it's the kind of story that is cumulatively shaping their lives. I look down on the Avenue, where so much history has marched – triumphant war-lords, foreign invaders, victorious revolutionaries. Of course it's just a march of abstractions through my mind; the image before my eyes is an empty stretch of roadway. But in a moment it's apparent that the road is never really empty, even at this late hour. Something – some pedestrian, cyclist, taxi, van, or truck, with breath or exhaust fumes whitening in the frosty air – is always moving silently across my field of vision, in endless irregular procession through the city. At the other side of the road dark masses of buildings huddle; beyond them the city lights twinkle away into the distance. 'And all that mighty heart...' If Wordsworth had wanted to notice, he would surely have seen a few struggling souls, abroad very early or very late, to mar his great image of peace. But then, my own image is still troubled by the beggars.

Next morning as my taxi makes its way to the Writers' Association office, the procession of vehicles along Chang'an Avenue is now nose-to-tail, and my air-conditioned capsule comes to a frequent halt, surrounded by crowded buses. The Chinese faces at the windows are much like the faces of commuters anywhere, especially the British perhaps, a people similarly ungiven to the public expression of feeling. They register the milder forms of abstraction or anxiety, or simple tiredness, and any eyes that happen to meet my own, glance quickly away. But as we wait at a red light, a middle-aged woman, strap-hanging in the aisle of her bus, seems to return my gaze. She looks the typical urban wife and mother, preoccupied but alert, her mind on one problem while watching out for others. Her thoughts are mostly now perhaps on shopping, but for the moment one of them seems to have lighted on me. And I suddenly see myself through her eyes – the rich foreigner in a car. She is no longer separated from me just by two panes of glass; a gulf yawns, and this time it is I who avert my eyes.

In part the gulf is truly material; I'm here in the taxi, she's there on the bus; a paradigm of Mammon's pervasive influence. But such gulfs of course are largely of the mind. This doesn't make them unreal – 'Hold them cheap...who ne'er hung there'. It means however that the mind can largely bridge them. I look at her again. She has raised her right hand (which is holding her bag) to push back the coat cuff from her left (which is hanging onto the passenger-strap), and she is frowning up at the watch on her wrist; but her eyes remain calm in her square yet feminine face. I can instantly identify with her gesture, her expression, her situation. The twinge of snobbery and guilt that made me look away is easy enough to control, and there is nothing to obscure my perception of our common humanity.

Rather different from last night and the episode of the beggars. I sink uneasily back into the upholstery. The other day I dropped into a picture-shop on Chang-an Avenue. The moment I entered, a young woman in a fashionable dress advanced towards me with a smile. I was evidently the only customer, and being a westerner I was by defi-nition rich. For me this was a novel experience. In this kind of place in Europe I'd get the bum's rush – in some politely modulated form of course.

She ushered me towards the paintings – tasteful blends of the tradi-tionally Chinese and the internationally modern, skilfully executed, easy to look at, and priced mostly at around three thousand pounds – then hovered at my elbow, gently waving a catalogue. In a shop of course it's beguiling to be treated as though you're rich; you feel that for once you're being valued at your proper rate. The assistant was charming, too, and her English had the musical cadence with which the women of Beijing are said to speak any language. Unfortunately her grammar was something of a wreck, but, having been a teacher in China, I could piece most of it together. At length I asked her whether they had any work by women. She replied regretfully no, but then she led me into a room with easy chairs and a big low table strewn with art-books, and began happily showing me reproductions of paintings by some of the 'famous' (her default adjective) women-artists of Beijing.

It was all so thoroughly nice, I had to remind myself sharply that it was really all about money. But this in turn felt rather cynical. Buying and selling, grotesquely over-rated though they are by the shopping ethos, are pleasant enough human transactions. So I indulged myself in ten minutes of her company – though I knew I couldn't really afford to buy – and emerged from the gallery in a rather complacent glow.

As I sit brooding now in my taxi, the cynicism returns. For her I was surely just a socio-economic construct – 'rich westerner'. But on reflection I'm not so sure. 'The rich,' Fitzgerald famously remarked, 'are different from us.' But the Chinese, I think, incline on the whole towards Hemingway's dry corrective – 'Yes, Scott, they have more money' – with its insistence on a common humanity. George Orwell somewhere says that in East Asia he never met the 'touch me not' gulf between between rich and poor that he felt in England – the gulf between the righteous and the damned. It is perhaps no accident that it was largely the English who developed the very language – abstract and analytical – that allows 'socio-economic man' to be constructed. And it is a language by the same token blind to both individual and universal man, because incapable of recording the necessary data – the particular recognitions and encounters in which our common humanity is revealed.

But Hemingway himself was a little too pat. Money can obviously create real barriers; and I myself, being residually English – class-conscious in a miserable working-class way – am sometimes inclined to exaggerate them. As my taxi pulls into the kerb in front of a modest building faced with polished brown stone, I begin to see myself as an intruder, indulged by the Writers' Association only because I have hard currency to disburse.

The driver points interrogatively towards the building. A dusty brass plate at the entrance confirms his surmise, and in a few moments, in the dusty foyer, a painted sign directs me up a narrow staircase with dusty marble banisters. Dust – it's just accentuated here by the polished surfaces – is ubiquitous in Beijing. In the long dry spells it drifts in from the desert, hanging in the air and slowly settling. Together with the bright sunlight it seems to drain the city of all colour. By day even the red walls of the Imperial Palace look rather bleached, whereas at night, especially in the lamp-lit side-streets, they seem to be painted with blood.

At the top of the staircase an anxious-looking clerk directs me into a room that might be either lounge or foyer; as I sit waiting, other clerks criss-cross it through various doors, but it's very fully furnished. Huge armchairs upholstered in grainy black plastic and adorned with embroidered antimacassars are arranged four-square around a low table. In the centre of the table's marble top, like some ceremonial apparatus, stands one of those elaborate chromium-plated ash-trays that are a feature of modern China – you press a plunger and the lid spins round and down, depositing your stub in a cylindrical container and whirling a little cloud of ash into the circumambient air.

But this last is of no consequence, since everything in the room, from the varnished floor-boards to the heavy black frames of the Chinese ink-brush paintings around the walls, is already filmed with dust. As I gaze through the window at the dusty courtyard, its soot-blackened tree as yet untouched by spring, a small gloom descends upon me. I think of the dreary rooms of old, where one used to sit, before and after visits to model factories, listening to the ritual lies of the local Party secretary. Will my interviews with these writers be like that?

At last the main door abruptly opens to admit a young woman, who launches, even while closing it, into rapid, slightly flustered, speech. Though occasionally wayward her English is very fluent, and it strikes an ambiguous note – somewhere between apology and accusation – that leaves me unsure whether she's late or I myself am early. But it's clear, at any rate, that she's going to be my interpreter. Clear too that she's a woman of some resource. As she takes off her white trench-coat and black beret, hanging them on an ornate Victorian hat-stand in a corner, and talking briskly all the while, I can feel her quick glances taking me in. When she finally introduces herself – her name is Cheng – she seems more relaxed, but in her grey suit with a white silk choker at her throat, and her hair gathered to one side in a big jade pin, she is still a very poised and definite presence. She's good-looking, too, in a pale, high-foreheaded way; her profile, half-turned towards me from the next armchair, and showing an aquiline nose and slightly hooded eyes, is rather arresting,

She seems used to being admired, but is businesslike too, and quickly grasps the sort of interview I have in mind. Interpreting for visiting writers, it appears, is her regular job. She drops one or two international literary names – to put me in my place, perhaps. My sense of being an outsider returns. I have always felt the impertinence of my project. I can read no Chinese at all, and speak it only in the form of very basic Cantonese. And now I feel like the provincial academic stumbling into a metropolitan literary scene. But a moment's reflection makes it seem more likely that Cheng was puffing herself up a little rather than putting me down; at any rate, we're on quite easy terms by the time the door opens again – to admit this time a rather tall slim man with an alert but affable face.

Cheng introduces him as Deng You Mei, my first interviewee. His dress – a blouson jacket with blue and grey stripes, a lilac shirt, a blue-spotted maroon cravat, and light grey slacks – rather belies his peasant origin; and his dark hair and easy movements certainly belie his sixty-five years. But with his air of quiet confidence he looks exactly what he is – a man successful in his world, an eminent novelist and president of the Beijing Writer's Association. A success no doubt made sweeter by earlier trials; like many artists he was condemned as a Rightist in the 1950s and like all he had to endure the Cultural Revolution.

In an obvious recoil his stories have turned to dwell on the 'old Beijing' of his childhood; a district of artists and craftsmen, opera singers and their admirers, gourmets and song-bird fanciers, poetasters and calligraphers, *flâneurs* and connoisseurs. And his characteristic 'heroes' are the hapless, helpless, cultured scions of the Manchu gentry, the Bannermen, marooned by history.

Of course I know his work only in English. His translator, Gladys Yang, is one of the band of foreigners with socialist sympathies who have spent most of their lives in China (some went straight there from the Spanish Civil War), teaching, writing, and translating – and occasionally languishing in jail; they haven't been merely privileged outsiders. In the past few years, like socialists elsewhere, they have experienced certain mental difficulties. Those with unassuagable radical and missionary zeal have switched from socialism to feminism, as the only progressive vehicle now capable of creating an impression of rapid movement. But Gladys Yang has taken a more general moral line. It shows in her preface to Deng's *Snuff-bottles and Other Stories*. These tales, she remarks, hold up the sons of the Manchu gentry as a warning to the spoilt children of modern Party officials.

There's clearly some truth in this. China has a long tradition of seeing its history in terms of the recurrence of moral ideas – 'the sort of thing that happens', as Aristotle put it when discussing the typicality of good plots. But Deng's art doesn't really feel didactic at all. Something in him just seems to respond to these sad Bannermen. Not that he seems remotely 'decadent'. Facing me now he looks the image of contentment and success; and his stories contain no modish admiration for marginality in itself; he sees his 'heroes' open-eyed, with all their weaknesses as well as strengths.

The latter are mainly the strengths of the artist, and they are felt to reflect a certain credit even on the parasites of the art-world. They're epitomised in 'Snuff-bottles', when an artist threatened with having his hands cut off, still refuses to paint flattering portraits of the Japanese conquerors.

What attracts Deng is the resistance of art against power – a lesson evidently drawn (and perhaps a little late) from the Cultural Revolution, when art didn't resist at all. Deng's own key memory of those unhappy days, he is now wont to relate, is of an old artisan who began painting snuff-bottles to raise funds for his commune, only to find himself branded as a 'reactionary element'.

Snuff-bottles are a minor art-form of a classic kind. They seem to have been made from everything on earth; wood, bone, tooth, shark-skin, shells, pearls, nuts, gourds, fruit; almost any kind of stone – jadeite, nephrite, lapis lazuli, turquoise, marble, tiger-eye, amber, agate, chalcedony; not to mention every imaginable combination of metal, enamel, ceramics, and glass. An exhibition of them seems altogether a display of the manifold materiality of the world, its sheer variety of matter. And any particular artefact, in its texture, colour, consistency, and shape, has an acute and various sensory appeal, a 'thinginess' unobstructed by any idea – the idea of snuff-bottles (the convenient dispensing of snuff) presents a negligible interpretive challenge even to a modest intellect.

That evidently applies to all 'collectables', no matter how highly wrought, and needless to say Deng's stories are art of a more significant order. But they too exhibit some excess of image over idea. Their main theme – of art as resistance and self-respect – is clearly capable of great development, but it is somewhat limited by Deng's focus on art of the snuff-bottle kind, and his own art becomes a little like it; his scenes are sometimes simply decorative, and the narrative mode is leisurely, inconclusive, always leaving room for more decoration if the story-teller feels so inclined.

My own criterion here – the integration of image and idea – is of course Coleridgean again, and these days it may seem somewhat limited, being based on the 'classic' literature of the west, and apparently rejected by post-modernism. But in essence it is simply a reflection of perceptual process. When I 'see a cat' I am integrating a new image to an old idea. Perception is merely baffled if an image finds no idea at all, and rather mechanical if the idea is found too readily. The function of art is to keep perception active and healthy; to remove from our eyes, as Coleridge said, the 'film of familiarity and selfish solicitude'. And in fact this is just as true of post-modern art, which, different as it might seem from Deng's, springs from a similar impulse: a reaction against the dominance of the idea – the dominance of 'theme', that is, and 'meaning'.

Soon after the Cultural Revolution ended I heard a famous actor called Zhao Dan describe the wooden triumph of 'the idea' in the revolutionary theatre. Actors were permitted only three gestures. Arm pointing to the horizon, face resolute: 'forward with the revolution'. Arm pointing to the boards, face grim: 'down with the capitalist running-dogs'. Arm raised to heaven, face reverent: 'up with the Great Leader'.

Some years later I spent a few pleasant days visiting all the temples marked on my tourist map of Beijing. It wasn't so much a pilgrimage as simply a device for seeing the city, and my memory of most of the temples is now rather dim. The one I still recall most vividly wasn't even on the map, and it was quite the most depressing.

I caught sight of it by chance in the southern part of the city – the equivalent of London's east end – while en route from a Taoist temple to a mosque. Its ghostly grey tower stood up tall and slightly bulbous on the nearby skyline. The problem was to get to it. It's first line of defence was a warren of old houses with narrow lanes and tiny courtyards. Trying to penetrate this at various points, I was always – as I expectantly rounded some corner with the tower looming close – stopped short by a high brick wall. This difficulty, together with the tower's ruinous appearance – the more apparent the closer I got – made me the more determined.

At length I struck upon a particularly promising lane, slightly wider than the others and a little less devious. And indeed it ended not in a wall, but in a great double gate; two solid sheets of rusty iron, some ten feet high and secured in the middle by an enormous padlock and chain. As I stood there staring at it, three boys in western-style school uniforms came walking past. I stopped them and pointed towards the gates. Smiling a little, but still respectful, one of them gave a negative shake of hand and head. We looked at each other for a moment, then I shrugged, and they moved on.

I wheeled my bicycle up close to the gates and peered through the gap. There was an extensive yard, presumably once the temple precinct, dotted with stacks of drainage pipes and bricks. Next to the temple was a long low shed with dirty steam coming out of a vent. There were no workers in sight but it was evidently some sort of brickworks, set up perhaps in The Great Leap Forward, when everyone's back-yard was given over to Industry. As for the tower itself, its pale stucco was streaked with grime and had crumbled away in patches, exposing a loose grey brickwork; but its graceful shape, like a great slender vase, remained to attract the eye and accentuate the surrounding ugliness. Its present state seemed to embody all the speed and violence of change. Imagine England, if the Reformation, the Industrial Revolution, and the decline of religion had been compressed into fifty years.

But the Taoist temple I had seen earlier in the day had survived the attentions of the cultural and economic commissars. It had become, ironically enough, a tourist attraction. Some of the younger monks strolling in the cloisters, with their wispy beards, grey cotton smocks and leggings, and their Taoist air of *dolce far niente,* weren't averse to posing for the camera. Nuns were passing in and out of a dormitory-building, and from the upper windows, screened by an ancient tree whose limbs were propped up by iron crutches, their chatter and laughter spilled out into the courtyard. Some local elegants, in black leather, blue denim, and expensive shoes, were rather self-consciously burning sticks of incense at the altars – tiered structures of red silk and gilded wood, crammed with urns and bowls of fruit and old bronze gods.

A Taoist purist would no doubt have shaken his head at much of this. But how infinitely preferable to the débâcle at the brickworks. And the temple must have survived – how else? – through the efforts of individuals on the spot. A local resistance, as Foucault used to insist, is more authentic than a central revolution. But how odd of Foucault then to proclaim the 'death of man', and so to deny, in effect, that the very qualities required for such resistance – courage and stubbornness and faith and hope and guile – are common to humankind. It is a resistance closely related of course to the resistance of art depicted by Deng Youmei in *Snuff-bottles*; it springs from local perceptions of the kind that supplied the temple tree with crutches, and is naturally more conservative than radical.

But the commissars who had their way at the brickworks, believing like Foucault in the 'death of man', saw nothing in the way of imposing their wonderful new industrial idea. 'Je m'en fou du passé,' poor Edith Piaf used to sing, to please the existentialists; 'Je depars à zéro.' Her ravaged face and plangent voice suggested that the news hadn't reached her body. And the brickworks temple reveals a similar rift in the continuum between body and mind, between nature and art. To simply erase the past, inscribed as it is on the physical world, is to make not a new start but a shambles.

But China has at least come off more lightly than Russia – a country ravaged by theorists of the left, then of the right, and finding continuity only in the culture of cynicism that Conrad portrayed so profoundly in *Under Western Eyes*. The Chinese have both a longer history and a more tenacious memory. And in Deng's stories of the Bannermen, for all the nostalgia, this makes itself felt as an essential sense of balance.

Leaning forward now in his black plastic armchair and discussing the economics of the Chinese literary world, Deng himself seems easily balanced too. A system of royalties is starting to develop, he tells me, but writers are still paid a living wage. He grumbles mildly about greedy publishers but concedes that newspapers pay well for articles; the essay, he adds, has ousted the short story as the form most in demand. And he seems just as much at ease when he speaks of social changes; his own household, he observes with a twinkle, is really ruled by his daughter. But interpreter Cheng smiles rather coolly at this, as though unconvinced that the patriarch has dismantled himself so affably. And when we talk of change in literature, Deng begins to show a conservative edge. At my mention of Wang Shuo – a younger writer who made his name with unmoralising stories about Beijing's new spivs and has now declared himself simply a 'technician in words' – he waxes rather emphatic about the 'cynicism of the younger generation'.

It intrigues me, naturally, to see these familiar quarrels going on here, and it is clear why Deng, whose fiction aims to retrieve a real history, should reject the belief that all is 'words, words, words'. But again I feel uneasy. Interpreter Cheng – she is of the younger generation herself – still has that critical look. And Deng's conservatism, I can see, may indeed be rather self-serving, just as his liberal twinkle may have been rather false. But I have no idea how his ambivalences may have issued in action; whether and how his no doubt considerable literary influence has already touched interpreter Cheng or even Wang Shuo. I'm beginning to feel the strain of trying to keep up even a facade of intelligence, and I'm not sorry when Deng starts glancing at his watch.

With a routine handshake he disappears, and interpreter Cheng starts putting on her coat. There is only an hour before the next interview and, suddenly loth to go out foraging alone, I suggest that we lunch together. I mean of course that I'll pay for us both, but I don't quite like to say so, for fear of implying that she's poor. She looks at me uncertainly. 'Are you inviting me?' she says, with a little flash of annoyance. 'Yes,' I reply, annoyed in turn that my false delicacy has compelled her to ask outright. And she had of course to make sure. The sort of place she would want to take a foreigner like myself would be beyond her own means. But we soon seem to recover from this socio-economic stumble, and in a few minutes we're studying the menu in a place just round the corner.

High-ceilinged and formal, with square black marble pillars, grey carpet, and crisp white table linen, the restaurant is rather deserted. It reminds me, I tell Cheng, of the old days, except that then the few diners would have been hard-faced senior cadres, whereas now they are evidently businessmen, looking rather flushed and excited, like bookmakers after a good day at the track. She nods. The problem confronting her own generation, she says, is to adjust to a world where money is replacing office as the route to privilege.

She herself, I can't help thinking, seems to be adjusting very well. She came to Beijing, she tells me, from Hangchow, to study at the Broadcasting University. Her ambition was to be a TV anchor-woman. Sent to work instead for the Writers' Association, she's decided to become a writer herself. At present she's translating Doris Lessing's *Golden Notebook*, to develop her skills and start making a name. Clearly her work has already given her an inside view of the literary world; and in Chinese culture this world has a traditionally sanctioned place in the world at large. There is nothing of the poet-in-a-garret about Cheng. She is a woman building a career. A lot, she sagely remarks, depends on 'contacts'.

I look at her and think once more of art as resistance. She is plying her chopsticks in a rather languid fashion, but that doesn't mean very much; young Chinese women all tend at times to affect the fantas-tical-genteel. If the Red Guard – or any other shade of thought-police – were somehow to return, how far would she 'adjust'? Would the individual strength that lurks in those hooded eyes reveal itself? I suppose that she herself wouldn't know until the event.

Fiction once thrived on such uncertainties. Though Cheng doesn't look remotely like a victim, I think for some odd reason of Cordelia; and then of Edmund's surprising attempt to save her at the end, with all its cruel suspense.

But uncertainties like that depend on plots, and plots of course, along with all the other patterns we think we see in events, have been latterly dismissed as merely arbitrary impositions on the great unut-terable. Hume on causality and Heisenberg on the indeterminate have been much invoked, to reinforce Saussure. And the patterns, we are told, are sinister as a rule. *King Lear* itself, it's been suggested, imposes on the world a 'pattern of apocalypse' that prefigures the Nazi Holocaust.

In some narrow sense, I suppose, interpreter Cheng – now delicately broaching a steamed prawn – may indeed be an unutterable shimmer of whimsical quarks; so may the prawn. But the pattern of digestive events she is setting in train isn't something that she arbitrarily imposes. In broad outline it's quite easy to predict, though not of course with temporal precision. In short the world in which people live and writers write, exhibits both pattern and uncertainty. The chaos theorists may have discovered this only recently, but storytellers, like other common folk, have always known it.

In *Lear* again there are various causal patterns – of parental whim and filial greed, and so on. But Edmund's decision to save Cordelia seems fortuitous, triggered in a strange and unexpected way by the deaths of the terrible sisters who have loved him. And once the decision is made, our sense of chance grows painfully acute. Evil has largely destroyed itself, and everyone now wants Cordelia saved; but the message to the gaol is just too late. So far from the blank imposition of a pattern, there is a poignant sense of how different the pattern might have been. Hence Dr Johnson's distress at Cordelia's fate, so nearly averted and so unnecessary.

An important function of stories, it was once believed, is to convey this disturbing uncertainty of life – without indulging either in Hitchcockian exploitation or Hardyesque paranoia. But with the advent of modern criticism in the 1920s, dramatic uncertainty was reduced to 'ambiguity' of 'meaning'; theme replaced action as the principle of structure. And in the fullness of time there appeared post-modern narrative, where life's brute contingencies have dwindled to the bookish 'indeterminacies' that agitated Hume and Heisenberg.

In further pursuit perhaps of her digestive pattern, Cheng at length excuses herself, and as I wait to settle the bill, I think about our next interviewee. His name is Chen Jiangong. Born in the *annus mirabilis* of 1949, he has lived through 'interesting times', as the Chinese call them, in which chance and pattern are both intensified. I will simply ask him to tell his own story.

The lounge-cum-foyer feels just the same as in the morning; the sun, it seems, never falls on its dusty windows; and Chen's story too is as one might expect – for modern China. He tells it in an even voice, detached, with an occasional smile lighting up his square but sensitive face – he is as handsome as a film-star, though his rather tired-looking clothes (brown suit, white shirt, and sober tie) seem more appropriate to a middling official, which indeed he also is, being Secretary of the Beijing Writers' Association.

His father, the story begins, was foolishly honest. In the 1950s he gratuitously confessed to an Anti-Rightist Committee that a man just exposed as a Nationalist spy had once been his friend. The committee seemed to let it pass, but in fact set out to destroy him. Jiangong himself, then still a schoolboy, became a universal butt. Only his talent for writing essays preserved him a remnant of self-respect – he pauses here and looks at me – and when the Cultural Revolution started he was happy to escape from school by being sent to work in the coal-mines. But conditions in the pit were so harsh that when he sustained an injury to his chest, this in turn seemed like a lucky escape.

And this time it really was. While convalescing he got to know the caretaker of an old library that had eluded the Red Guards' attentions. The books, he remarks with an ironic gesture, not only saved his sanity, but when the radical madness passed, enabled him to qualify for university. He wrote his first novel (about the mines) while still a student, but the Writers' Association admitted him straight to their ranks; and... well, here he is. His dry smile seems to acknowledge that his narration has been perfunctory, but at the same time suggest that it's quite adequate to the occasion.

As indeed it is. It reflects credit both on himself ('the writer who suffered and survived') and the government ('the bad old days are over'), and these are proper impressions to give to an inquisitive foreigner. It seems a true enough story too. It could of course be differently told. He could recount it as a drama of choice and chance, or as a comedy, or even concede a point to those who think the old days weren't entirely bad. The variations would reflect various purposes, audiences, points of view.

And this, a neo-Saussurean would triumphantly claim, in fact confirms that they all arbitrary impositions. But the claim itself is founded on what Whitehead called the fallacy of simple location. What is at stake here is clearest if we think of the story-teller and the audience face to face. In my own case this means the air-raid wardens' post on a council housing estate in the Second World War; a concrete block-house where a handful of middle-aged men, including my father, used to while the nights away around a coke-fired stove. The nearest bombs that fell were on Sheffield, several miles away, but the rumble of the aircraft overhead, the distant dull explosions, and the sulphurous smell of coke, all thickened the atmosphere, whatever tale was being told. For a five-year-old of course it was pure paradise.

No doubt I was absorbing a good deal of nonsense, but, for good or ill, I was also starting my career as a critic, as I learned from the adults whether to take a story seriously or with a laugh, with a nod of approbation or a hoot of disbelief. When the audience was divided, as it often was, the arts of critical controversy were vigorously displayed; and I was beginning to acquire even then a sense of which listeners had simply missed the point of the story, and which of them had got it but were feeling differently about it, and for what reasons. The variety of response didn't dissolve the story into uncertainty, but thickened it into a richer experience, a rich location, as Whitehead would say, not simply in the mind of the storyteller, or of any particular listener, but somewhere amongst them.

The deconstructionist, on the other hand, perusing a critique of a critique of a critique of a printed work, thinks naturally of Pierce's endless chain of meaning. There is evidently no simple location; any central 'meaning' he tries to put his finger on just dissolves; and sitting at his solitary desk with his eyes on his silent book, the idea of a rich 'between' simply doesn't occur to him.

But in fact even Derrida's notorious lectures, as accounts of them make clear, are richly located. Like my evenings in the wardens' post they are evidently ritual occasions, with the words tailored to suit. On the page his clotted flow is merely opaque; given vocal utterance its effect is variously potent. Some of the audience are put to sleep and some walk out. The disciples remain content; for them the obscurity is a true profound, while the enemy are presented with an impenetrable tale, proof against hostile questions.

As for my own tale of Chen Jiangong, I sense that interpreter Cheng would tell a more critical story. The key to getting on with any writer, she observed over lunch, is that he'll regard himself as the biggest talent in town. Perhaps she has seen a little too much, for someone so young, but of course there's some truth in what she says, and it may be true of Chen.

When I suggest to him, for instance, that China will soon begin once more to produce writers of world stature, he replies abruptly that perhaps it's already started, and he rather seems to have himself in mind. An egomaniac? But later he generously compares Wang Shuo's street-life stories with the early work of Mark Twain – a life-giving breath of air in a stuffy literary world – and he evidently intends it as the highest praise, given without hint of reservation.

I look at his handsome, open face. What is he 'really' like? He is of course like Edmund in *Lear*, or all the rest of us, or like history itself for that matter – a bundle of ambivalent potential, a matrix of various ideas and images. A story about him would leave you aware of this, but it would still determine his actions at the point of crisis. Hamlet – to take the most ambivalent case of all – stabs Polonius through the curtain and from this act all the rest of the drama flows. If Shakespeare had simply wanted to brood on his hero's indeterminate essence, he would have chosen some other literary form.

My own form here of course is the 'report', so nothing dramatic need happen at all. At length Chen simply departs, taking his bundle of potential with him and leaving me to settle with Interpreter Cheng. As she carefully pockets the US dollar bills, she asks me whether her work has been satisfactory. It's one of those pleasant moments when one can be both complimentary and sincere, and as we descend the dusty staircase to the street, she still looks pleased at the double yield of smooth words and hard currency. For her the day's story has a happy ending, and if this is the sort of thing that generally happens, her career as an interpreter will be a great success.

My final view of her is from a 'cheap' taxi – little box-like vehicles, locally made, that you creep into virtually on your hands and knees. She ducks her head to look through the window and wave goodbye. I wonder if she'll become a well-known writer? As the taxi pulls away from the kerb, I wave back, and wish her well.

In most cities you'd assume that the steel grille around the taxi-driver's seat is to protect him from muggers; in Beijing, so I've been told, it's to prevent the driver from robbing the passengers. Can this be really true? My own driver is lean-faced and tanned, more like a peasant than a city-dweller. He'd look the part on the Great Wall in Manchu warrior dress. But his radio – as in all 'cheap' taxis – is blasting out the latest pop. The lyrics are in Chinese of course, but it's clear that even the driver can't really hear them. Hunched in fierce concentration over the wheel and continually switching lanes in pursuit of some advantage invisible to me, he seems simply driven by the pulsing beat, like one of the Great Khan's horsemen riding to drums and trumpets. But the rhythms here come straight from Motown, and his rattletrap vehicle is sadly unlike a horse.

This is the kind of split image that currently fuels debate about China's cultural future. An unpredictable, perilous future, so we are told; after the deep wounds inflicted by the cultural commissars perhaps commercialism will now deliver the death-blow; and there is no 'master narrative' with which to even weigh the possibilities.

I think of interpreter Cheng again and of her literary ambitions;

and then of her digestive system. Cultural systems are no doubt more complex, but they too are 'chaotic' unfoldings of pattern and chance. And on China's cultural stage it seems quite clear which stories will unfold: an avant-garde will posture while traditionalists rage – and vice-versa; some genuine talent will be ignored and some acclaimed; a number of charlatans will emerge and some be exposed; much bad work and much good will be done for money; we shall see public hatchet-jobs and private stabbing of backs, oleaginous sycophants and the odd honest critic.

This isn't just to say that 'plus ça change...' The old stories will puzzle us with new images. And of course for any individual the brute uncertainties of life remain. Which stories, for instance, will feature interpreter Cheng? What contradictory potential in her will be put to what test, and with what results?

Some stories will no doubt be more important than others in shaping the cultural history of the age. But who can say which ones? Even after the event they'll still be in dispute. To look to some 'master narrative' for guidance here would clearly be a waste of time. On the other hand, as with digestive systems, there are always useful *rules*; eat your greens, don't bolt your food, take exercise. The rules of literary behaviour are just as easy to state, only rather more difficult to apply. Pope's *Essay on Criticism* – a work on literary principles worth attention now that 'theory' is in retreat – is a great compendium of them. Some are simple moral rules: keep a sense of proportion; work hard; know your strengths and weaknesses; be less envious, more generous; and don't tell lies. And the more literary rules are equally simple: study the master-works and learn the craft; be wary of mere fashion; avoid above all the plague of pedantry.

With regard to the last, it's the neo-Saussureans of course, with their doctrine of the arbitrary sign, who are currently displaying the classic symptoms – a morbid attraction to laboured word games and a predilection for the fragmentary and obscure. In China, with its traditional fondness for subtle and difficult art, this syndrome could be a serious hazard. Some Chinese film-makers who have been taken up by the international critics are already beginning to succumb.

The 'cultural' wing of the neo-Saussurean movement might be more dangerous still. Even in the affluent West, the cultural critics, having lost the 'master narrative' (i.e. the kit-set of socio-economic abstractions) by which they felt they were charting their universe, now fear that we're sailing off the edge of the world. Their epitome is Fredric Jameson, who set out boldly in Los Angeles to locate the position of The Westin Bonaventure Hotel in cultural history, and had trouble even finding the entrance to the building – his head too full of ideas to admit an image.

China, in the throes of profounder change, can't afford this kind of self-indulgence. To negotiate their current cultural straits they need to fix their eyes not on some master narrative – or on its absence – but on the Popian rules of navigation. And the best of luck to them, for that will be useful too.

The taxi stops. I'm home, and unassaulted by the driver. But it's broad daylight of course and I'm a foreigner. What if it were dark and I were a local? As the driver turns to collect my fare through the grille (surely what they say is just a joke?), he smiles with a flash of dark eyes and gold fillings, his teeth very white in his swarthy face. The spring sun, intensifying through the wind-screen, makes me suddenly aware of the heat of life beneath his greatcoat. He looks warm-hearted but perhaps a little wild; you could fit his image to either idea; which of the two would emerge in any crisis of action would no doubt depend on how you dealt with him.

How uncertain life in China suddenly seems, compared with the old socialist days. But no, it isn't true. The old days were uncertain in the extreme for those who disagreed with Big Brother. Even the cosseted 'foreign guests' were in danger from his lies, and most of us succumbed in some degree. Life is always uncertain, dangerous, one way or another, and especially so, perhaps, when it seems most dull and safe; that's why we need the story-tellers to clear our eyes of the 'film of familiarity and selfish solicitude', by revealing the dynamic of old stories and new events, old ideas and new images.

Hong Kong Revisited

A grey, luminous, spring day, already humid. Clumps of bamboo frame a view of rugged green hills and a silvery bay. The shoreline is all coves and headlands, and from here the sea looks enclosed, like a lake. I could be an old Chinese scholar gazing down from his mountain pavilion. But 'here' is in fact my mother-in-law's front door-step, in a Buddhist retirement village in the New Territories, a few minutes drive from the city.

It's reassuring to find that Hong Kong still has its quiet places. When my wife and I were courting in the sixties, a ten-cent ride on a ferry or a short drive in a car would always take us to some beach or hill that felt like the Outer Hebrides. And I still have a vivid memory of swimming, one hot summer's day, just up the coast from here, with two colleagues from the university. We basked in the warm sea, flopping over occasionally to dive to a cooler depth; there was no sound but the murmur of the waves on the shore; between the glow of the sky and the glitter of the water the world seemed melting to a spaceless, timeless haze; a lotus-eating sort of day. But our floating dreams were abruptly disturbed by a deep hollow 'boom' – a sound rather felt than heard, a vague, powerful force that gave the whole surrounding body of water a sudden push; then left everything just as before.

More puzzled than alarmed we trod water and peered about. A hundred yards further out, three figures in baggy black pants and jackets and straw lamp-shade hats stood gesticulating on a rocking sampan, their voices startlingly clear across the water. And in a moment, between them and us, white shapes began silently rising to the surface – a few at first, then hundreds. Fish, belly-up, either dead or stunned. The sampan was fishing with explosives. We beat a hasty retreat, half-expecting another blast. Safely back on shore we shouted and shook our fists at the piscatorial bombers – who paddled hurriedly away, abandoning their catch.

The shock of different worlds colliding. 'City of Contrasts', the travel posters used to say. The post-modern version, it seems, is 'City at the End of Time' – the title of a paperback I'm carrying in my pocket. A book of Hong Kong poems, in Chinese with English translations, it has an introduction by an old student of mine, and this afternoon I'm to meet the poet – Leung Ping-kwan, or PK, as everyone seems to call him. I take it out and look at the glossy cover – an aerial photograph of the city, like a computer mother-board, but with fragments of Chinese painting half-transparently superimposed: incense rising from an urn, bamboo in an archway, ladies with flowing robes and refined but earnest faces, jewelled combs in their hair and cherubic infants in their arms. The whole collage is suffused with a smoky orange glow, suggesting burning.

Perhaps there is something in Chinese perceptions that accommodates post-modernity rather too readily. The view from my mother-in-law's doorstep is a valued feature of the place, but just next to the clump of bamboo that frames it, stands a discarded fridge. There seem to be three ways of looking at this. The aesthetic discord may upset you; or create a certain piquancy; or the view and the fridge may just be seen as separate.

My mother-in-law's way, I'm sure, is the third. On our way to her rooms we stopped to look at the Buddhist temple at the entrance to the village. A new and imposing edifice, four-square on a little hill, its green-tiled roof sweeps ponderously down, to rise up again at each corner, elaborately carved and gilded, like the prow of a fantastic ship. It's prize possession is a jade reclining Buddha, and this too turns out to be imposing and new. Of rather dull stone, and rather crudely worked, it sprawls stiffly amongst a clutter of ornaments and offerings, casting a stony eye down on the ceremonial instruments – bronze bells and gongs and drums – at the foot of the altar.

But in my own eyes, I must confess, a very different feature of the temple loomed much larger. Arranged symmetrically just inside the main doors, identical in size and shape, stood two six-foot metal cabinets, one green, the other red, automatic dispensers of Seven Up and Coca-Cola.

To my mother-in-law they evidently didn't loom at all. She has a sure eye for form – despite her eighty years she is still a fine calligrapher – and she was critical of the jade Buddha in itself, but she clearly felt no urge to connect it with the soft-drink machines. Her vision is less 'totalising' than mine; less sensitive to disjunction. She's lived a long time in this 'city of contrasts'. But there's a traditional modesty at work too, I think. Old scholars who couldn't afford a mountain pavilion, developed the art of miniature landscape – mountains in plant-pots, complete with wind-swept pines. Never mind that they stood on little tables in cramped rooms; they were there to give a sense of liberation, not of irony. The scholars, being 'unscientific', had never expected the whole world to conform to one idea; enough if one corner of it did. And the poetry book-cover suggests no irony of failed absolutes; its fragmentations seem more decorative than disruptive, the orange glow more glamorous than apocalyptic.

I slip the book back into my pocket and go into the house. My wife and her mother and a distant relative – a woman of sixty or so who lives next door – are talking about religion. My mother-in-law likes the retirement-village but is growing disenchanted with Buddhism. The monks, she says, are rather grasping and careless landlords. And since two of her daughters once attended convent-schools, she is now drawn by the idea of Christianity.

She approaches all this in the spirit of Pascal's wager. If she has an immortal soul, then the Buddhists will look after it; and as long as they are competent to do this, then Coke machines inside the temple are neither here nor there; her view is pragmatic, not aesthetic. And the Catholics will serve her purpose just as well.

In any case her deepest beliefs remain Confucian and family-centred. Her ancestral shrine, with photographs of her parents and her husband, hangs on the wall – just above her telephone and fax machine which keep her in touch with her children and grandchildren, all driven overseas by China's impending take-over of Hong Kong.

Are the electronic and Confucian worlds in collision or in collusion? The medium, McLuhan famously said, is the message; the technology determines everything else; and in the academies his word still largely holds good. But my mother-in-law's fax machine is really a wonderful medium for transmitting her calligraphy to a family dispersed around the world. And the MTR – the underground railway system – helps her to keep in touch with her own generation, her sisters and cousins, who have mainly chosen to stay in Hong Kong. When I went into town with her the other day, she was delighted to show me how to work the ticket machines and barriers.

Technologies set constraints, no doubt, but within them our freedom is very great – perhaps infinite, if the chaos-theorists are right about enclosed infinities. My mother-in-law and I are on friendly terms but her English and my Cantonese exist at the same humble level and our communications are usually rudimentary. The ticket machine is an opportunity we are glad to seize. It allows *her* to be gracious and *me* to be grateful; and the success of the enterprise (presto, out pops the right ticket) proves that communication has really occurred – an outcome that in our case remains often in doubt. The machine, in short, is the occasion for an exchange quite undetermined by the technology. Academics, though keen advocates of large and abstract liberties, tend not to notice freedoms of this small and daily kind; uncovenanted, they defy easy classification.

Freedom of course entails uncertainty. My mother-in-law was free to leave Hong Kong, but chose to stay; and this led to some anxiety; it was hard to establish a viable *menage* for her. But the problem was solved by another chance element – the distant relative. She too was suddenly left on her own, and with enough money to set up house next door. A younger woman, energetic but even-tempered, she has become an indispensable companion.

The introduction to my book of poems dwells much upon the uncertainties of Hong Kong, but says nothing at all about chance. This isn't surprising. My old student adopts a leftish, cultural-critical stance, rather scornful of the 'bourgeoisie', and occasionally prone to rap the poet over the knuckles for straying from 'history' into 'idealism'. On the other hand he sees the Frankfurt school as naive, and would claim, I suppose, to take a more subtle view than the old Marxists. The 'aggregate of accidental events' in a story, said Lukács, for instance, constitutes a 'poetic necessity', and this might seem to soften the social-determinist line; but Lukacs quickly reconverts the 'poetic necessity' into a 'deep-seated social necessity', and thus shuffles both chance and freedom out of the game.

And 'freedom' is still a word my student avoids. He speaks instead of Hong Kong as a 'heterogeneous cultural space', which one must 'negotiate', turning its 'cultural and historical differentials to positive use'. He sees 'freedom', in effect, as the prerogative of those in a position to manoeuvre between different cultures; a definition to appeal to the post-colonial ego.

He and I have kept in touch over the years, though in a desultory way. Middle-aged now, and himself of complex ethnicity – including, I think, Chinese and Indian – he has done his share of cultural negotiation. I recall him as an undergraduate describing the delicate conduct required in restaurants if he happened to see a Moslem relative dining on pork chops. When it became clear that the British government wouldn't honour the British citizenship of Hong Kong citizens like himself, he was angry and disturbed. He felt no identity with China, and saw himself becoming stateless. But he has since come to regard Hong Kong as a real locality, a home; this is the burden of his introduction to the book of poems.

His negotiations in all this are obviously social and historic. But even more they presuppose a negotiating power. And in the end this power is simply the instinct for balance and coherence that sustains any living organism, caught as it always is between its two fundamental and conflicting needs – to assert its independence, and to relate to the multifarious 'other' of the world. The power that Coleridge called the 'primary imagination', and that Michael Polanyi christened 'tacit thought'. In my student's case, the word 'balance' reminds me that he once belonged to a fencing club called 'The Toledo Blades'. This too was evidently a 'cultural negotiation', and of a youthful kind; he idolised Mel Ferrer, as I recall, a film-star duellist; but at the same time he really looked the swordsman – tall, lean, and dark, with straight eyebrows and narrow eyes. Here lies the physical source of all his freedom to negotiate.

No longer a swordsman but a theorist, he now sees the human animal as a merely socio-linguistic creature. This is scarcely any advance on the crude Marxist model, and it comes of course, via Bakhtin, from the old Soviet psychologists who severed language from its roots in animal perception. 'Generalisation,' said Vygotsky, for example – and he was implicitly speaking for them all – 'is a verbal act of thought, and it reflects reality in quite another way than sensation and perception reflect it.' But in fact it's clear that animals generalise, as Mary Warnock vividly shows in her book *Memory*, when she describes her horse acquiring the general idea of a 'horse-box' – and taking a strong dislike to it. Indeed Vygotsky's own experiments point to the same conclusion: language simply extends and refines our animal powers. But 'social scientists' – of left, right or centre – naturally prefer to see humanity as a social construct; it boosts their own profession.

My mother-in-law's 'negotiations' might *seem* almost entirely social. She is, you could say, concerned with 'keeping up appearances', but you have to give the phrase a certain weight. My student would perhaps dismiss her as 'bourgeois' – one of the legion who keep Hong Kong's tailors, cooks, and hairdressers in employment. And so she is. But she is also a beautiful old lady – a category beyond the merely social, though it presupposes a high degree of civilisation. See her, for instance, late at night, brushing her long white hair and chatting in a desultory, intimate way with one or other of her daughters. She seems so much at one with them, yet so entirely herself. It is in this contradictory space between self and other that freedom has its origin, not in the spaces between heterogeneous cultures.

Catholicism having been duly considered and approved, the negotiation now taking place in her sitting-room is about travelling into town. Since there are four of us, a taxi will be as cheap as public transport, and in a few minutes I'm reviewing the Hong Kong landscape from the front seat, while the others sit in the back discussing lunch.

'Mountains are slow to change', as the Taoists, with their love of the profoundly obvious, like to observe. Lion Rock still couches at the centre of the mountain-barrier between Kowloon and the New Territories. The road that used to wind so deviously round, now drives straight through it, a motorway in a great fluorescent tube. But transformations like this have been world-wide of course. One of my childhood haunts in Yorkshire was a stream that rippled over pebbles and beneath alders, past a little coal-mine whose pulley wheels just showed above the tree-tops; the pit-ponies were sometimes brought up from underground to sun themselves in the fields. When I first went to Hong Kong as a young man in 1960, the stream still wandered on, in the old Lawrencian way; when I returned home four years later, it had become a concrete drain beside the M1. But, like these Hong Kong hills, the whole dale had kept – and keeps – its beautiful contours, its northern scarp still climbing up to the town, its southern slope rising gently to a dim horizon.

When we emerge from under the hills into Kowloon, the city reveals some of its own enduring features. From a distance the older tenement blocks look like a grey scurf on the landscape, but once amongst them of course, you become aware of each local stretch of pavement with its restaurants and dry-cleaners, grocery-stores and beauty-parlours, punctuated by the narrow entrances to the flats on the upper floors. Typical Chinese city streets; tidier than Canton, less antiseptic than Singapore, more westernised than Taipei; its hard to put your finger on exactly what makes them distinctive, but something does, and the children who pass continually in and out of the entrances know not only that, but also what makes their particular stretch of pavement quite different from the next.

The power of close observation, says a Chinese proverb, is most highly developed in small children and small dogs. But it's a matter of activity too. As a child I knew every inch of the neighbourhood streets because they were the field of action, where our chasing and hiding games were played; to know a dark corner or a gap in a wall could seem a matter of life and death. And the Hong Kong street I still know best runs past the block of flats where my wife lived with her family before we were married. I can still smell its vivid smells – leather from the shoemaker's tiny shop under the slope of the ground-floor staircase; glue and camphor-wood from the furniture factory next door; the street-market just round the corner, with fruit and vegetables, beef frying with garlic, joss burning somewhere. I was scarcely conscious of these perceptions at the time, but they were the background of action – of courtship and marriage, and they return now not as random perceptions from a lost time but as part of a continuing story.

In its current episode my wife is now disappearing with her mother amongst the crowds of a roaring Kowloon street, en route to a family lunch, leaving me to make my way across the harbour to the university, to meet the poet. Having time to spare I decide to take the ferry instead of the underground, and I'm soon standing in the bows, watching the island's great phalanx of skyscrapers drawing near, with I.M. Pei's Bank of China in the van.

Pei's building, say the locals, has played havoc with the 'feng shui' – the geomantic harmony – of the business district. Sharp and gleaming, with broad criss-cross belts of steel, it's seen as a communist knife at the city's heart. The specific allusion of course is to the take-over, but the general habit of metaphor is ingrained in popular geomantic thinking. The Hong Kong and Shanghai Bank, which resembles a rocket-launching tower, is said to be a kit-set structure, to be dismantled if the take-over goes sour.

I went once with a Hong Kong family to a sea-side spot in New Zealand called Castle Point – a Pacific beach, with a natural harbour and a lighthouse – and within minutes of arrival I was told that the long low headland forming the harbour-wall was itself a ship, and the crag towering over the entrance a giant guard-dog, its paws resting in the water. Protection is a common 'feng shui' theme. The big pines and gums at the end of our garden, my wife is wont to say, are sentinels, our tutelary deities.

To see nature not as 'unknown modes of being' but as bearing on some human enterprise is evidently a Confucian rather than a Taoist or Wordsworthian habit. It links the environment with action rather than contemplation – a 'bourgeois' strategy, perhaps, but a strong agent for binding the human and the natural together.

At the ferry terminal I catch the number 3 bus – the same number as it was thirty years ago. It still skirts the central square – once a cricket ground for the colonial gentry, now a park where Filipino housemaids congregate on their day off (the only folk who seem to actually enjoy the city centre) – and it still labours up Garden Road to the mid-levels. The apartment buildings here are far taller than they used to be, but the streets themselves – narrow and winding, with local shopping centres and the occasional tree – still have their old suburban, almost intimate feel.

The bus stops at the university's original centre – and the setting for one of PK's poems, 'An Old Colonial Building'. On its steep, cramped slope, the university, like the city at large, is in a state of continual demolition and construction, and the poem opens with scaffolding, noise, and dust. But as I get off the bus it's already Saturday afternoon; the rock-drills are silent, the dust has settled, and the place feels quite deserted.

A handsome three-storied structure of red brick and cream stucco, its tiled and lofty corridors are separated only by balustrades from the inner courtyard with its palm-trees and fish-pond. The pond is the poem's main image. Its surface reflects the building's tower so clearly that the gold-fish, 'swirling orange and white, their gills opening and leeching', seem to be swimming in and out of a round window in the cupola. And PK sees this water 'riddled with patterns of moving signs' as a symbol of ambivalence.

I walk round the first floor corridor, peering over the balustrade, until I can see the same image. It's just as the poem says. But my own impression is one of density rather than uncertainty. The reflected cupola simply adds to the visual interest. And this is further thickened by a dash of narrative interest, as I wonder whether to report my impression to PK.

The modernist habit of scrutinising an image until it yields an ambiguity – which of course it always will – is really, I think, the mental equivalent of looking at an object until one sees it double. I stare at a dark fleck in the stone of the balustrade just next to my index finger; fixed focus quickly leads to a loss of focus.

Ordinary vision of course entails a continuous stream of movement and adjustment, as we integrate our two retinal images into one dense, three-dimensional picture. And for organicist thinkers like Whitehead, Polanyi, or Merleau-Ponty, this epitomises mental process; perception and thought exist only through time and action; as does reality itself. There is, as Whitehead put it, 'no nature at an instant'. The 'instant' – that pinpoint on which you feel you might touch the 'really real' – is in fact an abstraction, immensely useful but deeply illusory in the end. Mistake it for reality and the world itself turns to illusion.

And this is where modern scepticism has arrived. PK surveying a gold-fish pond feels a curious obligation to re-enact Heisenberg trying to fix both the position and velocity of a particle – and being driven to a sense of 'indeterminacy'. This procedure may admirably advance the cause of physics, but poetry, as Aristotle said, needs to move; it shows us not the moment of existence, but the sort of thing that *happens*.

As I continue my way up flights of steps, across courtyards, and through further buildings, towards my hostel at the top of the campus, I stop for a moment outside the library, where a student is standing guard over a cardboard architectural model. This, I assume, is connected with a poster on the library door advertising a lecture-series called 'Hong Kong: City of Vision'. But in fact, he tells me, it's a plan for the development of Chang An Avenue – the main thoroughfare of Beijing. He's evidently just taking the model somewhere and has paused to rest.

I look at his space-age construct, all white and gleaming, with its dynamic unity of flowing and soaring lines; and then I think of Chang An as it actually is – the long, dusty straggle of old and new and half-finished buildings, in every style from Ming to post-modern. The discrepancy between the actuality and the student's idea is very gross, but what strikes me now is that P.K.'s *City at the End of Time* is built on a simple reversal of it. 'An Old Colonial Building' for instance rejects the city centre's 'tall buildings of chrome and glass' in favour of the ambiguous, marginal pond. A variant of the metaphor occurs in 'The Leaf at the Edge', where the 'beauties at the centre' of the pond, the lilies, are rejected in favour of the 'under water', where 'roots grow together, new leaves furl in the heart'. And this contrast between a showy but sterile centre and obscure but fruitful margins – the real 'heart' – pervades the whole book.

Fruitful because 'individuality', as my student's introduction puts it, can only be 'negotiated in the mixed cultural space of the margins'. And in a metaphor he sees as appropriate to Hong Kong, he compares the process with 'arbitrage' in the money-markets – the extraction of profit from shifting rates of exchange. He calls it 'the ability to find movements and discrepancies in a situation that seems to be fatal and foreclosed; the ability, to put it in another way, to see the humour even of a deadly situation.'

The claim that virtue resides in the cultural margins has a venerable history. Empson examines its chief variants in *Some Versions of Pastoral*. Pastoral of course is the genre of the agricultural margins, but the old pastoral writers could be sceptical about the claim to virtue. As Empson observes, a work like *The Beggar's Opera*, yoking pastoral with satire, shows the politicians at the centre and the highwaymen in the margins as about equally corrupt.

For a migrant like myself, my student's more simple view has an attraction both obvious and insidious. Take the point about humour. In a poem called 'Lucky Draw', PK sees life as a lottery and contemplates the winners rather wryly:

> He gets two rich aunts,
> and a parrot...
> He gets a self-cleaning filing-cabinet,
> an alarm clock that never stops ringing.
> He gets his own investigating committee,
> formed by two dozen Englishmen...
> She gets a canned husband
> and a bunch of motorized relatives...
> She gets four crocodiles that can sing...
> a rhinoceros that waits at the corner of the street.

As for the poet himself:

> I am empty handed...
> I buy a newspaper
> and miss my ferry...
> I wait for the next train
> at the wrong station...

and so on. The English translation, I'm told, blunts the playful edge even more than one might expect, but the general effect is clear.

All comedy is evidently carnivalesque, but it flouts convention in many different ways. PK's strategy here seems self-mocking rather than aggressive – 'see what a funny misfit I am' – but it also mocks the ridiculous prizes at the centre, and implies that the apparent loser is the real winner; he not only survives outside the conventions but remains pleasantly amused by the whole business.

Dave Barry, the vastly popular American humorist, deploys the same strategy quite routinely. Lamenting his ever-broadening girth, for instance, he observes, in Twainian style, that towels are increasingly the only garments he feels happy in, and he goes on to consider getting himself a black one, for wearing to funerals. To acknowledge that life is more comfortable outside the conventions is itself of course a convention, but even comedy as conventional as Barry's helps to keep its audience aware of the limits of the social; it confirms the capacity for detachment which is one of the hallmarks of being human.

Since my student thinks that social limits can only be transcended in the margins, he in effect denies the centre a sense of humour; the denizens of the gleaming tower-blocks are as unwitty as they are acquisitive. This is the traditional attitude of the 'wit' towards the shopkeeper. What is curious is it that the 'wits' have adopted this social scientific style – 'negotiating the heterogeneous cultural space' and so forth. It seems not only unwitty but ineffectual. The 'wits' of old were successful insofar as they really seemed more free and flexible, more centrally human, than the leaden money-grubbers. This of course entailed a central use of language, with all its powers of feeling and tone, its subtle variety of resource for addressing 'the other'. And to use such a language is of course to assume that the audience, even the money-grubbers themselves, can become human too; it is to be, as Wordsworth put it, 'a man speaking to men'.

And PK himself generally is. In an interview at the end of the book, he declares that he writes 'like a clown speaking on television, like a cab driver speaking in the front seat'; and in 'Lucky Draw', the marginal poet in fact makes a friendly approach towards the hurrying prize-winners in the centre – but 'they think I am trying to catch up/and walk all the faster'. This feels rather Chaplinesque (PK is evidently fond of old films); the friendly tramp is cold-shouldered by the uneasy 'toffs', and we feel that the 'toffs' lose more by this than the tramp. PK is here the wit, in the central human position, but the prize-winners are human too; we sense their anxiety and loss, and they are linked to the poet by his regret as well as his amusement. Poetry, as Wordsworth added, creates community.

'Theory', on the other hand, creates 'interpretive communities', each one cut off from the others. My old student's merely social definition of freedom divides the 'heterogeneous cultural space' into enclosed compartments. And his critical idiom of course enacts his self-ghettoisation. Though not heavily jargon-ridden by current standards, his work is accessible only to initiates. And in the dreary wastes of contemporary 'theory', it is hard to discover any other voice than this, mumbling away in the caverns of obscurity.

On the final staircase to the hostel, I stop for a moment, in the shade of a great glossy-leaved magnolia, its white flowers half-opened, and recall PK's voice on the phone, when we arranged our meeting. He sounded perhaps a little offhand. Will he turn up on time – or even at all? Or is he a stereotypical 'artist', his social habits as free as his poetic voice?

The steps end in a courtyard next to the dining room, and I see that I'm in time for the lag-end of lunch. The place is almost empty and I take a seat by the window, for the view. The hillside, dropping all the way down to the waterfront, is studded with tall, slender apartment blocks. The constraints of terrain and population have given them all a certain regularity of height, mass, and distribution, and they have an oddly natural look, like great groves of buildings.

Beyond them the sea carries its usual traffic – a string of long black barges behind a tug; two slim grey warships, like toys; cargo-boats moored on the open water, each with its attendant cluster of junks and sampans. Beyond that again the blue hills of Lantao stretch away across the Pearl River estuary towards Macau. But the big down-town office-blocks are obscured by a building just below the hostel; the view seems without a centre. And how naturally the eye seeks one. The traveller, as the plane descends, looks down past the quivering wing-tip, towards the assembly of gleaming cubes that signifies 'city'. If you approach at night of course the whole place seems like a centre, a glittering field of light in the void; but soon you're homing in on a brighter core; and after the plane has run the gauntlet of the Kai Tak tenement blocks – great honeycombs of light so close to the plane that you can see people cooking in their kitchens – it's disappointing to be taxi-ing back along the dark nowhere of the runway, with its dim lights and dark shapes of hangars. But of course you quickly look towards your next centre – the concourse, the hotel, the people you'll be meeting.

Poetry, said Coleridge, improving on Aristotle, not only moves, but shows the best way to travel; like the snake, it coils itself together, making *everywhere* the centre, though still journeying on; the reader wants to dwell thus on each line, and yet is drawn to the next. A model for a full life, every rift loaded with ore.

Can I turn the view from the dining-room window into a many-centred thing? The night I arrived at the university I went walking in those same streets down below. There were still people about and the local stores were still open. From one of them a man with a plastic bag of groceries emerged into the pool of fluorescent light on the pavement. He glanced round, then crossed the road, where he unlocked the steel gate at a shadowy entrance, collected his mail from a row of boxes in a tiny foyer, then disappeared up a dimly-lit stair-case. It was all routine behaviour of the most insignificant kind, yet, to me just then, it seemed curiously vivid. The man was elderly, one of those delicate small-boned Cantonese with stooped shoulders and fine features who look scarcely more substantial than their own cotton jackets, and who tend to make Europeans feel rather powerful – or gross. But my sudden odd awareness of his physical being made him a presence at the centre of his world.

I try to think now of the thousands of such centres in the streets below. But of course it doesn't work. My imagination isn't up to it. The view remains an undistinguished panorama, with the mere idea of 'rich centres' just tacked on – like one of those cheap prints entitled 'Rue de Paris'. But the idea is still valid in itself. For the imagination there are no margins. An obscure goldfish pond is a vivid centre, but so are the downtown blocks, the stock exchange, or the Governor's dinner-parties.

My own centre is suddenly required to adjust to the arrival of two others – a British couple, but long resident in North America, and currently in Hong Kong on sabbatical leave. We have only a nodding acquaintance, but can place each other with insidious ease – Anglo-Saxons in the provincial academic leagues, from different generations and social backgrounds, perhaps, but about equally immersed in career and mental conceit. Of course there's more to us than that, but we've no occasion to seek it out; it's easier to stay at the level of academic chatter, and as in most negotiations between self and other, self remains largely in hiding. So we chatter our way through lunch, until they go off to negotiate with each other at tennis, and I to my less predictable encounter with PK.

My uncertainty is compounded when I find the college office deserted and locked. How will he find out my room-number? I scribble a note, and pin it to the office-door with a thumb-tack lifted from a nearby poster. As I walk away, already beginning to worry whether he'll notice my notice, a figure appears at the main entrance to the courtyard. Fortyish, of compact build, wearing an open-necked shirt and grey slacks, and carrying a supermarket bag, he isn't at all the sort of *outré* figure I'm half-expecting, but his air of looking for someone he doesn't know suggests that it's the poet; and when he sees me in turn, his affable, unremarkable face reflects a similar sequence of thoughts. In a moment we've met, and this abrupt resolution of our slight uncertainties gets us off to a friendly start. He soon suggests that we go down-town to a bar called (it really is) The Fringe Club.

Despite the name it's in the central district, and as we enter I am vaguely prepared for 'bohemian' manifestations, but my expectations are met in an unexpected way. The place is oddly shaped and on several levels, as though randomly formed by the edges of other structures – an impression strengthened by the raw concrete walls, exposed wiring, and by the tables and chairs, which, though uniformly bleak and unlovely, come evidently from a variety of sources. But the suggestion of a bare and improvised existence is rather negated by the well-appointed bar, with its prompt, polite bartender, and by the clientele, who are mostly male, sitting talking in pairs and small groups, and looking as comfortably conventional as PK and myself.

All this soon prompts me, when we're settled over our beer, to raise directly the question of centres and margins. Surely, I say – after reporting my impression of the fish-pond – we all of us belong to a number of centres, or 'circles', to use the more common word. A home circle, a work circle, a sporting circle, and so on. And we're outsiders with respect to many others.

PK readily agrees, but remarks that in China, for instance, there is a sense of a national centre, which Hong Kong lacks. In part he's clearly thinking of 'the take-over', but I suspect he has literature in mind as well as politics. To the mainland Chinese literati, 'Hong Kong poetry' is a phrase with the same oxymoronic resonance that 'Australian poetry' still has in some retarded English ears. As things stand now, Hong Kong is a distinct entity, with a unique post-colonial profile and its own niche in the international news. Its poetic pond is very small but, as the book in my pocket confirms, PK at least gets enough oxygen of public attention to keep him swimming. He is bound to feel nervous of being swamped when Hong Kong goes back into the great sea of China.

So I can understand his need to see himself as marginal man, with unique messages to deliver. And up to a point of course he *is*. His view from Hong Kong will continue to be special; but only if he remains a man speaking to men. If he puts on airs of marginalist superiority, he might soon find himself not just in the margins but completely off the page.

I glance at him as he lifts his glass. He gives an overall impression of sturdiness, but his features are finely modelled, and his gaze, though level, has a beautifully limpid quality. I like him, and he seems to like me too, but we aren't getting on quite as well as I'd hoped. Did I broach the question of centres and margins too abruptly? Perhaps he himself is uneasy about his dual literary personality – the poet and the cultural theorist – and is aware that I'm aware of it.

He is, you might want to say, a 'site of discursive conflict', but that phrase itself of course exemplifies all the defects of the neo-Saussurean mode. It assumes that the 'subject' is merely a 'space' where 'discourse unfolds'; it denies him an individual will and intelligence; and it leaves him of course dependent on the wisdom of the theorists, who, like the Marxists of old, assume that their own ideas somehow transcend the socio-linguistic forces that determine everyone else's.

But after all PK is surely more poet than theorist; he has that air of immediate awareness, of being where he's at. It's my old student who is more the cultural critic. The last time we met he was about to fly off to New York for a conference on post-colonialism (he's there again now). Hong Kong, he remarked, is currently a 'sexy topic', but despite his ironic tone he had the bright-eyed, distant look of a being from a realm of seminars and 'papers'. Of course he's a very intelligent man, himself a free individual, but the international groves of academe are still pervaded by a miasmaɫ social determinism the more contagious for being vague.

I recall a recent review – in a prestigious literary weekly – of some contemporary 'proletarian' British fiction. Its working-class protagonists, the reviewer remarked, have 'degraded minds', with 'hardly anything else in them but the images and gestures of mass urban culture'. They are in short 'what their time has made them', and even when one of them commits a brutal murder, it is 'in a sense, a correlative to the debased contents of his mind'. Evidently it's this sort of thinking – or failure to think – that once drove Mrs Thatcher to assert 'There's no such thing as society'. Silly of course, but no sillier than to say, 'There's no such thing as the individual'. The reviewer's implicit reservations ('hardly' and 'in a sense'), and the evasive word 'correlative', acknowledge this of course; but they are no more than tokens; the steady drizzle of fashionable verbiage – 'the discursive site upon which the subject is constructed', and so on – has fatally dulled his conception of individuality.

Fatally? It seems hardly too strong a word. Anyone with a functioning memory, a vestigial conscience, and a comfortable salary, may well feel guilt, amongst other things, about the new 'underclass'; but to absolve its members therefore from all individual responsibility, even for murder, is a woeful abnegation of responsibility in itself. Before 'theory' began to exercise its numbing influence, of course, literature was seen as precisely the place to look for a more intelligent view of 'the individual and society'.

The relations between PK and his society are evidently various. He has a job at the university, his poems get published; and at six o'clock (he tells me) he has to go to visit his mother – the plastic supermarket bag, laid carefully on the table beside his beer, contains his gift of food for her, I'm sure. Described like this, his social profile suddenly reminds me of Philip Larkin – though he shows no signs of Larkin's morbid, maudlin propensity to blame his parents for 'fucking him up'. The Chinese family system, of course, does have its darker side; in the 1960s many of my students were anxious to escape and become 'western individualists'; but PK seems rather a witness to its virtues. A Chinese 'clan' includes not only female and male, old and young, clever and dull, nice and nasty, but also, as a rule, both rich and poor. And this keeps them all aware of both human variety and identity (for they are all undeniably 'family'), of the individual and the universal – the two vital human elements ignored by the sociologising cultural critics.

The other day I went with my wife and mother-in-law to see Ah Yau, an old woman who spent all her working life as their family servant. Now retired she lives in a new town beyond Kowloon, in one of the enormous housing blocks that themselves seem almost as big as towns. It was my first visit, and as we made our way through the building – in a metal box of a lift and along bare concrete corridors punctuated by the steel security grilles of the apartments – my misgivings grew. It seemed more like a prison than a home.

We were expected, and the door opened promptly at our knock to reveal Ah Yau's diminutive figure and smiling face. She looked scarcely changed from thirty years ago, when she used to laugh out loud at almost anything I did, especially when I was enjoying her cooking. It was nothing personal; she was simply delighted, over and over again, to see that foreigners eat and drink, and so on, like other human beings.

She shares her flat with a woman who was also a servant – in the old days 'amahs' were mostly unmarried and stuck close together. The friend hovered now in the background and was smiling too; indeed the whole apartment, small as it was, seemed to wear a smile; bright with light from a big window, it was crammed with all the treasures – crockery, ornaments, calendars, photographs in shiny frames – with which ordinary Chinese folk like to fill their rooms.

Ah Yau was not only happy to see us but, as she told us over several cups of tea, happy in general. The block was well-maintained, with shops and restaurants on the ground floor; she had enough to live on; and she had her friend.

That no doubt sounds a touch 'Dickensian'; and Orwell, I remember, used to complain that Dickens never achieved any comprehensive social vision; his idea of the good life was a happy family living next door to another happy family – relatives, preferably. But we now seem to have reached the opposite extreme; the cultural critics have a social vision of such breadth that it not only blinds them to actual people but renders them sadly prone – so gloomy and grand are the socio-economic abstractions clouding their minds – to mild but chronic fits of megolomania and despair.

Is my own notion of 'society' here too modest? In one of his last stories, D.H. Lawrence imagines a people who are spiritually, socially and physically so at one that their religious devotions, at morning and evening, seem as spontaneous as the wheeling flight of a flock of birds. A beautiful ideal – a poetic version of the Leavisian 'organic community'. But the story is frankly presented as a fantasy – and it was never finished. In any case, the way the world is now, we must surely learn to be content with a greater gap between ideal and reality.

But I'm still not quite happy with the gap between PK and myself. It seems one of those odd Forsterian junctures, when everything feels propitious to a moment of real human contact, but nothing happens; some element is lacking; 'the universe doesn't want it', Forster would have said; which here may simply mean that beer in the afternoon sits uneasily on my stomach. PK himself looks content enough, and perhaps he is. Forster, I recall, was also wont to feel that 'the East' tends to mistake social form for authentic meeting; the quotidian reality for the rare ideal. But his own conception of the authentic as something rare and evanescent seems in turn peculiarly western – a product of the urge to nail reality to an instant. The Chinese are more inclined to see the truly human as a formal creation, and one that takes a good deal of time.

I must try to be more Chinese; I start talking to PK about Hong Kong in the 1960s, when Repulse Bay, now a mini-city, was just a quiet hotel and an avenue of flame-trees running down to a beach, and when Giancarlo and his band played the 'twist' every night in the Blue Heaven – which must, I remark, have been virtually on the spot where we're sitting now. PK was still a schoolboy then, but he recalls the period with enthusiasm, endowing it with the mythic quality that we give to the era of our childhood. He dwells with particular affection on the old Lee Theatre, where he evidently spent far too much of his time, and acquired his passion for the cinema. One of my wife's maternal uncles, I tell him triumphantly, used to own it; and I'm pleased to sense that this gives me a touch of mythic status in his eyes. He is, in short, being very gracious; and we both know of course that this is all a nostalgia game; no communion of souls – but none the less an enjoyable enough encounter of self and other.

And a casual encounter; it's not likely that we'll meet again. But still we are busy weaving each other into the patterns of our experience. PK is now connected with my memories of Hong Kong – the Blue Heaven, Repulse Bay, the Lee Theatre. And our meeting in the first place isn't entirely random. I have a long interest both in poetry and in this particular city; and that a British scholarship boy of the 1950s should go to work in Hong Kong, marry a local scholarship girl, and revisit the place from time to time, falls into a number of quite obvious larger patterns – including some of the humble kind beloved by Samuel Smiles. There are of course chance elements. The last time I saw my old student, it happened that *City at the End of Time* had just come out, so he gave me a copy. Had I visited him at another time, I might never have seen the book nor, consequently, PK himself.

How can systems that seem both patterned and random, predictable and uncertain, be best described? Chaos theory is a current scientific attempt. A typically modern poetic attempt is Craig Raine's *History: The Home Movie*. The poem hangs on two clear frameworks. First, a conventional outline of modern history – the Russian Revolution, the Depression, the world wars, and so on. Second, the genealogies of the Raines and the Pasternaks – the crux here is that Eliot Raine, Craig's uncle, married Lydia Pasternak, a sister of the famous Russian novelist. The whole poem covers the years from 1905 to 1984 in some ninety brief episodes (mainly incidents from family history) and we are told the year in which each episode occurs. But within these overall patterns the uncertainty is radical. The relation between incident and framework is always elliptical and often enigmatic, and there is no sense of sequence between the incidents themselves. In short, we have the familiar modernist techniques of discontinuity, though deployed in the service of a more disengaged post-modern mood.

But although the whole idea of a 'master narrative' is being implicitly rejected, the poem itself in fact feels like one – like a *demonstration* of life's discontinuities, rather willed and insistent. One can see of course why a poet, especially one like Raine, might be loth to dwell on continuity and pattern – they tend to be obvious, and 'obvious' is next door to 'boring'. But next door on the other side is 'profoundly true', and simply to ignore this seems a passport to triviality, a pursuit of striking effects, rather than an attempt to explore the world.

Chaos theory is evidently a serious exploration. It acknowledges, as we clearly must, both randomness and pattern, and its focus on action – on *changing* pattern – is a crucial hint for literary critics, too long preoccupied with static structures of 'symbol' and 'theme'. But like all science of course it has a rooted aversion to individuality. It is happy to recognise the mysterious symmetries in, say, the changing patterns of a population, but will tell you nothing of an individual caught up in their uncertainties, an individual moreover who feels free to choose.

PK and I might choose to linger here in The Fringe Club, but he's arranged to meet his mother, and I my wife, and we have no good in view to outweigh the evils that attend domestic unpunctuality. Our conversation is pleasant but not compelling. We empty our glasses and PK takes up his shopping bag.

We walk together to the Central MTR station and stand chatting at the entrance – PK, I sense, is curious to meet my wife. The evening is drawing in and the crowds of shoppers are turning into crowds of pleasure-seekers. At length my wife appears, looking glad, as people do, to have achieved a rendezvous in a busy city centre. She and PK take to each other immediately, and are soon engrossed in identifying the few 'old' buildings that remain in the neighbourhood.

At length we say our farewells, and PK makes for a taxi-rank across the road, where a huge office-block, designed with a slight bulge in the concrete at every floor, seems to be muscling its way up into the smoky light of the zenith. Down here in the streets the neon and the traffic are growing more insistent. Night-town awakes. But for my wife and myself it's home to mother. And tomorrow we return to New Zealand. Our son and daughter are flying in from China and we're travelling on together.

Next day, as I wander restlessly about the departure lounge wondering whether our children will arrive in time for their connection, my eye is caught by an odd procession. At its head, dressed in a tracksuit and 'trainers', is a serene-looking old man with white hair and a beautifully clear light brown complexion. At its centre is a gilded wooden shrine, carried on two poles, like a sedan chair, and emitting clouds of smoke from clusters of joss-sticks. The line of people before and behind it – are they a Chinese minority group, or Nepalese, or what? – is moving in a purposeful way that draws my own aimless steps to follow. And naturally I'm curious. Here's a community so organic that they carry their church about with them. Do they hope to board a plane with their incendiary tabernacle?

They pad steadily across the carpeted expanse, attracting almost no attention – the crowds of travellers are either familiar with the phenomenon, or just engrossed in duty-free shopping – and pass at length into a shabby annexe overlooking a concrete yard full of rubbish bins and caterers' vans. The smokers' ghetto. The votaries lower their smoking altar gently to the ground, and as I smile to myself at this oddly appropriate behaviour, some of them produce packs of cigarettes, light up, and start puffing away.

But some just flop into chairs and gaze vacantly into space, and some pace restlessly about; the leader, perhaps less serene than he likes to appear, is one of the smokers. And these small tensions of individual difference are found of course at the centre of any community. The hymns in a church, the roar of a football crowd, the applause at a Party Conference, may seem to come from a single mind, but even a casual eye can see the signs of straying – the shuffling of feet or hymn-books, the glance at a watch, the look of wary appraisal. Perhaps a wheeling bird-brain is all-absorbed by communal flight, but as a rule the human mind has some spare capacity – for detachment.

I wander back into the departure lounge to find that our son and daughter have arrived and that our flight is ready to board. I shall never know what happened to the shrine; I suppose they just snuff out the joss-sticks before they embark. Then, as we start moving forward with our queue, we find that our 'children' – they are both in their twenties – have no seat-numbers on their tickets. No one, they say, reminded them. They rush off to the enquiries desk, and are sent downstairs to 'Transfers'.

My wife and I carry on queuing. But of course as soon as your 'children' are in difficulty, even of the most minor kind, the inverted commas disappear, and old anxieties begin to stir in your breast. Genes are thicker than water – though to say so isn't to agree with the crass reductionists who claim that we are nothing more than our genes. This business of the seat-numbers drives all thought of the shrine out of my head. That was merely a random glimpse, this is part of my life; perhaps there'll even come a time when the 'children' start to worry about me in the same ridiculous way. At any rate I'd like to think so. And this of course is the way we do most of our thinking about our lives, weighing self against other, groping for patterns of events and thus creating them; a social and cultural process, no doubt, but primarily moral and individual. And to keep a due balance at the primary level is to hold the centre that really matters.

Our son and daughter return just as we reach the gate. They've been duly allocated seats; but not next to ours; and we're all, I think, quite relieved at this, to be flying home together but a little apart.

In Pursuit of Pleasure, or
a Night at the Pictures

Some years ago, when cinema-going was at its nadir, we used to park
in a street of shuttered shops, then huddle in the empty expanses of
the Hollywood-Egyptian theatre balcony (the stalls had long been
abandoned to the mice.) Now we pursue our cinematic pleasures in
a 'multiplex' of course – 'Cinema Eight' – reached via a lift from the
car-park and a stroll through a shopping-plaza lit by the sort of
wattage said to act directly on the wallet. It exerts its most striking
effect in the Games Arcade, where the joys of the screen are 'inter-
active' – and they clearly go beyond the pleasure-principle; the faces
absorbed in feats of electronic destruction look almost as grim as the
cartoon alien at the entrance. (Are death and shopping as inseparable as the moralists say? The plaza-girls' 'Shop till you drop' a
self-betraying battle-cry?) And then come the food-bars – Italian,
Chinese, Indonesian, Turkish – ranged round a tiled court with rows
of tables, an altar-like ATM, and a cascade of gleaming escalators,
whence wafts the buttery smell of popcorn from the eight shadow-
caves upstairs. The whole place is one of those 'landscapes of popular
pleasure' that Stuart Hall thinks the intellectual left must learn to
accommodate; a battery of stimuli for human 'desiring machines'
and their neural 'pleasure centres', on the anti-Oedipal model
conceived by Messieurs Plug-in and Turn-on, aka Deleuze and
Guattari.

As for me, queuing now for the early evening show, after a hard
day's teaching, I simply want to sit back, eat chips (my wife is downstairs buying a carton), and let the moving images wash over me. But
this vulgar pleasure is becoming harder to indulge. Like everything
else in New Zealand, the university that employs me is being 'restruc-
tured', and English is 'merging' with Media Studies – whose staff
may perhaps indulge an occasional smile at the absence of presence
('the cinephile gains pleasure from the never-quite-closed-gap
between imaginary presence and real absence' as one pundit has it),
but they tend to regard the more common forms of cinematic enjoy-
ment as capitalist opiates.

Yet I've been anxious for the merger to succeed. The alternative (Media Studies to 'merge' with Sociology) would be too much of a triumph for the culturally studious left – the new Platonists who'd like to banish poetry from the commonwealth altogether (except for hymns in praise of the correct), and who are, moreover, competing with us for students.

Since the films currently showing include *Batman and Robin* and Branagh's *Hamlet* the queue is rather a motley, with blank-faced teenage couples, 'senior citizens' (who get cheap rates at the early show), and children clutching buckets of popcorn. We've opted for *Hamlet*. An uneasy choice. As a boy I naturally enjoyed some bits of Shakespeare. I found Nym and Bardolph (though not Falstaff) wildly funny, and conceived a bookish adolescent's adoration for Beatrice and Rosalind. But L.C. Knights and company soon taught me to regard 'character' and 'plot' as a distraction from what really mattered – 'concrete realisation of the over-mastering theme' and so forth.

Later, in Hong Kong, when I saw a local audience – avid cinema-goers but still familiar with old forms like Cantonese opera – give vent to a collective 'Aaaahh!' of dismay when Caesar's ghost appeared before Brando-Antony, I recognised a genuine responsiveness I myself had lost, and began a long campaign to recover it.

But surely there are different kinds of 'genuine'? I glance at the teenagers in the cinema-queue. My own current crop of students love Steve Perani's *Romeo and Juliet*. In part of course it's just the pop music and the spectacle, and the relief at not being simply bored by yet another 'great work'; but this also encouraged their 'concernment' – to use Dryden's word – their involvement in the story. The actors, needless to say, simply murder the poetry; but this is a perennial complaint; think of Hamlet's own diatribe against the Thespians. Or think of Dr Johnson, who saw Shakespeare's tragedies as notable not for their language but for their 'incidents' – and my students certainly respond to those. Heresy to the modern critic, for whom language reigns supreme, and especially to the deconstructionist, for whom there's nothing outside 'words, words, words'. My uneasiness grows. *Hamlet* is already ruining the prospect of a simple image-bath and media-massage.

My wife and I share our chips and our workday news while the adverts are showing; when at length the screen glows dimly with a night-time long-shot of a neo-classical pile resembling a Ruritanian Blenheim Palace, my thoughts stray to other cinematic Elsinores – Olivier's towering cliffs and tempestuous sea, Nicol Williamson in a maze of prison-like walls, Kozintsev's fortress with dark waves rolling restlessly in, Zeffirelli's castle on a green hill by a sunlit beach. But this sort of connoisseur's pleasure always erodes 'concernment', and when Branagh himself appears, with a hint of self-consciousness, even narcissism, in his bearing, I struggle not to think of other Hamlets. At least there isn't the distraction of abridgement; the film is to follow the complete text. But the cinematic deployment of sheer material, so to speak – furniture, décor, extras, uniforms, dresses – though impressive in its way, is rather overwhelming, and it's only with the scene in which Polonius orders Ophelia to stop seeing Hamlet that I begin to feel the pleasure that Aristotle saw as one of the two cornerstones of art: the pleasure of realism – of recognising, to use his own simple and Athenian-sexist phrase, 'that it is he'.

It's evidently a recognition of types – the father patronising and dictatorial, the daughter obedient and good. But not an easy recognition. 'Do you believe his tenders, as you call them?' Polonius asks contemptuously, and the rather careful, precise inflection of Kate Winslett-Ophelia's reply ('I do not know, my lord, what I should think') has a two-fold implication: 'I'm inexperienced; instruct me' and 'I know one must be careful, but I remain open-minded; he might after all be sincere'. The first seems pathetically submissive; the second suggests a certain independence; and the contradiction makes us wonder what she might be concealing (we learn later of course that she's already in love with Hamlet).

This active integration of individual with type is a renewal of the powers of perception, a removal of the 'film of familiarity and selfish solicitude'. It's also an integration of feeling and thought; we respond to the tone and rhythm of the careful-hesitant inflection and we ponder its meanings – which are by the same token dramatic possibilities as to what might happen to this interesting girl. Our perception is heightened by our 'concernment'.

Ophelia exits, and in a moment we see Hamlet on the dark battlements with Horatio, waiting for the ghost, and inveighing eloquently against Danish drunkenness, as he listens to the noise from the hall below. Can this be the rake just portrayed by Polonius? And the question evidently exerts a subtle pressure on the unfolding story. But this is also one of those moments when Hamlet seems a plot-free being, a keen and various observer, inclined to expatiate on human affairs.

This condition – the simultaneous independence and integration of character and plot, of part and whole – has been traditionally seen of course as yet another mark of aesthetic unity. Like the unity of feeling and thought, or of image and idea, it's a balance between relatedness and resistance to a wider structure. It's thus a variable, not an absolute. In Kozintsev's version, for instance, the scene between Ophelia and her father is drastically shortened, and Hamlet is shown eavesdropping. This weaves the scene more closely into the plot, tilting the balance away from the part and onto the whole. But there still remains an intrinsic interest in the father and daughter and their relationship.

For Aristotle, unity was the second great source of aesthetic pleasure – and this has been variously glossed. The culturally studious left of course see it as a 'fetishizing' of 'organicism'; sensibilities fragmented by capitalism, they say, will cling to the illusion of being unified by art. Another typically modern (i.e. negative) gloss is Freud's explanation of pleasure in terms of dreams and the death-wish – which, like some other Freudian ideas, continues to influence literary thinking by default, even though their inventor has gone largely out of fashion.

Freud began by believing that dreams are born simply of the pleasure-principle, and then he encountered the nightmares of shell-shocked war veterans, compulsively repeating their original trauma. How to reconcile this with 'pleasure'? An expected shock, Freud argued, brings 'anxiety' and thus resistance; unexpected, it brings sheer 'fright', pre-empting resistance and penetrating deep into the psyche. The soldiers' nightmare repetitions were attempts to turn 'fright' into 'anxiety', to relive the painful experience in order to resist and control it. And this, Freud added – the control of dangerously powerful impulses – is the ultimate source of *all* human pleasure.

An obvious enough conclusion, one might think, and also obviously applicable to art, which had always been seen as an aid to painful recognition, an instrument of self-awareness and wholeness, of realism and unity. *Too* obvious perhaps. At any rate Freud ignored the usual application to art, and then simply asserted (it seems no more than that) that the pleasure of control foreshadows the pleasure of death, the end of all disturbing impulse, the quietus we can make for ourselves with a bare bodkin.

But surely the pleasures of control have various sources. Up there on the screen, for instance, the ghost has fled from the approaching dawn, and Branagh-Hamlet is warning his friends that he might, on occasion, 'think meet to put an antic disposition on'. This was a tactic later employed by Muhammed Ali, and for the same reasons – to disturb his opponents and to release his own tensions. These impulses towards control – of self and of others – are evidently geared not to death but to survival.

The death-wish, as Hamlet elsewhere amply shows, is in fact a desire to abandon control – 'Oh, that this too, too solid flesh would melt.' Control is the essential life-wish. Coleridge's 'primary imagination' or 'esemplastic power', Polanyi's 'tacit thinking', or the modern biologist's 'genetic codes', are all versions of the organising power at the heart of physical being. D.H. Lawrence (more recently echoed in this by Jonathan Miller) saw it as the 'true unconscious', and regarded the Freudian 'unconscious' as a mere by-product of consciousness – as 'the cellar in which the mind keeps its own bastard spawn'.

But disbelief in the unifying power has been an essential feature of modern literary thought. The Freudian doctrine that the self is radically disorganised becomes at length the self-contradictory dogma of the Lacanian 'mirror stage', asserting a basic rupture in the very genesis of the self (though in fact it assumes the existence of a self already fully organised – capable, that is, of recognising not only self and mother but their reflections in the glass.) The same Freudian prejudice colours Barthes's distinction between 'pleasure' and 'bliss'; the former rational and calm, the latter dark and disruptive. And though anti-Oedipal Deleuze and Guattari make frequent appeals to Lawrence himself, their 'desiring machines' are as far from his 'true unconscious' as from the Freudian cellar. The tacit processes are neither disruptive nor mechanical, but the agents of organic unity.

Freud himself of course – and here too his influence still lingers through inertia – saw art as giving pleasure not through the recognition of reality, but through its evasion: 'Man, as we know, makes use of his imaginative activity in order to satisfy the wishes that reality does not satisfy.' *King Lear* for instance is seen as a variant of the fantasy in which the inevitability of death becomes the freedom to choose a beautiful woman. This might seem a 'wish-fulfilment' too wildly at odds with reality for even the most devious to indulge, but it 'offers no serious difficulty', Freud remarks, 'to the work of analytic interpretation'; the mechanisms of 'reaction-formation' and 'condensation' can convert anything whatever into its opposite.

Cordelia, then, is Death, and when Lear carries her body onto the stage at the end of the play, 'Eternal wisdom clothed in the primaeval myth bids the old man renounce love, choose death, and make friends with the necessity of dying.' A resounding conclusion; but how 'wish-fulfilment' has contrived to become 'eternal wisdom' remains unexplained. And so far from growing wise, Lear is in fact still trying to convince himself that Cordelia is alive. He does so, needless to say, because he himself is finally responsible for her death, as for many others; it is this, conveyed by the play with such painful realism, that he has 'to make friends with', not some sentimental-mythological 'necessity of death'.

One of my early cinema-going memories is of Trevor Howard playing Mr Morel in *Sons and Lovers*. Two minutes into his first scene, a squeal of delight and dismay came from a girl just behind me, 'Eee! He's just like me dad!' The painful pleasure of recognition. New Zealand now, with one of the world's highest suicide rates for young males, would derive – so one might think – a more serious shock of recognition from Hamlet, the proverbial 'young man sick of life'. Yet the local reviewers saw the film as 'literary' and 'irrelevant to contemporary life'.

In a small town near here a year or so ago, when suicide seemed almost epidemic, a young woman spent an evening in the pub with friends, then went off and made her own quietus (though not with a bare bodkin), leaving a note to say how much she'd enjoyed her 'farewell party'. But her friends hadn't been aware that's what it was, and one of them later expressed public anger at her 'irresponsibility' – her inability to see or care how her actions might affect those around her.

Hamlet evidently has a similar incapacity. It comes out now as Branagh delivers the great suicidal speeches, full of self-reproach for his own ineffectuality. But they're counterpointed by clear signals that his strategy against Claudius is in fact working. The first ('O what a rogue and peasant slave') is immediately followed by the king's worried reference to his nephew's 'dangerous lunacy', and the second ('To be or not to be') is immediately preceded by the king's guilty aside – 'How smart a lash that speech doth give my conscience'. After eavesdropping on Hamlet's encounter with Ophelia, Claudius decides to send him away to England; and then we see Hamlet coaching the actors in the speech he has written to expose his uncle's guilt. Again Branagh vividly conveys the sense of Hamlet as a plot-free being, a man with emphatic opinions about art and life. But there is also a gathering momentum in the action – of which Hamlet himself is still unaware.

His sense of futility clearly springs not from events but from a crisis of self-hood. D.H. Lawrence – in his wonderful account of an amateur production of the play in *Twilight in Italy* – sees this as a failure of the balance between 'sympathy' and 'assertion' fundamental to any living organism; the balance between dependence on the non-self – for love, food, oxygen, and so on – and that radical *in*dependence without which organic life simply fails. Hamlet wants pure 'sympathy', wants his 'too, too solid flesh' to melt back into the all. But he also wants to be like his father the king, a great self-assertor. His 'To be, or not to be' reflects this dilemma, the Renaissance crisis of the self, that was really a crisis of the body, triggered, Lawrence surmised, by epidemic syphilis.

Lawrence liked to project his ideas onto large back-drops; he sees 'assertion' as 'Paganism' or as 'God the Father', 'sympathy' as 'Christianity' or as 'God the Son' – with the Holy Ghost as the 'true unconscious', the power that holds the balance, keeping the organism organised. But he was also a down-to-earth man – good at cooking, sewing, and odd-jobbery – and his view of the self clearly answers to common experience. Indeed, baldly stated it sounds like the sort of truism that gets 'discovered' by 'social science'; it's in the imaginative exploration of particular cases that Lawrence's genius shows – as it does here, in his suggestion that Hamlet's problem lies in the Holy-Ghost-unconscious, rather than the Freudian cellar. His view of the self also answers clearly to the experience of New Zealand's young suicides, who, whatever else, are organisms whose formative years have been unbalanced by a national lurch from left-liberalism to right-monetarism, from a 'sympathetic' to an 'assertive' ethos.

Hamlet's blindness to the effect of his own acts is repeated, with less excuse, by modern academic criticism, which, from its inception, virtually defined itself by its lack of interest in action of any sort. In the 1920s critical interest shifted from plot to pattern, symbolic or thematic. Pattern reigned supreme for the structuralists, that hypertrophy of synchronicity of which Jacobson's definition of 'the poetic' was the paradigm; while any interest in the actions of individuals was yet further extinguished by the Marxist belief that in the unfolding pattern of history only mass-action is effective. One eventual reaction to this sort of thinking was the 'Thatcher revolution', with its slogan of 'the responsible individual'; another was postmodernism, rejecting pattern not for responsibility but for randomness.

But good stories clearly depend on all three terms – pattern, randomness, and responsibility. And so does the natural world – at least according to the chaos-theorists, with their vision of reality as composed of systems highly organised but in fine balance, and tipped one way or the other by individual and unpredictable events.

Whether in life or art, the essential feature of chaotic systems is suspense – as is exemplified now, in Hamlet's use of the travelling actors to assure himself that the 'something rotten' in the state of Denmark isn't simply his own 'foul' imagination. Will his violent interjections during the Play expose Claudius or ruin his own scheme? And is Claudius even guilty? (We ourselves aren't sure until we see him at prayer.) A small random event that helps tip the balance, is the Player-king's coarse acting. Jarring on Hamlet's wire-taut nerves ('pox, leave thy damnable faces, and begin'), it sparks the outburst ('you shall see anon how the murderer gets the love of Gonzago's queen') that in turn puts Claudius to flight.

But here Hamlet strikes too soon of course, and the suspense carries over into another poised chaotic system. The king may have been simply frightened by his nephew's wild behaviour; this is how Claudius presents it when he reappears – and how the courtiers choose to see it. But his conscience has been sharply pricked – as we see when he tries to pray. And this tension will drive him to send Hamlet to England to be killed – 'for like the hectic in my blood he rages'.

Chaos begets the pleasures of concernment. But my own pleasure just now is running ahead of the film. With the king's exit and Hamlet's feverish excitement, the screen has faded and the lights have come up for the interval. My media-studies colleagues of course (are there any of them here?) would see my pleasure as naïve, élitist and irrelevant. I glance warily round, like Hamlet looking out for Rosencrantz and Guildenstern (the stock vices of the academy are those of Elsinore, are they not? Poison in the ear and the knife in the back).

But that's ridiculous; like Hamlet I should be worrying instead about my own paranoia. In fact our last merger-meeting was amicable enough. One film-studies lecturer in particular, an American woman, pale but strong-featured, with grey eyes and jet-black hair, whom I had seen as an explosive mixture of tragic heroine and militant feminist, emerged as a reasonable negotiator with an engaging smile and wry sense of irony.

The culturally studious themselves, however, would say that I'm just switching the individual woman from one stereotype to another; and here lies the essential rejection of unity that they share with the deconstructionists – though of course they're less inclined merely to smile at the eternal absence of presence. Adorno, for instance, according to Eagleton, thinks that 'individual particulars will never rest content under the law's yoke' and that 'the central tenet of traditional aesthetics' is therefore 'a lie'. The tenet is undeniably central; since our perceptual response to an 'individual' is also the source of our feelings about it, the integration of individual with type includes that of emotion with thought. But a 'lie'?

In fact the integration of particular and universal, image and idea, isn't just a 'law' of 'aesthetics' but of all perception. It's an integration I perform every time I 'see a cat'. Of course the idea may simply overwhelm the image, and prevent us from really seeing it. But the reverse may also occur. In *An Anthropologist from Mars*, Oliver Sacks describes a notable artist of 'individual particulars' – an American-Italian who painted, with hallucinatory accuracy and vividness, scenes recalled from his childhood village in Tuscany. He seems to draw his visual straight up from the well-springs of perception, pure and unmodified – and unmodifiable. And this last is Sacks's point. Their vivid particularity is untouched by any maturer conception; for all their power, the paintings feel strictly limited, indeed rather obsessive.

In narrative (and all poetry is narrative of one kind or another), aesthetic integration suspends the particulars between more than one idea (should we see Ophelia's reply to Polonius as 'submissive' or 'shrewd'?) The particulars thus remain free, and are carried on the current of the action not towards a determination of their 'meaning', but towards a dramatic resolution of their possibilities. They don't have to 'rest content' under any 'law's yoke'; they move with the living flow in which all perception occurs.

One feels the more need to insist on all this, because to lose the idea of integration is to lose a basic critical tool – whose use can be conveniently demonstrated on Eagleton's own prose: 'If a brutal asceticism is one aspect of capitalist society, its inverted mirror-image is a fantastic aestheticism. Sensory existence is stripped to skeletal need at one level only to be extravagantly inflated at another. The antithesis of the blindly biologistic wage-slave is the exotic idler.' Representative, I think. Some readers – especially the Marxist *flâneurs*, anxious to cultivate both their principles and their pleasures – claim to derive aesthetic satisfaction from it. And indeed, to a casual eye, it presents a sort of cartoon vigour – simple outlines, colour boldly laid on.

But on a closer look it dissolves, to reveal routine antithesis and alliteration, inept metaphor and inert abstraction – reminiscent altogether of bad eighteenth-century verse, though deployed in the service of a tired politics rather than a tired morality. The 'skeleton', for instance, lends some of its metaphoric half-life to the dead metaphor of 'inflated', which then conjures up the stock image of a Michelin-man plutocrat, greedy and gross; but of course this doesn't really fit the stereotype of the 'exotic idler'. The only integration one might claim is that the weakness of the imagery matches the conventionality of the thought.

I look round at the denizens of this 'landscape of popular pleasure', now straggling into the foyer for the interval. 'Wage-slaves' or 'exotic idlers'? Obviously neither. Stuart Hall is right about this at least; the 'left' needs to put these folk in a better story.

Eagleton ends with an attempt to retrieve 'the aesthetic' by turning it into 'the progressive'. The fusion of universal with particular for instance translates into the fusion of 'equality' with 'individual rights': it's 'just every individual's equal right to have his or her difference respected'. This is clearly well-meaning and it gestures, albeit vaguely, towards an important truth – that an artist's imagination may be as fired by a beggar as a king. But to convert the artist's imaginative power into the beggar's political right betrays the usual equation of artistic quality with political correctness. The Red Guards are still with us in spirit.

I glance round again, no doubt with narrowed eyes; still no culturally studious enemies in sight – beneath whose undermining mines I might delve one yard and blow them at the moon. But there's a fresh source of pleasure. The cinema where high-brow films like *Hamlet* are shown has its own separate foyer, where the patrons get free coffee, instead of the over-priced fizz and popcorn foisted on the groundlings in the main lobby.

As we queue for it my wife tells me more about her day. Not good, it seems. Like my university, her polytechnic is being 're-structured', and of course this well suits staff who're more interested in politics than in teaching. Court-politics, that is, immediate and personal, though somewhat less deadly than those practised at Elsinore – and very different from the historico-socio-economic politics that engross the students of culture. There's a connection of course; the 'restructuring' in my wife's polytechnic is being driven in part by the current market ideology. But these connections are never straightforward. A socialist ex-colleague of mine, for instance, wrote to me recently from England, in a state of high excitement about some academic 'league tables' – not, as I at first assumed, because they reflected an abysmal market mentality, but because they rated his own university's 'research output' equal with Oxford's. Social philosophy overwhelmed by academic pride. Thought and feeling disjointed.

It's a universal problem of course. My wife has just remarked that the coffee is weak, and I'm suddenly aware that I've been simply guzzling it, groundling that I am, too preoccupied to notice. Donne's thoughts were always at the tips of his senses, said Eliot, yearning for the same. Did Donne, I wonder, ever guzzle? My wife never does. Brought up in a middle-class Chinese family, serious eaters but unsnobbish, she's as judicious about hamburgers as about Peking duck. I think of Hamlet's contempt for his own theatre's 'landscapes of popular pleasure', with their 'inexplicable dumb-shows and noise'. Leavis-like he equated the popular with the 'unrealised'.

But realisation surely starts at a more humble level. I let the taste of the coffee come into consciousness; yes, it's weak. No great intellectual feat to recognise it. In fact the most commmon obstacle to realisation is explicit thought, overwhelming the tacit powers – the senses, feelings, intuitions. This is Hamlet's problem of course; 'what a piece of work is a man', he enthuses, and yet 'what is this quintessence of dust' to him? He remembers the idea of good coffee but has lost all pleasure in the taste.

I remember a recent television broadcast of a Kiri Te Kanawa concert in the open-air on the Auckland waterfront. A warm summer night, a popular show, a huge crowd – Te Kanawa is virtually royalty in New Zealand. Some of the wealthy had paid to moor their yachts in a basin below the stage, an opportunity for self-display enhanced by television, with frequent shots of the champagne-sipping, camera-conscious *ton* – rather irritating no doubt to real music-lovers. Then suddenly a lingering close-up of a boy, perhaps the same age as Huckleberry Finn; legs dangling over the side of a boat, toes trailing in the water, he seemed oblivious to the cameras and deeply absorbed in – what? The cool water on his skin? The glamour of the music? The reflections of the stage-lights in the glassy depths? At any rate he seemed to embody a wonderfully pure pleasure of the senses. Of course the pleasures of the show-off adults are real enough too. The joy of assertion, of absorbing the world into the self – like Hamlet's father, or the shopping-plaza girls. The boy however seemed an image not of assertion but of interplay – that taking of the world into the self and projecting the self out into the world, that underlies all our perception; a Wordsworthian boy, I thought, exemplifying the 'grand elementary principle of pleasure' by which we know and feel and live and move.

Meanwhile the great suprano was pouring her heart out in song – well, at rather low pressure in fact, and perhaps understandably so, given the nature of the audience. Yet who knows? Amongst all those dark heads and shining faces turned towards the brilliant stage, there were doubtless music lovers too. And even at half-steam Te Kanawa is a reminder that the pleasures of perception are at their keenest in music – in the sheer richness and diversity of sound, from strings softly plucked ('pearls dropping into a jade bowl', said a Chinese poet), to the cry of a horn – or Kiri's own voice now, soaring into the etherealised version of the Maori song 'Po Karekare Ana' that has latterly become the commercial anthem of Air New Zealand.

Myself, I like voices with more throat and chest in them; Elaine Page, Celine Dion; the sirens; for of course music is also the art closest to sex, where assertion and sympathy, and all the pleasures, are at their most intense. I recall another summer evening, years before, driving home with my family along a country road, and becoming gradually conscious of a vague glare cast up into the night, from behind the dark hump of a hill. As we turned a corner, our headlights caught a group of policemen and women, with their brilliant blue and white cars, at the entrance to a side-road; and then I remembered – the open-air rock-concert, held annually here on somebody's farm. I dipped the lights and changed down, and we could hear the waves of music beating out from beyond the hill. The pleasures of the dangerous impulse controlled – just – with the help of the Platonic police.

But that's a Hamlet-ish view again – of the kind I first remember adopting as a teenager in Larkin-land in the 1950s, a New Orleans jazz purist, inclined to imagine the local *palais* as the scene of Dionysian abandonment, and to despise and envy its groundling clientele. And so it remained when I became a Leavisite undergraduate, convinced that a truly 'popular culture' had been destroyed by industrial capitalism.

But I've long since joined those who see the 'modern waste land' syndrome as the Leavisian weakness, as a simple refusal to acknowledge that the fifties *palais* or the Edwardian music-hall, the medieval church or the Cambridge English School, would all more or less equally have contained the brutal and the sensitive, the wicked and the good, the assertive and the sympathetic, have contained, that is, every individual variety and degree of the 'realising' power – or the lack of it. In every village I visit, said Confucius, there are people at least as intelligent and virtuous as myself, though I've never found anyone as dedicated to study. Leavis seems to have fallen into the habit of thinking that intelligence and virtue, the true *mens sana*, were to be found only in the 'trained sensibility', in the dedicated few, that is, who contributed to *Scrutiny*.

His recent commentator, Gary Day, seems to echo his blank opposition to 'the modern world', and compounds it with a misunderstanding of what Leavis meant by 'realisation'. 'Akin to psychoanalysis,' says Day, 'it makes manifest what is latent.' But a 'meaning' hidden 'behind' the immediate experience is surely the opposite of what Leavis had in mind. He saw 'realisation' as a heightened consciousness of the experience itself; his conception belongs with phenomenology rather than psychiatry.

And though he failed to realise how much 'the masses' realise, he was always clear about what the process is. This is why he saw analysis as strictly limited, and why he came at length to endorse Michael Polanyi, whose whole philosophy of 'tacit knowledge' is designed to show that we always 'know more than we can tell'. Dr Day, intent on turning 'realisation' into yet another academic device for bypassing the image in order to get straight to the idea behind it (a by-pass guaranteed to lead you astray of course), fails even to mention Polanyi.

A depressing thought. Is the literary-academic enterprise really so lost in the deserts of theory? But the way out is easy enough to see, in theory at least – or rather in *principle*, for the old word seems increasingly preferable, and the relevant principle here is that 'poetry is the best words in the best order'. Which can be defined in practice as 'what Eagleton's words plainly aren't', or as 'what Shakespeare's words plainly are' – as I find myself thinking when the film starts again after the interval.

''Sblood, do you think I am easier to be played on than a pipe?' Hamlet, the embittered idealist, is caught between contempt and regret for Rosencrantz and Guildenstern, and is excited by the acuteness of the tension; the pleasure of a barely kept control. When he spares Claudius's life a few moments later in the chapel, he's caught in a similar conflict, between his unconscious inability to murder a man at prayer and his conscious desire to send him to hell. The bitterness and idealism reach fever-pitch in his golden memories of his father and his disgust at his mother's sexuality.

This tension draws the action forward. We have just seen Claudius's growing desperation – 'like the hectic in my blood he rages' – and this makes Hamlet seem the reverse of ineffectual. Now, in quick succession, he kills Polonius, wrings his mother's conscience, and explores her complicity with Claudius. (His 'As kill a king good mother' elicits her evidently genuine astonishment, and his sharp 'There's letters signed. Do you know that?' her evidently innocent dismay.) He is not only redeeming her but driving a wedge between her and Claudius, and at the end of the scene his sense of happy anticipation is intense: 'O, 'tis most sweet/When in one line two crafts directly meet.'

But again it's a wild Hamlet-excitement. Can he maintain the control he showed earlier, resisting Gertrude's suggestion that he is driven not by her 'trespass' but his own madness? And can she keep her promise that she 'has no life to breathe' what he has told her?

'Come sir, to draw towards an end with you.' The little joke might be a sign of unusual control or of imminent breakdown. As Hamlet drags Polonius off, I glance round at the audience; rows of dark heads and shining faces again, turned up towards the screen as to an oracle. What are they all thinking? Not very much – if we believe Michael Cohen's *Hamlet in My Mind's Eye*. The reader of a text, Cohen argues, can dwell on all its ambiguities, but a mere spectator, forced by the press of events on the stage or the screen, must at any given point choose just one meaning. The reader may attribute Gertrude's oath of silence, for instance, to various motives – her shame at her own role in the story, her fear of revealing just how mad her son really is, or her recognition of her husband's guilt. A subtle and persuasive analysis. But surely the spectator's 'concernment' is in fact a balance of all these possibilities, as we check the nuances of her language against what has happened and what might happen, against her character and the unfolding story.

In short her words are the best, and in the best order, because their ambiguities are geared to the suspense. And our dwelling on them while at the same time casting to and fro, is the movement of the imagination that Coleridge figured as a snake, always gathering itself together in order to move forward.

This movement entails no more than the mental powers – chiefly tacit – with which we conduct our daily life and language; but in poetry the powers are more sharply focused. It is thus, of course, that poets 'purify the language of the tribe'. And the record of their attempts is in the 'national literature' – a phrase that degenerates either into a slogan or a joke, if we lose sight of these elementary principles. 'Elementary' implies 'education', and the reconnection of ambiguity with suspense, of poetry with narrative, is particularly needed in the classroom; it will generate a modest and specific style of analysis, helping students equally to resist the polysemic vapourings of the 'post-structuralists' and the megalomaniac abstractions of the culturally studious.

It will also make them alive to the sort of poetic drama unfolding now, as Hamlet leaves his mother's room. Taunting first

Rosencrantz and Guildenstern and then the King, he seems both powerful and vulnerable; he makes Claudius feel privately desperate, and himself look publicly mad. The death of Ophelia widens the rift between Gertrude and the King, but its effect on Laertes then endangers Hamlet. And the suspense quickens of course with Horatio's receipt of Hamlet's letter.

Like other directors Branagh can't resist reading the letter voice-over, against some footage of nautical derring-do, and the poetry drowns in the plot-filler seas. But the dark heads of the audience still seem intent. I feel a Prufrockian desire to see their nerves thrown in patterns on the screen, a revelatory brain-scan, such as I.A. Richards might have dreamed of, showing how wonderfully the organism is organised by poetry. But it would show nothing of course – except the incalculability of art. Who can 'measure' the effect of a play? Or, by extension, the influence of a Shakespeare or a Dickens? We can only generalise from their effect on ourselves – on our 'concernment', quickening our sense of language in full and subtle human action – and then ponder the significance of this for a whole society, over generations.

I'm thrilled, as always, when Hamlet reveals himself at the burial: 'This is I, Hamlet the Dane', and 'I loved Ophelia'. But the thrill is complicated by the extravagance: 'Woo't drink up eisel? eat a crocodile?/I'll do it.' Of course Hamlet's self-mockery is really mockery of Laertes: 'Nay, an thou'lt mouth,/I'll rant as well as thou.' And its edge is attractive. But it also strikes the self-conscious Hamlet-note – which then echoes clearly in the futility and disgust of his 'but it is no matter', as he stalks off.

A part of my mind strays back to my first acquaintance with the play, a teenager readily identifying with Hamlet's extravagance and disgust; too readily, as I realised later, since his feelings are Renaissance-full-blooded not post-Victorian-furtive. These thoughts are still lingering when Branagh reappears with Horatio, still recounting his exploits at sea, and he seems suddenly repellent – his complexion yellow-ish, his blue eyes rather bulging. But this vagary of my personal 'response' (yet another line of theory that has thrived on the disconnection of ambiguity from suspense) has no effect on the course of the plot – which is now quickening to its crisis.

The decisive moment comes with Gertrude's 'I will my lord; I pray you, pardon me', as she rejects Claudius's plea, and drinks from the poisoned cup. Cohen as usual lists alternative 'readings': she is simply being playful, and her 'rejection' is thus a gesture towards family unity; or she has guessed that the drink is poisoned and is sacrificing herself to save her son; or, being a woman of strong appetites, she is simply excited and in need of a drink. But as usual the audience, like Gertrude herself, can take all these in its stride: a sudden inkling that her husband intends to poison her son, will give the gesture towards unity a dark ironic edge; but it will also bring relief, in a sense of death as the only way out.

The action not only unites the alternative meanings, it gives them a structure, as in the counterpoint between the conventional phrase ('I pray you pardon me') and its tragic implication ('Forgive me for betraying you and not my son'). It gives them a hierarchy too. My own recent flicker of Hamlet-disgust, for instance, has made me receptive to the thought of Gertrude as a woman driven by appetite; but to see this as the sole or chief meaning would be clearly grotesque; it finds a minor place in the whole effect, as her sense of grim satisfaction that this is the last drink she'll ever feel the need of.

In a few moments the betrayal comes, with Gertrude's 'No, no, the drink', contradicting the King, and triggering Laertes' confession, without which Hamlet's story would never have been credited; and this of course is Hamlet's great concern:

> As th'art a man,
> Give me the cup. Let go. By heaven, I'll ha't.
> O God! Horatio, what a wounded name,
> Things standing thus unknown, shall live behind me!
> If thou didst ever hold me in thy heart,
> Absent thee from felicity awhile,
> And in this harsh world draw thy breath in pain,
> To tell my story.

Branagh gives the speech its due urgency. In the intensity of 'wounded name' and the exaggeration of 'draw thy breath in pain' we're still aware of Hamlet's self-consciousness and disgust with life. But the real harshness of his world largely converts these flaws into their corresponding virtues – self-respect and self-awareness.

'Good night sweet prince…' But even here at the height of our feeling for him we're still prompted to further reflection. His curses as he stabs the King and then forces the poison down his throat – 'Thou incestuous, murderous, damned Dane' – are still ringing in our ears and make us wonder about 'sweet'. And when Fortinbras enters, to remark in quick succession that corpses, though out of place in the great hall, look well on the battlefield, that Hamlet himself would have made a good soldier, and that this, by the way, seems a suitable moment to claim the kingdom, we can imagine the 'sweet prince' making some bitter observation.

So when the lights go up I'm still in Elsinore, still absorbed by the image of a Hamlet both sweet and bitter and unexhausted by either category, the heart of his mystery still unplucked. The sudden world of popcorn, muzak and chatter is disconcerting. My wife seems to sense my mood, and we make our way home saying little.

As we drive up Mountain View Road towards our suburb, the city comes into view below, lights glittering in the dusk, the huddled masses of buildings still visible; and beyond it stretches the dim plain, with dark clumps of trees and the occasional farm-house light; and a hundred miles beyond these again, on the far horizon, stands the mountain itself, its volcanic cone etched black against the dying sunset. All seems portentously vivid and real. Concernment, especially when it issues in a tragic death, heightens the senses and the sense of life. I recall the dim-witted profundity of the scullion in *Tristram Shandy*, with her cry of 'So am not I', on hearing that Bobby is dead. The pleasure that there is in life itself.

Not that I can credit myself with such fine simplicity. The view there before me, with its contrasts of city, plain, and mountain, of light and dark, reminds me rather of a print by Hiroshigei that hangs in my living-room. Life imitates art. Perhaps too much so, in my case. Walking home from work each day, I cross a wooden bridge over a stream that runs through some native bush; a conventional scenic image, but if I stop to gaze at the dark ripple of the water, glittering green and silver from the light-spangled canopy overhead, it looks like some Warhol trick with a photographic negative. Yet these borrowed images neither determine nor exhaust the scene; they explore and are explored by the something in it that lies 'beyond text'. Life itself is an art, a story with images, and with corresponding pleasures, but it's still none the less life.

And the art is well or badly executed. As we climb the the hill, with the evening drawing in, more lights coming on, and smoke rising softly from the chimney-pots, the Hiroshigei-view takes on a more domestic tone, and this mingles with the quiet presence of my wife, in tune with me. Or is she? I glance at her dark head over the steering wheel, intent, unknown. My life-story wobbles into uncertainty – of the everyday kind (I trust), not the 'purposes mistook/Fall'n on the inventors' heads' that mark the Hamlet story – though I recall that the most recent 'carnal, bloody, and unnatural act' in the city down there below was a domestic homicide triggered by an illegible shopping-list.

At the top of the rise we turn away from the city lights and the sunset, and into the dim suburban street. Awaiting me at home is an MA thesis to be examined; I've put it off and put it off until it's become a guilt-laden thing. Hamlet again. 'Procrastination is the thief...' Poor Cowper. And foolish me.

It seems natural to seek refuge in the darkening evening from these nagging thoughts; 'and each day dies with sleep'. But no; the solid flesh isn't ready to melt. Resisting the death-wish pleasure, I think of dinner instead. Stir-fried chicken noodles, yes, I'll cook them, eat them, enjoy them – with sweet peppers, glossy red and green, and fresh mushrooms, those magical creations of earth, water, and air.

My art of living is crude no doubt; sloppy emotion overcorrected by conscious will. At my age I ought to be more adept. But the resistance works and the melting stops; 'the lost heart stiffens and rejoices'. And the Holy Ghost, I hope, is still in there somewhere.

Theorising Barnsley

Sunday morning; my New Zealand eye watches the English heart-land drifting past to the steady rhythm of the train wheels; thick hedgerows, stately trees, and rolling pasture; stone farm-buildings and churches. It's well into October, but with barely a trace of autumn, except for the slant rays of the sun and a suggestion of haze – even the glint of the railway lines seems mellowed. 'Season of mists...' – or is it just pollution? In any case, after a day and a half of planes and air-ports, plastic furnishings and fluorescent light, flickering screens and electronic voices, the whole scene looks time-less. But then, in a way, so did the piles of *Observers* and *Sunday Times* at the Heathrow newsagents, the dawn emptiness of the Underground, the echoing roofs of King's Cross station, and the soul-wearying straggle of tenements, warehouses, and factories on the way out of London. It brought back all my youthful journeys from south to north, home to Barnsley from the chimerical glamour of London or Oxford. How long it haunted me – haunts me still perhaps. When I went back to Oxford just a few years ago, the dreaming spires and college fronts seemed like cardboard cut-outs, without depth or resonance, but the fluting complacency of a College Fellow holding forth in a senior common room could still call up the ghost of old feelings of exclusion, inferiority, and resentment; and the gowned students in the High Street brought back the old seduc-tive sense of being one of the world's chosen, the cleverest. Contradictory feelings, but that's how it was.

When the train passes through Doncaster and into the industrial West Riding, I feel the same mixture of intimacy and estrangement. The red-brick houses and narrow back gardens of a mining village, where I used to deliver milk during school holidays, slide into view and then fall away, half-like a weird tribal settlement, half-like a dream of home.

At Wakefield, waiting outside the station for my brother, I fall into conversation with two railway-workers, a chubby, pink-cheeked teenager, and a man of forty-something, slight but active-looking, with pale, mobile features and inquisitive grey eyes. The boy is bashful, the man talkative. When he finds out where I've come from, he falls into anecdotal reminiscence, vivid and faintly *risqué*, of an encounter with a New Zealand woman in search of her family roots in Wakefield. He 'talks Yorkshire' but in complex sentences, and with a conscious mastery of both dialect and syntax. Is this a performance for my benefit, or is he always the raconteur? In any case his complacency is oddly reminiscent of the fluting Fellow. In a while, perhaps sensing my detachment, he seems suddenly to lose interest, and turns away.

In his poem 'At Knaresborough', Donald Davie – himself from Barnsley of course and in my thoughts quite often on this journey 'home' – records a similar meeting with a loquacious Yorkshireman; but there it's Davie who turns away, repelled by the man's insincerity. Is there a significant difference of generation and 'class' between Davie and myself? His father, he tells us, was a small shopkeeper, who always voted Conservative. Mine was a moulder in an iron-foundry, a socialist with a conventional scorn for shop-workers ('counter-jumpers') and a conventional pride in his own dirty overalls ('clee-an muck'). One of my most vivid childhood memories is of the Labour victory in 1945 and the feeling that 'the working-class had come into its own'. But in fact my father's great-grandfather had founded the foundry – the old tale of 'from clogs to clogs in three generations' – and by the 1950s my father had struggled back out of the clogs and into the managing director's chair. And even when he was a moulder we saw ourselves as a cut above the neighbourhood's really 'rough' streets, whose children we feared and whose clothes we could smell in the queue at the fish-and-chip shop.

I was born in between Davie's generation and the 1960s 'left' that he came to oppose. Terry Eagleton, interviewed in *PNR* by Nicolas Tredell, recalled being 'alienated' by the 'confident and dominative upper-class style' of Cambridge. Asked about this later by Tredell, Davie said he found it a 'strange response'. Remembering my own experience at Oxford in the 1950s, I wouldn't call it 'strange', but certainly too simple. The 'dominative upper-class style' was there of course, and could feel oppressive, but even at that time it was widely seen – and by public-school boys themselves – as an object of ridicule. And to ridicule such superior attitudes made one feel even more superior of course; there was more danger of conceit than alienation. 'Class-feelings' no doubt take root in 'the economic base', but they're just local varieties of universal passions – mainly pride and fear – weeds that thrive in all conditions, both social and individual. And the real differences between Davie and myself are clearly of an individual kind. I have neither the poetic nor the scholarly gifts, for instance, that made him feel at home in Cambridge. I'm more easy-going too, I fancy – hence my greater tolerance for the stock talkative 'Yorkshire tyke'.

In a moment some more social history appears, in the shape of my brother in his Jaguar. The foundry he took over from our father in the 1970s, dependent as it was on the coal-mines, went bankrupt after the Thatcher-Scargill wars, but being a qualified engineer, he found work with another local company – now owned, one need hardly add, by a German 'group'. As he levers his long frame out of the low-slung car, his pale, drawn face makes me think of his first arrival in the world, afflicted with an illness that seemed to presage his imminent departure. I myself was seven at the time, acutely aware of the tensions coming from the sick-room, but mainly conscious of myself neglected. Now, fifty years on, it's his wife, Trish, who has departed. Being the only immediate family-member left on either side, I've come 'home' for the funeral, that eventual 'end of history' – social or otherwise – for us all.

When my brother takes me to see the body next morning, the undertaker's wife takes us into her kitchen and goes off in search of the key for the 'chapel of rest' – it's just an extension of the house. With death so near at hand, the workaday home, smelling faintly of baking and comfortably untidy, seems rich with life. Lying on a table in the windowless chapel, the open coffin is lined with scarlet satin, and the body is in a winding sheet of the same colour, with a silver cord round the waist. They're colours Trish would have liked. A primary school teacher, her passion was teaching children how to sing; she liked jewellery and furs, Elizabeth Taylor and Italy – where she holidayed regularly and felt she was liked in return. Chemo-therapy took all her luxuriant hair, but when she died it was growing again, thick and black, without a trace of grey. In the scarlet coffin, with her dark cropped head and her features etched with the severity of death, she looks like a warrior queen. On a sudden impulse I bend to kiss her forehead; its coldness seems to stay on my lips all day. My brother is quiet and accustomed around the body, with the caring, slightly anxious look that was always in his character, inten-sified latterly by his wife's illness; it's clear that for him she's still alive.

It's the same when the priest comes to discuss the funeral service. My brother is attentive and precise about the speeches, the music, and so on, but he seems essentially aloof, as though none of this really touches what was, and is, between him and his wife. The priest, a brisk but sympathetic Anglican of forty-something, with sandy hair and a roundish freckled face, is clearly adept at catering for individual needs, but also anxious to remind his clients that this is a Christian ritual, not just a personal service. He talks about the journey to Emmaeus – the text for his funeral-sermon – and unconsciously slips into the pulpit mode; but he also happens to have – for me at least – a voice with a scalp-tingling, almost hypnotic, resonance, so soothing here in the hushed sitting room of a house where life has been fractured. To break the little trance I cast my eyes over the piece he proposes to read at the crematorium after the funeral:

> Death is nothing at all. I have only slipped away into the next room. I am I, and you are you. Whatever we were to each other, that we still are. Call me by my old familiar name, speak to me in the easy way which you always used.

And so it glides on, sweet consolatory prose for the death of a spouse, from the pen of a nineteenth-century Dean of St Paul's. It's so bland it sets me thinking of Dylan Thomas's contrary exhortation to 'Rage, rage against the dying of the light' – clearly bad advice, but at least it conveys death's bitter loss.

Why do I routinely prefer the bitter to the sweet? I think of the great cathedral's earlier Dean, who loomed so large in I.A. Richards's *Practical Criticism* – the book in which I first saw Victorian sentiment routed by seventeenth-century irony, in the war that established the modern literary tone. Sweetness was out, astringency in. And yet it was the seventeenth century itself that liked to speak, for instance, of 'sweet Shakespeare' – a phrase that sounds more sweetly in my own ears of late.

We've had a bitter literature, one might say, because we've had a bitter century. 'The world is rotten, unjust, and dying' – Donald Davie again – though in fact the words were from a left-wing publication he happened to be reviewing, where 'world' meant the 'modern bourgeois world'. Davie's point was that, 'as every Christian knows', the words are true of the world at large and at any time. The uneasy Marxist-Christian coalition. But the Christian, Davie adds, must also 'respect the world' as God's creation.

I remember once conducting a tutorial on D.H. Lawrence's poem 'The Ship of Death'. The students were 'extra-mural', middle-aged or older, studying literature mainly for love of it. I held up for their admiration the poem's closing lines, where the frail ship of the soul returns from the sea of death and re-enters the body, which has itself changed into a sea-shell on the beach; the whole image, I remarked, evokes a sense of great peace and beauty.

'It's not enough,' said a middle-aged woman with a pugnacious physiognomy. For a moment I thought she was referring to my exegesis, but her tone seemed more sad than querulous. 'You want more going on in the afterlife?' I asked. She nodded. 'You mean,' I prodded sympathetically, 'with singing, your family, angels, and so on?' She just nodded again, and I could extract nothing further; she had clearly been reluctant to testify at all, and was patently sincere. Lawrence's quiet, still image of resurrection just wasn't enough for her – as Davie's 'respect' for the world isn't enough for me; I want more expression of its sweetness.

My taste for the astringent was first acquired from an English teacher just down Cambridge. Pale and dark-haired, with piercing eyes under straight black eye-brows, he was Jewish in fact, though I was aware of this only vaguely at the time; working-class Barnsley boys, as Davie himself remarks, had little feeling about Jews – they were too rarely encountered. My teacher, it seems to me now, was a man of broad literary tastes, but he introduced me to the 'Cambridge school' and I soon became a doctrinaire Leavisite – for all the usual reasons: the sense of modernity, of intellectual discipline, above all of belonging to a precious remnant, cultivating an 'integrated sensibility' in a disintegrating world. For a shy, clever teenager like myself, this was a dangerous conversion, too fertile a ground for my youthful cynicism and idealism.

Look Back in Anger and *Waiting for Godot* – I got free tickets for both from the Charing Cross NAAFI Club while doing National Service – appeared fully to confirm that not only society but the universe at large were both hopelessly mismanaged; yet this failed to shake my belief that my sensibility was getting integrated; and these contradictions were held together by the routine of passing exams and winning scholarships. Much later in life, I came to identify with Dr Johnson for a number of odd reasons – short-sighted, hard of hearing, but chiefly that by the time he went up to Oxford, he was, so he said, more more or less out of his mind. I don't think I was ever quite as mad as the Johnson who was to make Mrs Thrale fasten manacles on him; my own remained mind-forged, though of course to loosen them has been – and is – a lifetime's struggle.

On graduating I went to Hong Kong, where I conceived an enthusiasm for Mao Tse-tung. This further contradiction was sustained vaguely by the Leavisian view of literary criticism as guerilla warfare, and more concretely by my junior lecturer's salary, which arrived monthly regardless of the incoherence of my ideas. And of course both Mao and Leavis presented me with convenient enemies in historically abstract form – 'the rise of capitalism', 'the technologico-Benthamite ethos' and so on. For me they were little more than verbal Aunt Sallies, and very welcome they were to a young man who felt power only over words; but needless to say it was the empty words themselves, the abstract formuli, that acquired power over me. It was only when I actually visited Mao's China in the 1970s, that I felt my verbal manacles begin to chafe against reality; but by then of course Marx and Saussure, respective prophets of the historic abstraction and the empty word, had become the talismanic names in the literary academies.

The day of the funeral is sunny again, but a breeze from the Pennines makes the air brighter, almost spring-like, with blue sky and white clouds sailing. In the mornings I've been breakfasting early and walking in the park of the local 'stately home' – now a university 'outpost'. (My brother gets up later – though he sleeps little, to judge by his face.) The mansion, built with a fortune made from coal, is lumpy Victorian-neo-classical, but the park has fine trees and a lake, set in a great amphitheatre of fields and woods that really draws the gaze upwards. English heartland again; but the grounds are also a Regional Sculpture Park. Strolling amongst the immemorial elms you come, for instance, upon two naked Japanese wrestlers, twice life-size, in glossy flesh-coloured resin, with purple loin-cloths, beetling eye-brows, and Genghis top-knots; huge cartoon-like figures, straining, one at each side, to hold up a life-size (perhaps actual) shipping-container. A few yards away stands an American West Coast Indian pole, with a totemic raven staring woodenly at the un-American landscape – and a real crow perched on its head, as often as not. And beyond that in turn squats a row of jagged metallic forms, like miniature ruins of dark satanic mills.

But I feel no sense of cultural fragmentation, either agonised-modernist or post-modern-cute. All the things in view speak to some part of my humanity; and the natural world – earth, water, sky, and trees – seems large enough to accommodate them all. I'm echoing Ezra Pound's view of culture perhaps – his 'cosmopolitan localism', as it's now called in environmentalist circles; 'thinking globally, living locally'. The view that turned the Poundian Davie against literary 'little England'. But it's really the essence of any poetry. When Wordsworth for instance thinks of his daughter, dead and buried, as 'Rolled round in earth's diurnal course/With rocks and stones and trees', he gives a sense of the local *as* the global; of the particular and the universal together, to use the Coleridgean terms.

Later in the morning the funeral party gathers at my brother's house. Mainly small business-people, stolid and unpretentious, from the unchattering classes, their talk, formulaic and broad ('It wer' a blessed release', and so on), seems to confess its own conventionality. They sip their glass of sherry and wait – and wait, since the funeral cars fail to arrive on time. But they wait without impatience, filling the gap with phatic communion, or, rather, without any sense of a gap to fill; the fact of the funeral is enough. I myself am more volatile, and when we're finally on our way, extravagantly late, I feel some nervous irritation – intensified of course by the cortège crawl.

The church, in a nearby mining village, is a Blakean experience – a box of soot-blackened stone without a spire and with an interior as near to shabbiness as perhaps Anglicanism can come. But it's full to overflowing, largely with staff and pupils from Trish's school, and the opening hymn breaks on the air with the sense of miracle, of Blakean innocence, you always feel when a motley crowd is transformed by the unanimity of song. It's a song about travelling through life into death with a wonderful friend, and it has a certain ambivalence; the friend is evidently meant to be Jesus, but, being unnamed, might be just a human companion, perhaps a wife, or a husband. So we can all safely join in.

A further innocence, or a sentimental evasion? Davie, I recall, praised eighteenth-century hymn-writers like John Newton because 'their fervour was always related to the literally true and the doctrinally exact'. A version of what Leavis called 'sincerity'; thought and feeling integrated. I glance round at the congregation. The Chairman of the School Board, a plumbing contractor with a hearty manner and a sensitive face, is looking nervous – his oration is to follow next – and there are one or two whose attention is momentarily straying, like my own, but the hymn is certainly being sung with fervour. Its essential 'thought' might be rendered as 'love conquers death'. From any Christian point of view this is surely true enough and doctrinally sound. But are thought and fervour 'sincerely' related?

In the eyes of the Cambridge school of course the great enemies of sincerity were 'cliché' and 'stock-response'. A cliché like 'love conquers death', they'd say, merely induces a vague emotional uplift – or vice-versa. In poetry the words are modified by the experience, and this was taken to mean that they come together at an earlier stage in the process of articulation. It was all in line with Eliot's account of 'Shakespearean' fluidity of language and with the Leavisian view of poetry as 'exploration'.

They were evidently quite right about the poetic product but, surely, quite wrong about the process. The effect of words – it's a mere truism to say – is to generalise, and the sooner they're brought to bear on a particular experience, the more thoroughly they do it. 'Nice tree over there,' I might say to myself, routinely classifying it as any tree of any kind. Crude 'identity-thinking', as Adorno called it. On a closer look, I might have said 'variegated elm'; still general, but far less so. Of course words always get into the act quickly to some extent, but the more they're resisted the more the experience survives and bends the words to its own shape – creating poetry. 'Put off using words as long as possible and get your meaning as clear as you can through pictures or sensations', Orwell advised the aspiring writer. 'His mind was more intent upon notions than words', said Johnson, attributing Shakespeare's poetic freedoms to his remarkable powers of putting-off. And, for all the neo-Saussurean denials, these are powers we all possess in some degree. My brother, for instance, will tell me afterwards that he had been dreading the funeral ceremony but that to his surprise he 'enjoyed' it. Though clearly a little embarrassed by the word, he just as clearly feels that it's the one he needs. A 'new' word for him in this context evidently, and discovered by keeping an eye on his experience.

But in a ritual new words aren't needed. I notice the small, sturdy figure of one of Trish's fellow-teachers. A strong-minded woman of quick feelings and intelligence, she was one of Trish's closest friends – was with her when she died. It seems almost curious to see her now, with her pale, resolute face, so absorbed in singing, for the song is without depth or subtlety of grief or consolation. It's in the energetic mode of 'Fight the good fight' but with a jollier tone and a bouncier rhythm, and of course full of cliché. But when people come together in a real sense of loss, the essential ritual feeling of community and transcendence can be carried by familiar, even superficial words.

The hymn finishes, the priest makes his journey to Emmaus, more words are said, more hymns are sung, and then comes a hiatus as the bearers step forward to take the coffin on the journey to the crematorium. The priest waits, impassive, rather pasty-faced, as four elderly men in not-quite-uniform suits get into position. I'm suddenly aware of the black iron hurdles supporting the coffin, and the bare, cracked flagstones underneath. And the sense of stark materiality quickly spreads to the stained rear wall of the church with its rough plaster patches, and the unstained glass of the high window, with its bleak, leaded rectangles. Even the coffin itself seems a mere container, a wooden box with fancy handles, for carrying the dead body into the church and then out again. In a natural recoil I think of Trish as she was in life – with her high colour and dark hair, and her grey eyes flashing nervously, perhaps friendly, perhaps dangerous; and for the first time I really feel my brother's loss.

Outside the church some children stand with tear-stained faces; and at the crematorium chapel, as the coffin finally slides through a curtained opening in the wall, to the voice of Ben E. King singing 'Stand By Me', one of Trish's favourite songs, my brother himself starts sobbing. I slip my arm round his shoulder – consoling myself perhaps as much as him. Ever since my arrival, I've felt that his friends, though really closer to him than I am, have been standing back a little because I'm 'family'. Now at least for a moment I can feel that blood is thicker than water.

Afterwards, at the gathering in the 'local', people are affable towards me personally, but there still seems a social distance. Is it 'class' again? When I find myself standing with the school board plumbing contractor and a motor mechanic who runs his own garage, the former talks (less 'broad' than usual) about 'the crisis in education', and this soon elicits from the mechanic an exhortation (quite savagely 'broad') to 'stop being so bloody painful'. A sharp collision of the two classic attitudes to anything 'posh'. At this point, luckily, we're joined by another man. Tall, lean, forty-something, with black wavy hair and dark blue eyes, he's one of the few guests I've met before. Philip by name and the husband of the school principal, he came with her yesterday to visit my brother, and the occasion was marked by a curious incident. The principal – also tall and good-looking, but with eyes of a lighter blue and shoulder-length red hair – spoke vividly of Trish, but Philip sat rather taciturn, and indeed seemed to have some difficulty in 'talking joined up', as it were. But in any case all conversation came at length to a halt, as the distinctive 'what-what' of a helicopter grew steadily louder, finally reaching a crescendo right over the house. Being seated nearest to the window, I stood up and looked out, just in time to see a young man scramble desperately out from under the hedge and dash across the lawn pursued by a policeman clutching some sort of weapon. It all looked so extraordinary that I stepped back, fearing shots might be fired. In a moment Philip had brushed past me, flung open the door, and, followed by my brother, was running towards the gateway, where the policeman, his tie ripped off and his weapon abandoned (just a truncheon, I could see now), was struggling with the youth down the gravel. Under the weight of reinforcements the fugitive soon succumbed, and on the arrival of a second policeman, was handcuffed and frog-marched down the street, protesting his innocence and yelling obscenities, past a gallery of half-lifted window-curtains.

Our speculations about the drama were cut short when the policeman came back for his tie; the youth, it appeared, was one of four who had stolen a car in Halifax, had been spotted and chased, and had finally jumped and run for it. As the policeman turned to leave, he apologised for the bad language during the arrest. Up to this point it had all seemed pure adventure, but now I suddenly saw myself through his hard blue eyes, as 'respectable', 'middle-class'; and this made me think of the young man in turn (I recalled his face, pressed down against the gravel) as perhaps from the 'under-class', 'a victim of society'.

Here in the pub the effect is curiously reversed. Seeing Philip again I think of him running down the drive, haunches working, eyes fixed on his quarry, and the web of class that I've been spinning round the other two men falls suddenly away; I see the human animal – the pale, sensitive-looking plumber, with his aura of bright, slightly nervous energy; the heavier-featured, darker-skinned mechanic, a little flushed, and giving off an altogether coarser charge. Class-feelings, like their parent-impulses of pride and fear, become cancerous unless kept in check by a deeper sense of humanity than the merely socio-economic.

Philip of course remains his taciturn self. Outdoing Shakespeare, he resists words not just till late in the process but keeps them out almost altogether. Though perhaps a virtue in a crisis, this seems more of a limitation in a pub, and I soon find myself drifting off to join a group in which a stocky, broad-faced older man is audibly offering less resistance.

He introduces himself as Albert Barlow, but despite the generic Coronation-Street name, it's soon clear he's a type that rarely features in 'the soaps'. A Miners' Union official who once ran against Arthur Scargill in the local elections, he radiates a fat man's *bonhomie*, but you sense more muscle than fat, and a deep shrewdness in the friendly grey eye. His wife seems a female duplicate of himself – they're strong pillars, both, of their shaken community, Netherton, a now mine-less mining village. Does he think, I ask him at length, that without the Scargill–Thatcher excesses the pits might have closed gradually, giving the community more time to adjust – a view I've got from my brother, who says his foundry could have thus survived. Albert agrees, and adds that Scargill was a revolutionary with no interest in negotiation (Scargill, I suppose, saw Albert in turn as a 'neo-corporatist', selling out to the boss-class);

but he goes on to praise 'King Arthur' the orator. This is evidently a practical man's genuine admiration for the visionary. But what a vision, I reflect, recalling its naïvety – though I don't say so to Albert. 'I know that we can produce a society,' proclaimed Scargill, 'where man will release his latent talent and ability and begin to produce in the cultural sense all the things that I know he's capable of: music, poetry, writing, sculpture, whole works of art that at the moment are lying dormant simply because we, as a society, are not able to tap it.' And of course his utopian slogans led him not only to delusions about art and society but to a fatal unrealism even about his own trade union. A born leader but a slavish thinker, half-genius and half-sloganeer, he was a classic product, it might seem, of a half-education; but the academics from Leeds and Sheffield who so influenced young pit-workers like Scargill in the 1950s were themselves no less slaves to abstraction – as indeed they and their heirs still are. For instance:

> The social relations and practices in which symbolic expression and exchange have historically been embedded cannot be known in some prior sense and then counterposed to the symbolic, for necessarily we are engaged in reconstructing those relations and practices when we endeavour to explore the contexts of the senses of historical experience which certain cultural texts or forms may be said to impart.

The reader peers through the verbal fog ('the contexts of the senses of...') at the wrecked metaphors drifting by('embedded', 'counterposed') and at length makes out the glimmer of a simple meaning – 'the past exists only through signs'. And this passage is from a recent 'moderate' work in 'cultural studies', protesting at the even foggier abstractions of current 'cultural theory'!

And we find Professor Eagleton, in his *PNR* interview with Nicolas Tredell, long after the collapse of the Soviet system, still talking just like Scargill about the socialist revolution. He isn't saying, he hastens to assure us, 'that forms of virtue will flow magically and spontaneously from certain kinds of material conditions', only that 'virtue has a chance to flourish when, for example, people don't literally have to fight each other for survival'. But how many generations actually is it, you ask yourself wonderingly, since the English had literally to fight each other for survival? And you reflect too of course that certain related virtues – such as 'decency', to recall

Orwell's favourite – have had a concomitant existence. To reserve these blessings for some imagined socialist future, is sloganeering even emptier than Scargill's.

But of course sloganeering was licensed by 'theory'. Adorno saw it, under the name of 'identity thinking', as an inevitable product of the deep 'reifying' pressures of a machine-and-money-power culture that reduces the world to manipulable stereotypes. Eagleton might accordingly reply that 'the left' can't avoid using slogans, and that they must be judged by their political effect. But the main effect here surely was to frighten people into voting for Mrs Thatcher, and, in any case, Adorno's theory itself is the merest sloganeering. In fact all human perception entails assigning individuals to a category; some degree of 'identity thinking' is thus unavoidable if one is to think at all. And language, again, generalises even further. But to recover at least some degree of individuality requires no socialist revolution; only the exercise of care with perception, memory, and words. The funeral ceremony in the church, for instance, as I've just described it, falls into obvious categories, and yet it just as obviously has its particularities. It doesn't achieve the fusion of particular and universal that fixes a really poetic image so vividly in the imagination, but neither is it blank generality. Like most writers I'm somewhere on the broad spectrum between genius and sloganeer.

Davie himself seems sometimes to regard poems as either 'achieved' or failed, saved or damned, with no in-betweens. This was the one area, he said in *These the Companions*, in which he was a Calvinist. Indeed he sometimes speaks as though all poems are damned:

> Names and things named don't match
> Ever. This is not
> A plethora of language,
> But language's condition.
>
> Sooner or later the whole
> Cloth of the language peels off
> As wallpaper peels from a wall,
> However it 'hangs together'.

No salvation either through 'election' or 'works'; only a shuffling of arbitrary signs.

But elsewhere he tells a very different story. 'It is true,' he confesses in the oft-quoted note in his *Collected Poems*, 'that I am not a poet by nature, only by inclination; for my mind moves most easily and happily among abstractions, it relates ideas far more readily than it relates experiences.' But, he adds, 'a true poem can be written by a mind not naturally poetic – though by the inhuman labour of thwarting at every point the natural grain and bent. This working against the grain does not damage the mind, nor is it foolish; on the contrary, only by doing this does each true poem as it is written become an authentic widening of experience.' The poetical elect are saved simply by being what they are, but the non-elect may earn salvation through strenuous works. This is as far from Calvinist predestination as from the Saussurean shuffle.

And Davie further attributes the gap between his words and reality to nurture rather than nature – primarily to his mother's loving encouragement of his bookishness: 'If I am so literary myself that I sometimes despair of breaking through a cocoon of words to a reality outside them, it is above all my mother's doing,' he says in *Trying To Explain*. 'And I am grateful; if my universe is verbal, so be it – I am happy in my glittering envelope, and will fight those who would puncture it.' He sounds more defiant than happy perhaps, but in any case this is surely the truer account. So far from being against the grain of nature, poetry is continuous, as Coleridge and so many others have said, with all our natural powers of perception. From experience into word, from the tacit level to the explicit, is a continuum that remains largely mysterious, but a continuum it must evidently be, with a constant flow of traffic to and fro between world, body, mind, and word. In a continuum like Shakespeare's the traffic moves mainly from world to word; and it's largely so in Davie's case too; and I don't mean just in the knotty and remarkable poems in which, against the grain of his training, he drives abstractions up against experience; it's true also of wonderfully 'easy' poems like 'The Evangelist':

> 'My brethren...' And a bland, elastic smile
> Basks on the mobile features of Dissent.
> No hypocrite, you understand. The style
> Befits a church that's based on sentiment.
>
> Solicitations of a swirling gown,
> The sudden vox humana, and the pause,
> The expert orchestration of a frown
> Deserve, no doubt, a murmur of applause.
>
> The tides of feeling round me rise and sink;

Bunyan, however, found a place for wit.
Yes, I am more persuaded than I think;
Which is perhaps why I disparage it.

You round upon me generously keen:
The man, you say, is patently sincere.
Because he is so eloquent, you mean?
That test was never patented, my dear.

If, when he plays upon our sympathies,
I'm pleased to be fastidious, and you
To be inspired, the vice in it is this:
Each does us credit, and we know it too.

The observers are as vividly observed as the evangelist, and the easy elegance heightens the incisive modulation of the last two lines. 'If this be not poetry, where is poetry to be found?' But Davie's *critical* bias was in favour of poems written, as he felt, against the grain. Leavis-like, he seemed to prefer, in the poetic no less than the moral sphere, the 'inhuman labour', the palpably difficult sincerity. But this all none the less entailed the very salutary belief that the poetic traffic between word and world could be quickened by study and effort; hence Davie's life-long preoccupation – as poet, critic, scholar, and teacher – with the language of poetry.

Adorno and company on the other hand see the road as blocked by 'capitalist reification', and a socialist revolution as the only way of breaking through. But what chiefly divorces the culturally studious 'left' from reality is evidently their own sloganeering prose. Hence the irony of their belief – as voiced by Eagleton to Tredell – that the study of literature must convert itself to 'cultural studies' if it is to remain 'relevant'. Like psychiatry in the old joke, 'cultural studies' are in fact the disease they claim to cure. What's needed is an injection of Davie's passion for poetic language, the only remedy against epidemic cliché and jargon.

That the 'rise' of highly abstract language, geared not just to recognising the world but to conquering it, is connected with the other famous modern 'rises' (of science, technology, capitalism, and so on) has long been argued of course, and with some truth. But to conclude that 'identity-thinking' will disappear if we destroy 'capitalism' is like saying that aggressiveness will disappear if we destroy modern weapons. 'Identity-thinking', like aggressiveness, is intrinsic to life ('truth is the kind of error without which a certain species cannot live,' as Nietzsche rather grudgingly put it). It needs likewise to be stopped from getting out of hand, and this is the function of poetic language, infusing abstraction with particularity, conveying a sense of actual life going on.

What's going on in the pub now is rather curious. Albert clearly regards my own language with some suspicion (I 'talk posh'), but when I demonstrate that I can still 'talk broad', my dialect is stronger than his own – which has lost some of its edge through years of politics, whereas mine is recalled straight from the streets of my childhood. He seems surprised. 'A coom thra' Barnsla, tha knuz,' I explain with sweet reasonableness, as though to say this is where the true dialect is to be found, not in outlying villages like Netherton; and indeed 'thra', for 'from', and the 'a' at the end of 'Barnsley', are the genuine article. A good-looking, well-spoken woman of forty-something – the wife of my brother's general manager – laughs in sudden amusement at my ironically inverted snobbery, and Albert looks slightly put out. I can see why of course. To be outsmarted, albeit in a trivial matter, and to see an onlooker enjoying it, is a very basic human annoyance.

This kind of annoyance and the kind occasioned by 'class' are evidently related in subtle and various ways. Was the conflict between D.H. Lawrence's parents – to take a famous example – a matter of 'class' or 'personality'? Both, evidently, but in what proportions not even Lawrence could say with certainty. What he gave us in *Sons and Lovers* was some sense of his parents as living individuals. And this is what literature and art of course are meant to give. To think about art in a generalising way is to miss the point – to be, as Blake remarked, an idiot. It is also, ironically, to ignore the most important sense in which art is political. 'He was naked, and saw man naked, and from the centre of his own crystal. There was nothing of the superior person about him. This makes him terrifying.' Thus Eliot of Blake himself, and this is the deepest egalitarianism, just as frightening to the socialist bureaucrat as to the society hostess or the politically correct academic.

In the days after the funeral, before I must return to New Zealand, my brother and I go off together in search of times past – the houses we lived in, the places we played. Some are gone of course. The foundry, for instance, where I hurried every day after school when I was nine or ten, to see the furnace being tapped, the molten metal flowing, incandescent yellow and angry red, and to watch my father and the other men doing dangerous work together in the sulphurous glare – it's been demolished to make way for a multi-storey car-park. But most of the old places survive, and many of them – the Grammar

School, the Globe cinema, the 'town-end', the cricket-ground – have figured in Davie's poems. Do any of *his* family still live here, I wonder? When I enquire at the Barnsley Literary Society, the man who answers the phone knows only of the poet's widow, who lives in Devon. But he's happy to give me the address, and I feel a sudden impulse to go; I can do it on the way back to Heathrow. Glorious Devon. It seems a far cry from Davie's Barnsley. But then so does Barnsley now, its unemployment and apparent affluence in stark contrast with the work, dirt and poverty of old.

When you leave the town centre, however, and drive out to villages like Grimethorpe, you see a new kind of decay. Perhaps every fifth house in the terraced rows has broken windows and the slates caving in; it looks like the beginning of the end. Then you notice the homes – and they are more than one in five – that still have scrubbed door-steps and white lace curtains. A mere show of respectability, or the outward sign of a real domesticity? The latter, surely, in some cases at least. I think of my mother of course, sitting by the fire in a house like these, and of myself at her knee, helping to 'brod' a new hearth-rug – knotting cut-up strips of old clothing into a piece of hessian. This would have been about the time of the Labour victory of 1945. Recalled now, the 'historic' event, with its 'we are the masters now' excitement, is tinged, like all memories of 'revolution', with amused or bitter irony. In the Blakean economy of the soul, it's in the realm of experience. The domestic event, my childish feeling for my mother and for the beauty of the rug – the bright colours, yet untrodden, the wonder of the growing pattern – returns not as nostalgia, but as a glimpse of a recoverable innocence, the economy's most precious element. And the mother remains a part of it of course. 'It's only in the revolutionary imagination that the dead can be recycled,' said Eagleton to Tredell; we live on, he means, only through our 'political contribution'. A poverty-stricken vision of humanity.

As my brother and I revisit childhood holiday-places by the sea and on the moors (where the bilberries are just finished), any Blakean thoughts dissolve into a mild Augustan sort of melancholy:

> Come autumn sae pensive, in yellow and gray,
> And soothe me wi' tidings o' nature's decay.

Then, one gusty morning, blowing showers from bright grey clouds and leaves from the church-yard elms, we take flowers to our parents' grave. My brother, holding a gay, flimsy umbrella that must have belonged to his wife, crouches to arrange the bunch. I stand back to take a photo and when he turns to the camera, his pale face, wet with rain-drops, looks so pure and vulnerable, so rinsed with pain, it puts my gentle melancholy to shame.

When the day of my departure comes, we both feel a little awkward; we've lived so long in different countries we really are strangers and brothers. But as we wait at the counter of the car-hire company all our attention is seized by an outburst from the manager – a lean, middle-aged woman with tight blonde curls and rather staring blue eyes. She's been called from her office to attend to three Indian men who're trying to blame the company's own parking attendant for a dent in their hire-car. As she rages, in open – and palpably racist – disbelief, their spokesman, an older man, stands impassive. The other two, keeping a little apart, let him bear the brunt. Strangers and brothers. The essential fact of human isolation, never far away, seems to harden in my consciousness. When my brother and I finally say goodbye, the awkwardness has gone; and all the way to the south-west, my mood holds, through landscapes looking suddenly more like autumn – leaves turning brown and dry, but not yet ready to dissolve back into the earth. In Tiverton – the town nearest to where Mrs Davie lives – the mood turns bleaker. The big, mouldering church and the bare-looking 'great house' – a tourist centre now, but closed for the day – speak not of mellowness but of decay, ways of life dead or dying. And when I check in at a nearby country hotel – idyllic thatch and white pebble-dash by the River Exe – the landlord, a sharp-eyed businessman, doesn't even attempt a 'mine host' façade.

Next morning, as I negotiate the narrow, high-hedged by-ways, the world is soft and grey with mist, but Mrs Davie's face, when she opens the door of her village high-street cottage, reminds me of my brother's – the same curious brightness, somehow like splintered glass. It's a year since her husband died, but my visit will have brought it all back. She talks about Donald and their life together; wartime courtship and marriage, happy times in Dublin and Cambridge, less happy at the University of Essex, where he became politicised against the campus-militants; then to the United States – where he was more appreciated as a poet than he ever was in England. She liked America, she says, especially Stanford, for the openness of the landscape and the life, and she now finds Devon, though her native county, a little constricting. I can believe it; when we talk about the world at large, she shows a quick and open interest, with none of the little-Englandism that her husband found the most depressing of Anglo-Saxon attitudes – especially in poets as gifted as Amis and Larkin.

She shows me his study, its ceiling brown with smoke from his beloved pipe. His sanctum, but their grandchildren, she adds, were privileged intruders. 'Grandad,' they would say, 'can we go into the study and play our game?' And in a while their shrieks of laughter would be heard from behind the closed door. What was the game? I ask. It was a secret, she replies, that she still doesn't know.

'I have been a coward before life,' Davie says in *Trying to Explain;* 'always, against the run of the evidence, I have expected the worst.' Fear was always, he continues, his 'strongest and most common emotion'. It may seem a feature of his class and time – the 'dour-miserable Yorkshireman'. I could say much the same of my father – or of myself. But it's surely just a northern version of the universal sickness against which 'faith' and 'hope' are the age-old antidotes. The games in the study with his grandchildren, it strikes me with a sudden poignancy, suggest a daily kind of sweetness, betokening more real faith in life than he allowed to appear in his harsh self-estimate – or in his poetry.

At length, I walk with Mrs Davie down the village High Street in the damp morning air, to the churchyard, and as she stands there by the grave – a grassy mound with flowers, without a stone as yet – her expression, preoccupied and remote, once more recalls my brother. Donald isn't really dead for her, and yet of course he is, and she's painfully working it out.

Lawrence's poem comes back to me again, with its exhortation to 'build your ship of death', and its vivid story of the body's dissolution and of the moment when the soul-ship must let go:

> Now launch the small ship, now as the body dies
> and life departs, launch out the fragile soul,
> in the fragile ship of courage, the ark of faith.

Life as a vale of soul-ship-making. Mrs Davie herself, feet together in the dew-silvered grass by the grave – standing to attention, it might almost seem – is clearly engaged in it. She comes from Plymouth, I suddenly remember, where so many brave ships have set sail.

I spend my last night in England with an aunt and uncle who live in Surbiton, convenient for Heathrow. My uncle is of Davie's generation. A Tank Corps NCO in the Second World War, then a civil servant for the rest of his working life. His house reminds me of Geoffrey Hill's *Mercian Hymns*:

Coiled entrenched England: brickwork and paintwork stalwart above hacked marl. The clashing primary colours – 'Ethandune', 'Catraeth', 'Maldon', 'Pengwern'. Steel against yew and privet. Fresh dynasties of smiths.

And like Davie he's marked by fear – 'coiled and entrenched'. In his case it appears as an occasional tendency to bluster and then capitulate. But in his seventies now, and subject to lapses of memory (forgetting, at shop-counters, what it was he went to buy), his fears have grown more open; and of course they're universal – Johnsonian fears of dying like Swift, 'a driveller and a show'. You can see them in his dark, still passionate, face and eye. Perhaps these keener fears will turn his bluster into courage. Ship-building, as the flood of oblivion starts to rise.

Next morning, he walks me round his garden. He's shown it to me often before, but still dwells with satisfaction on its extent, and on the public park beyond, and is still complacent (it used to irritate me rather) about having left Barnsley long ago for 'the south'. In short he's still enjoying the commoner sweetnesses of life – adulterated, as they generally are, with a dash of self. My aunt – tall, slightly stooped, grey eyes alert as ever (she plays competitive bridge) – is coming with me, in part to show me the way to the airport, in part to visit a friend. When we leave, my uncle stands waving and smiling, his burly figure framed by his Mercian blue front doorway. From the road, as I get into the car, he looks happy and young.

'Ripeness is all,' said Gloucester, old and blind; Hamlet, younger and sharper, settled for 'readiness', and of course there are many ways of launching your ship. To 'curse god and die' for instance – though that seems disproportionate to the common or garden demise. To rage, with Dylan Thomas, 'against the dying of the light' is not so much to set sail as to go down with all guns firing; this makes a fine noise, but, since the foe is plainly invincible and might even turn out to be a friend, it's surely better to use diplomacy instead. Montaigne's essay 'That to Philosophise is to Learn how to Die' is the great compendium of classical *tod-politik*, though it doesn't include either metempsychosis or ancestor worship, and indeed, with its deeply stoic cast, has little to say about the Christian heaven. The nurse's manual for the care of the terminally ill, said Philip Larkin, contains the complete truth about death. And this, I suppose, is a modern stoic view; but it evidently did nothing to alleviate Larkin's horror at the thought of annihilation; even Eagleton's street-named-after-you-in-Stalingrad seems a more sea-worthy ship.

Davie gets his ship from the Apocrypha. He tested it in *To Scorch or Freeze*, and it is to appear, Mrs Davie tells me, on his gravestone:

> and guarded by angels in profound quiet,
> they understand the rest that they enjoy.

This is the reward of the souls who constitute the 'fourth order' of the righteous, as described in the Second Book of Esdras. The greatest order is the seventh and last; they 'shall rejoice with boldness... and shall be glad without fear'. The sweetness of the afterlife for the fourth order is of a more modest kind. Perhaps Davie chose it because an *understanding* of peace implies that fear, its great enemy, even when finally defeated is still remembered.

Lawrence, I think, contrives to be both bitter and sweet, diplomatic and brave. 'Fragile', without any stoic copper-bottom, his ship is light enough to be propelled by a breath of faith; and since it seems reasonable to assume that faith will serve as well in death as it does in life, he isn't sailing 'against the run of the evidence'. The voyage is bitter – 'death is on the air like a smell of ashes' – but it ends as the sea turns pink with dawn, the sweetest of colours, and the most conspicuously absent, I should think, from modern poetry:

> The flood subsides, and the body, like a worn sea-shell
> emerges strange and lovely.
> And the little ship wings home, faltering and lapsing
> on the pink flood,
> and the frail soul steps out, into her house again
> filling the heart with peace.

Belief, said Lawrence elsewhere, is an emotion that has the mind's assent; and this is what his poem gives you, thought and feeling integrated, the spiritual idea in all its generality with the natural image in all its immediacy – the coming dawn, the receding tide, the shell left on the beach, the poignant suggestion of a butterfly 'faltering and lapsing' towards the shore; the old symbols all renewed. Religion, as Lawrence also said, is the imagination at its highest stretch.

At Heathrow, when all the queuing and waiting is over, and my plane accelerates with a roar into lift-off, tilting up into the unknown, I give Lawrence's fragile boat an imaginary trial – after an engine failure, say, and a long moment of fear, '*now* launch the small ship, *now* as the body dies... launch out the fragile ship of courage.' And it feels reassuring – more inspiriting than air-line Scotch, and with no dubious after-taste. But when it comes to the real voyage, as even the compendious Montaigne admits, a ship is only as good as its crew. Philip the word-resister, for example, will construct a vessel more rudimentary than mine, I'm sure, but I suspect he might prove a more resolute sailor.

A Post-colonial Excursion

When we remark that it seems quiet for New Year's Eve, the Indian waiter reminds us that its also the first day of Ramadhan, when any festive eating at all is frowned on by the Islamic community. 'Bunch of hypocrites,' he adds laconically – he's already discovered that we're from New Zealand and evidently assumes that we'll be no more sympathetic than himself to Moslem moralising.

In a moment he's taking a critical view of Singaporeans too, coming here flaunting their money more than ever now that the Malaysian ringit is going down. Slight of build, intelligent of mien, and elegant of dress, he seems a little anxious to impress; and it turns out that he's not just a waiter but the manager, and a graduate of a Swiss school for restaurateurs.

His restaurant, serving excellent Malay-Chinese food, is in one of the refurbished shop-houses that are amongst the tourist attractions of 'old Malacca'. Originally built by the Chinese traders who arrived here in the early fifteenth century, a hundred years before the Portuguese, they're like wind-tunnels designed to funnel any wandering sea-breeze through their seventy-yard-long partitioned interior and out into the street in front; a mixture of east and west, with classical pilasters rising to curled eaves and spiny dragons rampant, and, inside, carved wooden partitions, tiled floors, and sunken areas with pot-plants to catch the rain that comes through the ventilation slits in the roof.

After our Malaysian excursion, I'll be meeting Edwin Thumboo poet and professor at the University of Singapore, admirer of Conrad and Forster, and acute observer of the post-colonial world. What will he have to say about Singaporean arrogance? Or about the decline of the ringit? For the financial turbulence is already being called 'the Asian crisis', and the nervous smiles of politicians on TV portend a storm.

I sense it just for a moment in the café in the Portuguese quarter where we repair after dinner in search of New Year festivity. The fairy lights and neon in the twilight of the patio have an improvised, ephemeral look, and beyond the low balustrade lined with pot-plants, the darkening sea and the sunset smouldering down behind a smoky bank of clouds, look Conradian-ominous. I think of Captain Whalley, in 'The End of the Tether', going blind but still sailing these same tropical waters because the bank that held his life savings has failed, yet he must keep sending money to his daughter, married to a wastrel in Australia.

I glance at the folk sitting at the tables around the patio and listening to a local pop group. Audience, musicians, and music, are all 'Portuguese' – a long-matured blend of Chinese, Malay and Latin – and all are notable for humanity rather than elegance, the common run, threshed so often in the colonial mill of pride, power, money, and race. What will they do if *their* banks fail?

The atmosphere is more domestic than festive, with a steady murmur of conversation and an occasional burst of laughter or clamour of children above the music. The tiny front gardens of the houses in the Portuguese quarter are adorned with Christmas lights and plaster Virgins-and-child, but the New Year seems an unremarked festival – and tomorrow we have to catch the early train to Kuala Lumpur, so we retire before midnight, and get up for a pre-breakfast walk on the waterfront with its long jetty running out towards the sandbar.

The whole area is to become a resort marina, but like other big developments seems already halted by the financial uncertainty. At any rate the jetty is deserted except for a Malay in ragged shorts moving to and fro casting a fishing net, and a be-denimmed teenage couple who've parked their gleaming motor-bike beneath a sun-shelter and are engaged in a mild display of mutual affection. The fisherman at least, I imagine, might survive a collapse of the banking system.

Then at the end of the jetty another Conradian vision, as perspective seems to disappear, and the horizon becomes a mere thread separating the glare of the sea from the intenser glare of the sky. My heightened perception seems a 'making strange', a 'removal of the veil of familiarity', and in the phenomenenological style that Conrad also brought to bear on his observations of humanity.

When we return along the jetty the young couple are still billing and cooing but the fisherman has gone – leaving behind on the concrete a silvery trail of fish, too small, presumably, to be worth taking away. As we walk along I toe-end some of the gasping minnows back into the water, reflecting that tender feelings towards our fellow-creatures are the prerogative of the affluent. But suddenly the fisherman reappears, seeming to materialise from thin air (in fact from a flight of steps down the side of the jetty). Evidently his method is to shake out his net after each cast and gather his catch together later. He must have been startled to see them flying back over his head, and is clearly unimpressed, to say the least, by my piscine sensitivities.

I walk hastily on, apologising profusely and uselessly, a caricature of the western 'greenie' and leave my wife lagging behind to pacify the fisherman, who might, it seems, be provoked to downright violence by my European face, sublimely above the hard necessities of his life.

I remember my first venture into South East Asia in the 1960s, on a Yugoslavian freighter with a dozen passengers bound from Hong Kong to Venice. We docked for a week in a Djakarta seething with armed troops and with rumours of Sukarno's imminent downfall. The half-starved stevedores scrambled daily for scraps from the ship's kitchen and the ship's passengers made a daily pilgrimage to the Djakarta Hilton, where the smallest unit of any foreign currency was enough to buy the largest of cream cakes, and where page-boys in gold-braid-encrusted uniforms waited on American men with dark suits and hard faces – whose neo-colonialist exertions were later to bear apparent fruit when Sukarno's downfall was followed by a great 'purge of the communists' (i.e. the slaughter of half a million Indonesian Chinese).

Sukarno was replaced of course by the 'friendly' Suharto, who is himself now rumoured to be falling; and the dark-suited men in the Hilton will be brooding again – on the 'threat' of Islamic fundamentalism, I suppose, rather than 'world communism', though no doubt relieved, in any case, to have found another global enemy.

But my clearest memory is of a personal failure rather than a political event. The ship's captain, a pale slightly built man of sixty, with grey eyes and a careworn face, one day invited my wife and myself for drinks in the saloon. I'm not sure why we were thus honoured – perhaps because we seemed less obviously deranged than the other passengers, who had already been on the ship for several months (taking a cheap cruise in the form of a return ticket from Europe to Japan) and who had by now revealed all their foibles and developed various feuds.

The party in the saloon was a modest affair; besides the captain, another officer, and my wife and myself there were only two Dutchmen, who were evidently on board about some cargo. One of them, a stocky, red-faced man with glaring blue eyes, started talking about local politics, and soon revealed a typical set of prejudices. 'When an Indonesian smiles at you he means it,' he declared in his harsh and fluent English; 'a Chinese will smile at you and then stab you in the back.' I wasn't sure how much offence was intended. Perhaps the man was just being obtuse; but he should surely have realised that my wife was Chinese. She herself seemed unperturbed, but the captain looked uneasy; clearly some offence should have been taken, and by me; but – out of greenness, excessive politeness, timidity – I let the moment pass.

Later on of course I thought of various incisive rejoinders, and in thinking of them perhaps half-persuaded myself that they'd been actually uttered. In short I exhibited, though writ small, the essential psychology of Lord Jim – the inability to look a moment of failure in the face. And it was a moment with some of the complications to which Conrad was especially sensitive; my wife and I were only recently married and we still nurtured romantic racial stereotypes of each other. But that apart, my little story is just personal, unconnected with the political drama being played out.

The dark-suited men in the Hilton are also story-tellers in their way, and their interest moreover is in the connection between the political scenario and the individual protagonist; but of course they see the individual merely as an instrument for political ends. Again it's Conrad who comes to mind. Mikulin, the secret service official in *Under Western Eyes*, has a clear view of the student Razumov's type and of his precise usefulness, but takes no interest in the individual man.

Even for official purposes this seems too narrow a view; Mikulin fails to anticipate that Razumov might behave atypically under stress. And according to George Bundy's recent book, Henry Kissinger's chief shortcoming was his blindness to the individual differences between 'socialist' countries in the Soviet orbit, his crude stereotyping of them as 'satellites'. Bundy's point is that Kissinger's brutal neo-colonialist *realpolitik* – as in the destruction of Cambodia – was neither in touch with reality nor politically effective. He has the benefit of hindsight of course, and in any case Kissinger would no doubt dismiss his view as residual maundering from the East-coast foreign policy establishment, but the worrying thing, always, about the Kissingers is the obvious relish with which they spin their tales of cunning and power. They resemble, to compare great things with small, the theorist-radicals who were their cold-war contemporaries, would-be men in black, oblivious to individuality, 'interrogating texts' to expose the subtextual enemy, and leaving literary desolation in their wake – as exemplified by Professor Said's account of Conrad, criticised recently in *PNR* by William Rivière.

Said's motive is political of course, but it takes its licence from the neo-Saussurean theory of language as a system of mere 'difference', divorced from experience. If poets are simply manipulating conventional sign-systems and doing so (it goes without saying) to advance their own class-interests, then it's both inevitable and right for the critic to follow suit. Reader-response rules, and nowhere more so than in post-colonial studies.

In his recent writing about the Arab-Israeli 'peace process', Said in fact advocates the abandonment of 'politics' in favour of 'truth' and 'justice'; and even Derrida has declared in favour of the latter. They obviously realise, like everyone else, that a cold-war political cynicism will no longer do. But they've yet to acknowledge that any effective conception of truth and justice, whether in politics or in literary criticism, is simply impossible in neo-Saussurean terms.

The air-conditioning and tinted glass of the express to Kuala Lumpur seem to diminish the tropical world; the brilliant blue sky and billowing white clouds and lush vegetation all look deadened and dull. As we approach the city the Petronas towers, symbols of wealth, pride and power, dwarfing the ordinary skyscrapers and meant to challenge the west, even dulled look undiminished, but when we reach the city centre they become oddly elusive, and we soon find ourselves instead in one of Kuala Lumpur's marvellous malls – eight floors of shops overlooking a great semi-circular atrium with classical columns and black and gold wall-climber lifts on it's straight side. All the international brand-names are there, but we're in a small dress-shop that's clearly a local enterprise. Its special line is in clothes that give a modern look to traditional Chinese features – a high buttoned collar, say, or knot-and-loop fasteners, or a rich brocade material. My wife, very taken by it, chats to the saleswoman and her assistant, and in a few moments the proprietor – a pale, refined-looking Chinese with an easy manner, elegantly casual clothes, and excellent English – emerges from a back-room to join in the conversation. His wife, it seems, is the designer (she's in Europe at the moment looking at the new styles); he just takes care of the business. The sales assistant – a notably *soignée* young woman in a dress that's obviously from the stock – turns out to be his daughter; she's on vacation from university in Sydney, where she's studying computer science. She and her father are obviously proud of each other, and of the whole enterprise, as becomes even more apparent when he displays a scrap-book of press-cuttings – film-stars patronising the shop, his wife's award-winning creations, and so on.

The stereotypically successful Chinese family. Spurred a little by his complacency, I tell him that I myself will be writing for a magazine about my visit to Kuala Lumpur, and he shows such a keen nose for publicity, I feel obliged to add that it's a literary organ. 'Ah, heavy stuff,' he murmurs, with a raised eyebrow; he's clearly using his own set of stereotypes, with 'literary' as the marginalised opposite of 'commercial'; his interest visibly expires, and my own idea of the happy business family darkens a little in response. Even in such small currents of emotion do stereotypes vary. And it's easy to imagine, if the banks *do* fail, how violently the idea of 'successful Chinese' would darken in the mind of a Malay whose livelihood had been ruined by the vagaries of high finance. The very thought has the effect of making the shopkeeper and his daughter, so civilised and soft, appear vulnerable – and this restores my friendly feeling towards them.

The man is emphatic about the quality of their stock; it's superior, he says, to David Tan's, the Hong Kong entrepreneur who has cornered the market for similar clothes in the United States. His own workers, he adds, are more skilful, and he mentions in particular three elderly Chinese women who do the knotting for the traditional fasteners; brought up to the business from childhood, they've got the old dexterity and sheer strength of finger. The work's good for them too, he says – keeps arthritis at bay. By this time he's beginning to sound rather unctuous. One wonders what the old women would say about the blessings of labour. One also wonders of course what it all amounts to, this great business of manufacturing and shopping.

Only a few minutes earlier, in a women's shoe-shop, my eye had been caught by a young woman with a pale, unprepossessing face and short, fat legs, trying on and kicking off pair after pair of high-heeled gilt-and-silver sandals, and chattering all the while on a cell-phone; such a frenzy of social and economic activity that one of the cleaners who continually prowl the mall with dust-pan and brush began trying the shoes on too, as though caught in the spell; even a baby lying in a nearby pram, feet in the air and attempting, as babies do, to wrench off its socks, seemed desperate to join in. It looked like a sequence from a Chaplinesque satire against shopping.

A Lacanian would no doubt see it all as an attempt to furbish a false image of the self with the trappings of wealth and power: 'the narcissism of the Imaginary and its identification of an ideal ego'. The words are Homi Bhabha's, who has turned the Lacanian apparatus to post-colonial use.

But what a strange apparatus it is. In fact the self that needs wealth and power is rooted not in some arcane self-deception involving mirrors but in the simplest realities of existence. Any young animal is fragile and vulnerable; at the same time, by its very nature as an independent organism, it must assert itself against the non-self, the ubiquitous 'other'. It thus needs an assurance of safety and sustenance – which, in the human world, money can generally provide. And this is a richly adequate ground for all the excesses of fear, greed, and vanity, with their delusions about the self and reality, and with their drive to amass wealth and power beyond any need. But the effects of money-power may be real rather than illusory, and the failure to acknowledge it makes the Lacanians, like all the other neo-Saussureans, dealers in moral tales rather than close observation.

In Bhabha's post-colonial application the moral tale has an interesting twist. The chief device of racist and colonialist discourse, it's claimed, is the stereotype, and it has an ambivalent function, in part rational, in part emotive; to label someone a 'savage', for example, enables me to subject them overtly to 'civilised' mastery and covertly to lurid fantasy. Bhabha then supports this claim with the Lacanian scheme of the Imaginary and the Symbolic, and their provenance in the 'mirror-stage'. But the support really works the other way. The claim by itself clearly stands on firm ground, both psychologically and historically, and in fact lends credence to Lacan's highly speculative (now largely discredited) theory. All that the Lacanian scheme contributes is a veneer of intellectual fashion.

What the veneer obscures is that the stereotype – the assignment of an individual to a category – with its potential for both understanding and delusion, is the basic mechanism of all thought and language; and in combination with the raw emotions of the vulnerable organism, it creates all our bogeymen – 'filthy blacks', or whites, or communists, or protestants.

Once again we're confronted with more complexity than the Lacanian scheme admits. In its non-racial aspects the language of the colonist will be less subject to bogeymen; there will be patches of light and darkness, not an overall arrest of psychic development in some obscure 'realm of the Imaginary'. The need is not for a Lacan but a Forster, who can recognise, for instance, that as individuals the British in India had perceptions of Indians that they suppressed as a Club; recognise shifting degrees of verbal delusion in the shifting course of the story.

Forster's own emotions about the colonial officials vary accordingly. Pity, contempt, sympathy, amusement, indignation. And insofar as he is a good novelist they vary appropriately. Some have thought him inappropriately hard on the British officials. I suppose

Professor Said must think his Indians merely cardboard figures. Indian commentators themselves have thought otherwise.

But in any case emotional propriety can never be an absolute. Various kinds of story are already being told about 'the Asian crisis', with various emotions and various (though always emphatic) moral conclusions. It's being seen as a tale of crony-capitalism (a new version, this, of the story of the 'unreliable oriental' told by the old colonists). Or as a tale of the more general fecklessness of international bankers both east and west. Or of the painful but healthy discipline of the market. Or of predatory, even racist, currency speculators undermining national currencies. Or of the punitive market-force policies imposed by the IMF as part of an American plot to open the Asian economies to western domination. Or more generally still as a doomsday tale of Mammon destroying the world.

At one emotional extreme, the hard-bitten P.J.O'Rourke, in his *Eat The Rich*, expresses some appropriately satirical sentiments about the way academic economists tell their stories – 'at once puerile and impenetrable, *Goodnight Moon* rewritten by Henry James' – but when he strikes the same note about the beleaguered Asian economies, it sounds like western arrogance jeering, with a certain relief, at the wounded 'tigers'. At the other end is the intense concern of a Chomsky, expressing itself largely in statistics (which these days seem to have replaced rhetoric as the vehicle for moral indignation): so many millions of Indonesian rupiahs spent on American arms, so many more millions salted away in Swiss banks by the Suharto family, and in the end so many millions of starving Indonesians.

What all the tales have in common is the feeling that Mammon not only rules the world but does it in dramatic style. Even the satirical O'Rourke makes heroes of the New York stock exchange traders, the warrior-élite of the money-wars. And the whole picture is of great ebbs and flows of capital determined by market 'forces' (which may follow either deep economic law or mere investor whim) leaving some regions desolate and others rich, some lives fulfilled and others ruined by their passing.

* * *

The variety of stories creates no post-modern uncertainty; in general terms, it's easy enough to see them all fitting together in a narrative with the scope of a *Nostromo*. There's uncertainty of outcome of course. Will Malaysia, for instance, descend into the sort of anti-

Chinese violence already occurring in Indonesia? But this is the stuff of which narratives are made. And the Kuala Lumpur Chinese shopkeeper, who is no saint but evidently sells innocuous products and creates gainful employment, might appear as the 'good capitalist', perhaps made a scapegoat for the cronies, with their government loans and licences. His shop at any rate seems to present itself for contrast with the Kuala Lumpur railway station hotel, where we happen to be staying. An eastern fantasy of colonnades and minarets to rival the Gothic fantasy of St Pancras station in London, it's described in the guide-books as a 'heritage hotel', and indeed some (crony-capitalist?) money has been thrown at it in the form of new paint and décor; but it reminds me of hotels in China during the Cultural Revolution; the staff have the air of salaried officials and regard guests more as a source of inconvenience than of income. A succession of small frustrations erupts into crisis when they forget our early call on the morning of our departure. But luckily the platform for our train to the Cameron Highlands is only fifty yards from the hotel door, and as we drag our luggage out into the dawn light, my wife finds time for a volley of Parthian shots at the assorted staff lounging sleepily in the lobby – though her shafts make no impression on the solid wall of their indifference.

The detached observer, as opposed to the irritable tourist, might find more in the contrast between the the dress-shop and the hotel than the economic superiority of private enterprise over subsidised torpor, but it would take a longer story to explore it, and I don't have sufficient concern for the shopkeeper to make the intense imaginative effort required – as Conrad used to observe – for the understanding of another human being. Any imaginative spark in my own little narratives is struck out by the current of ideas rather than the characters.

The post-colonial theorists of course, good neo-Saussureans that they are, have reduced the imagination to mere 'difference': 'the appropriation of the English language is the first of a range of appropriations which establish a discourse announcing its difference from Europe'. This brisk complacency is as representative of *The Empire Writes Back* as the book itself is of post-colonial theory. 'How wonderfully well', it suggests, 'the revolution is going.' Obviously this is no more believable in the literary sphere than in the political or economic. There will be failed literary experiments in any variant English – as there are in standard English. But any conception of literary failure is ruled out not only by the tone but by the critical method. Each local 'discourse' is rendered as a list of the features (vernacular words and syntax, and so on) that 'establish' its 'difference' from standard English, and the difference is simply equated with success.

In a play by the Malaysian writer K.S. Maniam, for instance, an employer who speaks standard English is berated by an employee who speaks the local variant: 'You nothing but stick. You nothing but stink. Look all clean, inside all thing dirty. Outside everything. Inside nothing.' This is certainly different not only from standard English but also from any kind of speech I've heard during my – admittedly brief – sojourn in Malaysia, and I was relieved to find an expert describing it as a 'blending together of aproximations of pidgin and Malaysian English, the whole sounding more pidgin'. But of course the imperial responders (who themselves quote the expert) are undeterred by the dramatist's failure to capture any reality, since they reject the whole idea of 'representation' in favour of 'construction'. And what's being 'constructed' in post-colonial literature, they tell us, is a tension across the gap between the 'centre' and 'margin', the standard and the variant.

This might seem a reasonable proposition. My own post-colonial experience in New Zealand is of the settler kind, which hinges, the theorists tell us, on the inadequacy of the old language to the new place. And its clearly true that to a settler's eye the new place can present a wretchedly blank aspect, a gap between the 'centre' and the 'margin' that some migrants never cross; they either return to the 'centre' or feel forever exiled.

Even when the new place comes to feel like home, the gap may still be felt – in a sense of pleasure for instance in the new-ness of this *not-Europe* at the edge of the Pacific. But of course there's more to it than a sense of a gap, or of difference. My pleasure may arise, to take an obvious instance, when a spring southerly is blowing bright clouds across green hills running down to the sea; and it feeds mainly on thoughts of *similar* clouds, hills, seas, and springtimes, and on the sheer sensation of light and movement – which will include the differential 'meaning' of 'not darkness' 'not stillness', but can't be reduced to it. In sensation resides the 'other' of language, the grain of salt without which words lose their savour.

The neo-Saussurean attempt to ignore all this of course breaks down whenever a particular work is quoted:

Mas'r, is a heady night, this. Memory is pricking at me mind, and restlessness is a-ride me soul. I scent many things in the night wind; night wind is a-talk of days what pass and gone.

'Ou sont les neiges d'antan?' And every passage adduced to illustrate 'difference' in fact contains some common human theme; a group of men getting happily drunk but with a rising undercurrent of violence; a fearful glimpse of imminent collision during a mist at sea; a lament that we die alone; a little boy admiring men at work. To point this out is to be dismissed as a 'neo-universalist'. But one still has to insist on it. When we see a tree, we see its difference from plants and shrubs but also its likeness to other trees. And art vivifies perception by heightening this play of similarity and difference.

The little boy admiring the world of men at work, for instance, is Huck Finn:

> We slept most all day and started out at night, a little ways behind a monstrous long raft that was as long going by as a procession. She had four long sweeps at each end, so we judged she carried as many as thirty men, likely. She had five big wigwams aboard, wide apart, and an open camp-fire in the middle, and a tall flag-pole at each end. There was a power of style about her. It *amounted* to something being a raftsman on such a craft as that.

A raft is by definition one entity, moving all of a piece, a humble workaday thing, and a rather impromptu construction; a procession is by definition a series of entities, and a high ceremonial, not at all casual; but these differences between tenor and vehicle serve only to bring out the force of Huck's feeling for the one great point of similarity – the raft is truly as grand as any procession, the world of work as great as any high society display. The metaphor gives us what we expect from art; a sense of subjectivity not as some theoretic 'construct' but as the perceptions of a particular being at a particular moment. And since Huck's language so fully realises his world, the variant itself becomes a norm, self-sufficient. To see it as always trailing a pale ghost of standard English seems a peculiarly gratuitous insult.

In practice of course the criterion of the realising power is one that the theorists themselves (to their credit) have tacitly to admit. They describe the 'vernacular rhythm' of the night-wind passage, for instance, as 'consummate', particularly praising its 'fidelity' – which can only mean fidelity to the way people actually speak. The criterion of realism.

And (if the expert's account is accurate) the problem of the invented Malay-plus-pidgin variant is that it's too simply different; lacking 'fidelity', or similarity, it fails to give any 'shock of recognition'. Of course in all these cases, any judgement requires an intimate familiarity with the variant, but the essential grounds of judgement will be the same as for standard English.

The emphasis on pure 'difference' is meant to preclude any value-judgement, and of course the intention is political. The theorists' final belief is that texts in variant 'englishes' are all 'different but equal'. Unsurprisingly this is the same reduction of the imagination to politics that one finds in Eagleton, who translates the old idea that the imagination fuses the particular with the universal into the idea that 'every individual has an equal right to have his or her difference respected' – which sounds an admirable sentiment, but becomes nonsense when taken to require an equal respect for any text that exhibits some regional difference.

The dawn train that takes us from Kuala Lumpur to the Cameron Highlands is virtually empty. When the ticket-collector – a short burly Malay with a brusquely amiable manner and a gorgeous green and gold uniform – comes on his rounds, he shows us how to swivel our row of seats to face the next row, giving us more room to stretch our legs and a whole length of window to look through. He swivels several other rows too, partly to make sure I get the idea, but partly, it's clear, out of sheer *élan*, jabbing his foot on the release catch and spinning the seats round with a whirl of his arm and a fierce beam of a smile. When he's gone I can't resist a few whirls myself, and later on I proudly induct two new passengers into the art; I can't muster the guard's panache, but what we have in common is obvious enough – a boyish delight in the operation of a clever mechanism – shove, whizz, click – and in sharing the knack with somebody else. And it's as trivial as it's obvious; but it exemplifies none the less what Michael Polanyi called 'conviviality', our sense of common humanity at the deepest level, life recognising life.

'Homo sum et nihil humanum a me alienum puto.' The old humanist motto highlights the breadth of human sympathy, the capaciousness of soul traditionally seen as the great writer's gift. The theorist-radicals of course dismissed 'human nature' as a fiction designed to suppress 'deviance', whether political, sexual, or racial. When it became clear, however, that their own view of humanity in terms of mere 'difference' brought them embarrassingly close to the advocates of, say, 'ethnic cleansing', they began (with a good deal of internal friction) a revival of 'universalism', but with a looser,

Laclau-ian, relation between the 'universal' and the 'particular'.

Philosophically this seems sensible; it recalls Polanyi's theory of tacit thought, though it lacks his subtlety and comprehensiveness. Politically (which is what concerns its proponents) it simply means that any 'deviant' person or group is free to campaign for acceptance as a 'universal' – here synonymous with 'norm'. But with regard to aesthetics (which concerns people like me) it's quite laughably inadequate. 'Universals' in art aren't 'norms' in that sense at all.

This ticket-collector, for instance, embodies the 'universal' of a shared boyish pleasure in machinery, but this is determined by the particular circumstances of our meeting – the emptiness of the carriage, his mood, my attitude towards him. At other times, for other people, he will evidently embody quite other 'universals'. And indeed I can already see him as also embodying the freedom of art as opposed to the rigidities of the radical-theorists. Art lays its universals on the particulars with a light touch, leaving an element of the unknown, some room for 'another way of putting it' – to recall Eliot's definition of 'wit', which inaugurated a distinctively modern style of lightness. It's a lightness more generally evident in metaphor, which may allow a raft to be also procession, if the beholder is in the mood to see it that way. An artistic universal or idea doesn't exhaust the particular image as a stereotype does.

* * *

'On the whole a Chinese will be eighty percent effective, an Indian seventy percent, a Malay sixty percent.' A stock piece of old colonial stereotyping. 'Effective' means, roughly, 'good at running a shop – or a bank'. The twenty-mile journey from the nearest railway station to the Cameron Highlands is by taxi, and our driver is a middle-aged Indian, well upholstered and comfortably garrulous, rather like his car – a 1960s Mercedes that trundles stolidly up the winding road. Most of the taxi-drivers, we later discover, seem to be Indians; most of the hoteliers Chinese. As we climb higher, we occasionally pass the pole-and-thatch huts of a local people called the Orang Asli. Described as 'dirt-poor' by our tourist guide-book, they sell straw baskets and clay pots by the road-side, and I suppose they'd be rather less than sixty-percent 'effective' at running a bank; yet I'm struck by the fact that they very effectively settled in the best climate in the Malayan peninsula, the rolling tree-covered highlands, just high enough to be pleasantly warm by day and pleasantly cool by night, and completely remote until the British decided they were suited to growing tea. The plantations are still there, but the area is now chiefly a resort, and when we check into our hotel, I'm struck once again when I find a young Orang Asli woman effectively settled at the reception desk.

Bright-eyed, of fluent English, and coolly poised, she seems, to the tourist eye at least, a successful blend of the local and the international – like the hotel itself, whose wooden floors and exposed beams might equally seem Malay, modern or Tudor. In fact we're only in such an expensive place because the exchange rate is so favourable, and the room-rate so discounted in this town of half-built or half-empty hotels. A year or so ago, curiously enough, my brother's engineering firm in Barnsley made some haulage gears for the big rides at a projected theme-park near here. But they were never paid for; the project went bankrupt – as, shortly afterwards, did my brother's firm, a casualty of the 'market forces' that closed Yorkshire's coal-mines.

As we get ready to go out for dinner, television news begins as usual with a national politician exhorting the populace to keep their money in Malaysian banks; and it ends with a local item about a public-speaking competition for schools. The winners are a stage-full of teenage girls, Malay, Indian and Chinese, intoning in perfect unison and in florid English, a paean to their Malaysian identity – which seems already under stress from those same market forces.

But 'the news' is one thing, reality another. Downtown it's all very relaxed, though lively enough; the diners in the restaurants seem mostly locals, with a sprinkling of back-packers. The crowds arrive only at the week-ends, it seems, escaping the Kuala Lumpur heat. We enjoy a curry, then promenade the main street for a while, and listen to the backpackers chatting, in English with many accents but mainly one topic – how cheaply they managed to get this or that.

As we leave the town centre and walk back up the hill to the hotel, our eyes are caught by a flurry of activity across the street. It's some dogs emerging from a side-street; then some more; and then more; there must be a fifteen or twenty altogether. They're showing no interest in us, but the street is deserted, and I'm a little unnerved by the sense of their being out of human control but highly organised; silently following their leader at a sharp trot, eyes front, ears pricked, tails erect, and apparently on urgent business, they seem a glimpse of some sinister possibility. They disappear at length into another side street, and in a few moments there's a confused barking; purely canine business it seems.

Back in the elegant, deserted hotel lobby, the Orang Asli girl is still on duty. As she tells us with great charm and point about guided tours of the tea-plantations for next day, I'm still half thinking about the marauding dogs, the falling ringit, and potential trouble. My touch of imaginary concern for the young woman – felt more readily of course than for the middle-aged Chinese shopkeeper, and no doubt rather sentimental – makes me think of poor Jewel, Lord Jim's wife, and of the suspense at the close of the novel, when the white outlaws, set free on Jim's guarantee, kill Dain Waris. Will Jim succumb once again to the moral paralysis that let him abandon the SS *Patna*? Will Dain's father take revenge, or break the patriarchal mould? Will Jewel stand with Jim or with her own people?

The questions sound soap-operatic of course. Suspense in narrative, like metre in poetry, always runs a high risk of bathos – as is evident from the illustration that Coleridge borrowed from Dr Johnson:

> I put my hat upon my head
> And walked into the Strand,
> And there I met another man,
> His hat was in his hand.

Metre and narrative both heighten our sense of expectation – here conspicuously disappointed by the complete banality of the content.

What, generally speaking, is required to satisfy it? 'Complexity' of 'meaning' is the orthodox modern answer. For Empson – who established 'complexity of meaning' as the central term of modern criticism – the 'meanings' of a rich ambiguity exist in separation only in analysis. The actual effect is always a unity of the imagination. The pedants, as ever, ignored the latter and simply seized on the analytical method. In the case of *Lord Jim*, Hillis Miller, in his deconstructionist phase, offers a standard demonstration that Jim's 'character' can be variously 'interpreted'; and this is true of course; but all it means in effect is that there's room for debate about the extent of Jim's 'tragic flaw' – and to use the old-fashioned phrase is to recall how common such debates have always been in literary criticism. In fact the debatability itself is the main point.

At the end, Dain's father, with the whole village clustering round, shoots Jim point blank in the chest: 'the white man sent right and left at all those faces a proud and unflinching glance. Then with his hand over his lips he fell forward, dead.' We're aware of his courage, his sense of honour, and his incorrigible egoism; aware too that softer and harsher views of his case are possible. But, like a building that presents different faces as we walk around it, this creates no sense of 'undecidability', only a full realisation of the complexity of Jim's case, together with 'a sense of pity and beauty and pain' – to recall some of Conrad's own words about the imaginative quality he sought for in his art.

Some theorists of course denounce the imagination rather than simply ignore it. According to Fredric Jameson, for instance, the reader of *Lord Jim* is a victim of Conrad's 'aestheticizing strategy', which proffers a vividly realised world as a substitute for the 'real' world from which, not being a socialist-realist, he is 'excluded by history'. But if the non-socialist imagination is escapist then we would have to reject Conrad's highly realised and more-than-ever relevant picture of Russian cynicism in *Under Western Eyes* in favour of the Marxist orthodoxies about modern 'history'. As with Forster, there is no question here of some absolute of 'imaginative propriety'. Pain especially, I think, figures too largely in Conrad's vision, so strongly coloured by the unpredictability and destructiveness of the sea and the harsh life of the Victorian merchant seaman. But a genuine vision it is, not just a heap of words, and what it demonstrates is that realised work creates its own centre and transcends its historical circumstance, of which unrealised work is always a mere product and thus irremediably marginal.

* * *

Edwin Thumboo, I discover, when we return to Singapore, our Malaysian excursion ended, dislikes 'theory' quite as much as I myself. But I soon find myself thinking that he's avoided rather than confronted it; the problem of stereotyping he presents me with is professional rather than racial. Racially he seems part-European, part Asian, the same broad category as my own children – who are perhaps the people one is least likely to stereotype at all. But professionally he brings out the narrow Leavisite in me, the stern purist, the outsider who considers himself the real centre, one of the precious remnant. As he goes through a roll-call of people I might know (and mostly don't), takes an urgent phone-call from the Vice Chancellor, and gives instructions to his secretary (a very pleasant and competent young woman, also Eurasian and rather intimidated by him), there's something Singaporean, Lee Kuan Yu-ish, in the abruptness of his manner that calls to mind the Leavisian phrase 'academic ward boss', and when at length our talk turns to literature and he enthuses about Forster's humaneness and decency, I feel a certain doubt –

which seems rather mean when he goes on to invite me to lunch.

'This way,' he says, opening a French window out onto the roof. We're on the tenth floor, and there's nothing at all on the expanse of tarmac except the squat hump of a ventilation shaft. After a few brisk steps he pauses and gestures beyond the forest of cranes in the docks, towards a distant shoreline. 'Indonesia,' he says, as though that's where we're going, and strides on towards the edge of the roof. Having a poor head even for heights more modest than this, I feel a slight panic. Has he gone suddenly mad?

At the hump he abruptly halts, takes from his pocket with a little flourish – lo – a key, and opens a grey metal service door. 'Short-cut to the lift,' he beams, pointing down a flight of concrete steps. Does he realise how much he's disconcerted me?

We're to eat at a Japanese restaurant, but we call en route at a Chinese delicatessen; a bottle of sauce he bought there yesterday for his wife has turned out to be the wrong kind. As he bustles to over-come the shopkeeper's reluctance to exchange it, his abrupt manner returns, and it continues in the restaurant itself, a small local estab-lishment where he has his regular table and brings his own drinks – *sake* in black and gold aluminium cans, little works of Japanese art, which he produces from a plastic carrier bag. When he's sampled the *sake* and appraised the tray of sushi that appears with commendable speed, he gives me a quizzical look. He has to assert himself in public places like shops, he says, because they sometimes take him for a Malay and try to push him around. He sips his drink and peers up at me from under his eyebrows, his face suddenly transformed. The stocky bureaucrat with a hard-looking head on a powerful neck has turned into a goblin with sly eyes and a puckish smile. And when I take the opportunity to ask him about local racism he replies with an easy shrug that in any multi-racial society the majority group will tend naturally to dominate.

So we soon find ourselves talking not about race, or colonialism, or the the 'Asian crisis', but simply about family. How many chil-dren have we, are they boys or girls, what are they doing in life. Bureaucrat and goblin give way to 'the contented citizen'. 'Show me any ex-colony that's done as well as Singapore,' he says, and he clearly feels that his own achievements are in tune with the city's. Professor, poet, member of the National Arts Council, holder of the Public Service Star (and Bar). This public side of him appears in his poetry, in panegyrics on Singapore – whose youth, for instance, are

Earth movers. They tame mountains, swamps

Run oil-rigs, off-shore banks.
Shaping thus their better destiny...

But always, as here, the poetry seems rather abstract; an expression of pious sentiment; Thumboo's imagination isn't really fired by the things that have made Singapore what it is – productivity, business, money, and the powers that organise them. What modern poet's imagination has been? And without imaginative fire of course poetry is nothing.

Oh dear, I seem locked into critical thoughts about my kind host; and even when his kindness extends to insisting that he drive me home after lunch (I'm staying with my daughter, who works in Singapore), I sense that he's partly curious to see what sort of place she lives in. In fact it's a very fine place, in a cluster of white apartment blocks on a wooded hillside, with a swimming pool in its manicured grounds and a view of the downtown skyscrapers from its wide verandahs.

The poet swerves to a halt outside the security gate, with its burly Indian guard, and makes no attempt to drive in. Perhaps he doesn't want to risk being 'taken for a Malay and pushed around' – his car isn't quite the sort that usually comes sweeping up to the entrance. But as he leans forward and looks up through the windscreen at the apartments, the goblin look returns. 'Beautiful place,' he chuckles, in real appreciation of all the Singaporean symbols of urban and tropical affluence.

And I have rather the same mixed feelings. I like the Hollywooden glamour of it all, but I'm not sure I belong. There's an old colonial resonance, from years ago, when I worked in Hong Kong, a scholarship-boy uncomfortably elevated to the high life simply by virtue of being white.

He turns to shake hands and say good-bye. 'I enjoyed our get-together so much,' he says. 'It's unusual these days for me to meet someone new who's my own age.'

So he's stereotyping us by our years! 'Is not this the same box with a vengeance,' as Aziz exclaims to old Mrs Moore when they first meet. Aziz is exaggerating of course. That they both have two sons and a daughter is hardly a remarkable similarity. And his anxiety to stress it has ambiguous roots – in his earlier outburst against her, rooted in turn in his slight at the hands of the two Englishwomen who have taken his carriage. But it generates none the less the momentary glow of friendship that Forster saw as the only consolation of life on our wretched planet.

Well, Forster himself exaggerates perhaps, sets too much store by the spontaneous personal contact, too little by the formal social intercourse that he, in turn, thought over-prized by 'the East'. No one can claim an absolute propriety of attitude here either. But he still makes us warm to Aziz, as Aziz warms to Mrs Moore – and as I now find myself warming to Thumboo. No matter what box he's putting me in, his good-will is evident. I replace us in our professional box more convivially than before: two modest but worthy contributors to the modern 'English' academic enterprise. And the 'other' that I'm consciously excluding from the box of course are the neo-Saussurean theorists.

But the interplay of similarity and difference that shapes our experience is always provisional and always changing. What looms suddenly large, down there amongst the brooding tower blocks, is the 'other' of a monumental indifference to any literature at all. Poor Thumboo, charged with upholding the dignity of poetry against all those Philistines. And poor me, of course, for in the end all our concern for others is concern for ourselves – 'Tis Margaret you mourn for.'

But it's none the less crucial. Television news last night showed a Palestinian house bombed by Israeli settlers on the West Bank, that still-tormented post-colonial site. There were women weeping, the anxious faces of children looking into the camera. But the people sorting through the rubble and already starting to rebuild the house were both Palestinian and Israeli, and it was one of the former who said (according to the subtitles), 'If there's no mutual concern, there won't be peace.' Though I speak with the tongues of angels...

When I first began the formal study of literature I learned to admire 'irony' and to smile at the Victorian fondness for crying together over moving stories. Their sentimentality now seems preferable at least to feeling clever together deconstructing texts, or self-righteous together excavating sub-texts.

Of course neither the West Bank nor any other political world will ever be ruled by the pure voice of concern, but if it's altogether unheard, then Professor Said's truth and justice become the sounding brass of pedantry and legalism. What's saddening is that in the literary world, where it ought to sound most clearly, it's been drowned out of late by the tinkling cymbals of the theorists.